Urban Commons

D1343238

Dept of Architecture
Library

This book rethinks the city by examining its various forms of collectivity – their atmospheres, modes of exclusion and self-organization, as well as how they are governed – on the basis of a critical discussion of the notion of urban commons.

The idea of the commons has received surprisingly little attention in urban theory, although the city may well be conceived as a shared resource. *Urban Commons: Rethinking the City* offers an attempt to reconsider what a city might be by studying how the notion of the commons opens up new understandings of urban collectivities, addressing a range of questions about urban diversity, urban governance, urban belonging, urban sexuality, urban subcultures, and urban poverty; but also by discussing in more methodological terms how one might study the urban commons.

In these respects, the rethinking of the city undertaken in this book has a critical dimension, as the notion of the commons delivers new insights about how collective urban life is formed and governed.

Christian Borch is Professor of Political Sociology at the Department of Management, Politics and Philosophy, Copenhagen Business School, Denmark. His previous books include *The Politics of Crowds: An Alternative History of Sociology* (Cambridge University Press, 2012) and *Foucault, Crime and Power: Problematisations of Crime in the Twentieth Century* (Routledge, 2015).

Martin Kornberger is Professor of Strategy and Organization at Copenhagen Business School and visiting professor at the Research Institute for Urban Management and Governance at the WU Wien. He received his PhD in philosophy from the University of Vienna. Amongst other things, his work focuses on urban strategy and governance.

D307.1216
BOK.

Space, Materiality and the Normative
Series Editors: Andreas Philippopoulos-Mihalopoulos
and Christian Borch

Space, Materiality and the Normative presents new ways of thinking about the connections between space and materiality from a normative perspective. At the interface of law, social theory, politics, architecture, geography and urban studies, the series is concerned with addressing the use, regulation and experience of space and materiality, broadly understood, and in particular with exploring their links and the challenges they raise for law, politics and normativity.

Books in this series:

Spatial Justice
Body, Lawscape, Atmosphere
Andreas Philippopoulos-Mihalopoulos

Urban Commons
Rethinking the City
Christian Borch and Martin Kornberger

Forthcoming:

A Jurisprudence of Movement
Common Law, Walking, Unsettling Place
Olivia Barr

Placing International Law
Authority, Jurisdiction, Technique
Fleur Johns, Shaun McVeigh, Sundhya Pahuja, Thomas Skouteris, and Robert Wai

Urban Commons

Rethinking the City

Edited by Christian Borch and
Martin Kornberger

Routledge
Taylor & Francis Group

LONDON AND NEW YORK

First published 2015
by Routledge
2 Park Square, Milton Park, Abingdon, Oxfordshire OX14 4RN

and by Routledge
711 Third Avenue, New York, NY 10017

First issued in paperback 2016

a GlassHouse Book

Routledge is an imprint of the Taylor & Francis Group, an informa business

Copyright © 2015 Selection and editorial matter, Christian Borch and
         Martin Kornberger; individual chapters, the contributors.

The rights of Christian Borch and Martin Kornberger to be identified as
editors of this work has been asserted by them in accordance with
sections 77 and 78 of the Copyright, Designs and Patents Act 1988.

All rights reserved. No part of this book may be reprinted or
reproduced or utilised in any form or by any electronic, mechanical, or
other means, now known or hereafter invented, including photocopying
and recording, or in any information storage or retrieval system,
without permission in writing from the publishers.

Trademark notice: Product or corporate names may be trademarks or
registered trademarks, and are used only for identification and
explanation without intent to infringe.

British Library Cataloguing in Publication Data
A catalogue record for this book is available from the British Library

Library of Congress Cataloging-in-Publication Data
  Urban commons : rethinking the city / edited by Christian Borch and
  Martin Kornberger.
  pages cm. — (Space, materiality and the normative)
  Includes bibliographical references and index.
  ISBN 978-1-138-01724-5 (hbk : alk. paper) — ISBN 978-1-315-78059-
  7 (ebk : alk. paper) 1. Cities and towns. 2. Urbanization. 3. Public
  spaces. 4. Commons. 5. Sociology, Urban. I. Borch, Christian. II.
  Kornberger, Martin, 1974–
  HT151.U654 2015
  307.1'216—dc23
  2014036608

ISBN 13: 978-1-138-24163-3 (pbk)
ISBN 13: 978-1-138-01724-5 (hbk)

Typeset in Garamond by
Florence Production Ltd, Stoodleigh, Devon

Contents

List of illustrations   vii
Notes on contributors   viii

Introduction: Urban commons   1
MARTIN KORNBERGER AND CHRISTIAN BORCH

1   The city is not a Menschenpark: Rethinking the
    tragedy of the urban commons beyond the
    human/non-human divide   22
    JONATHAN METZGER

2   The false promise of the commons: historical
    fantasies, sexuality and the 'really-existing' urban
    common of modernity   47
    LEIF JERRAM

3   Sharing an atmosphere: spaces in urban commons   68
    ORVAR LÖFGREN

4   Producing, appropriating and recreating the myth of
    the urban commons   92
    PATRIK ZAPATA AND MARÍA JOSÉ ZAPATA CAMPOS

5   Managing the urban commons: Public interest and
    the representation of interconnectedness   109
    MARTINA LÖW

6   Mediated exclusions from the urban commons:
    Journalism and poverty   127
    GREG M. NIELSEN

7 Communities and the commons: Open access and community ownership of the urban commons 153

MAJA HOJER BRUUN

Index 171

List of illustrations

4.1 Waste pickers collecting recyclables at La Chureca 93
4.2 Intermediaries, sellers and buyers 96
4.3 Waste as a common: food, toys, material constructions 97
4.4 Protests at the dump 100
4.5 Obdurate waste picking at La Chureca 105
4.6 Waste picking in Gothenburg 106

Notes on contributors

Christian Borch, PhD, is Professor of Political Sociology at the Department of Management, Politics and Philosophy, Copenhagen Business School, Denmark. His current research focuses on crowds, financial markets, architecture, and power. His most recent books include *Niklas Luhmann (Key Sociologists)* (Routledge, 2011); *The Politics of Crowds: An Alternative History of Sociology* (Cambridge University Press, 2012); *Architectural Atmospheres: On the Experience and Politics of Atmospheres* (ed. volume, Birkhäuser, 2014); and *Foucault, Crime and Power: Problematisations of Crime in the Twentieth Century* (Routledge, 2015).

Maja Hojer Bruun is Assistant Professor in Applied Anthropology at the Department of Learning and Philosophy at Aalborg University, Denmark. She received her PhD in anthropology from the University of Copenhagen in 2012. Her research interests are in urban anthropology, organizations, politics, economy and technology. She is part of an interdisciplinary research project on contested property claims and social controversies surrounding the issue of squatting and the use of urban space.

Leif Jerram is Senior Lecturer in Urban History at the University of Manchester, UK. His research explores issues of materiality and the city from an empirical and theoretical perspective, and the ways in which things and people interact. His most recent book, *Streetlife: The Untold History of Europe's Twentieth Century* (Oxford University Press, 2011), uses space and place to understand the changes and continuities of modern European history from the perspective of the urban sites where they happened, and which may have, in fact, caused them to happen.

María José Zapata Campos received her PhD in sociology from the University of Alicante in 2008. Currently she is Associate Professor in Organizing and Environmental Sustainability at Copenhagen Business School, Denmark, and research fellow at the Managing Big Cities program at the Gothenburg Research Institute, University of Gothenburg, Sweden.

Martin Kornberger received his PhD in philosophy from the University of Vienna in 2002, followed by a decade at the University of Technology, Sydney where he worked last as associate professor for design and management and research director of the Australian Government's Creative Industry Innovation Centre. Currently he is a professor for strategy and organization at Copenhagen Business School, a distinguished visiting professor at Stockholm University Business School's marketing department and a visiting professor at The Research Institute for Urban Management and Governance at the WU Vienna University of Economics and Business.

Orvar Löfgren is Professor Emeritus of European Ethnology at the University of Lund, Sweden. His research is focused on the cultural analysis of everyday life and he has written on urban life, consumption, media, and travel. His most recent books include *The Secret World of Doing Nothing* (with Billy Ehn; California University Press, 2010), *Coping with Excess: How Organizations, Communities and Individuals Manage Overflows* (ed. with Barbara Czarniawska; Edward Elgar, 2014), and *Exploring Everyday Life* (with Billy Ehn and Richard Wilk; Rowman, 2015).

Martina Löw is Professor of Sociology of Planning and Architecture at the Department of Sociology at Technische Universität Berlin, Germany. Her current research focuses on the intrinsic logics of cities, space theory, architecture, and power. Her most recent books and articles include *Soziologie der Städte* (Suhrkamp, 2008/2010); 'The constitution of space: the structuration of spaces through the simultaneity of effect and perception', *European Journal of Social Theory*, 2008; and 'The city as experiential space: the production of shared meaning', *International Journal of Urban and Regional Research*, 2013.

Jonathan Metzger is Associate Professor of Urban and Regional Studies at the KTH Royal Institute of Technology. His research interests include spatial theory, the ethnography of planning practice and more-than-human perspectives on urban planning and regional development. His recent books include *Sustainable Stockholm: Exploring Urban Sustainable Development in Europe's Greenest City* (co-edited with Amy Rader Olsson; Routledge, 2013) and *Planning Against the Political: Democratic Deficits in European Territorial Governance* (co-edited with Phil Allmendinger and Stijn Oosterlynck; Routledge, 2014).

Greg M. Nielsen, Department of Sociology and Anthropology, Concordia University, Montreal, Canada, publishes in the areas of social and cultural theory as well as media and journalism studies. His current project concerns a study of how contemporary journalism is confronted daily with a growing list of citizenship controversies concerned with urban poverty, undocumented migrants and the 'reasonable accommodation' of cultural diversity in several large North American and European cities. He is author of *The Norms of Answerability: Social Theory between Habermas and Bakhtin* (SUNY Press, 2002); and *Le Canada de Radio-Canada: Sociologie Critique et Dialogisme Culturel* (Éditions GREF, 1994); co-author of *Mediated Society: A Critical Sociology of Media* (Oxford, 2012); and co-editor of *Acts of Citizenship* (Zed Books, 2008) and of *Revealing Democracy: Religion and Secularism in Liberal Democracy* (Peter Lang, 2014).

Patrik Zapata, PhD, is Associate Professor at the School of Public Administration, University of Gothenburg, Sweden. His research deals with the management of cities, waste management and waste prevention, sustainable organizing, scandalology, language in organizations and relations between organizations.

Introduction

Urban commons

Martin Kornberger and Christian Borch

Introduction

The aim of this volume is twofold, namely: (1) to rethink the city on the basis of the notion of the commons; and (2) to readdress discussions of the commons by taking them to the urban domain. We realize that this ambition might sound presumptuous, given the fact that reflections on both cities and commons date long back and constitute rich traditions. Yet an emergent literature can be identified which seeks to bridge these two traditions (e.g. Blomley, 2008; Harvey, 2012; Parker and Johansson, 2012; Susser and Tonnelat, 2013; Parr, 2014). We consider these attempts important first steps, but also believe that more work is needed to fully understand what it might mean to speak of urban commons, and what that term might entail for extant discussions of cities and commons alike – also beyond debates about the role of social movements, around which much current commons literature pivots. Providing some further steps towards such an understanding is the rationale for this book. Taking up the challenge of understanding urban commons will require us to address a host of issues such as collectivity, diversity, power, atmospheres, government, sexuality, inclusion/exclusion, etc.

Whilst this introductory essay cannot discuss all of these themes, it can set the scene for the chapters to come. We do so by focusing on four issues. In the first section, we present the key ideas about the commons as outlined by Garrett Hardin and Elinor Ostrom, two of the central voices in the commons discussions in the last half century. Much of their work centers on how to avoid overuse of shared resources through governance mechanisms provided by the market, the state or self-organization. In the second section, we critically discuss some of the limits of Hardin's and Ostrom's notions of the commons when applied to the city. In particular, we argue, classical work on cities, such as that of Ebenezer Howard, makes plain that a city is first and foremost a configuration of relationality and density where that which is shared, i.e. the commons, is not something that diminishes in its usage; rather, the use or consumption of a city adds to the commons itself. In other words, the urban commons is not a zero-sum game. In the third section we draw on

Peter Sloterdijk's and Gernot Böhme's discussions of atmospheres and explore how far this concept can provide an alternative vocabulary to analyze the urban commons. In the fourth section, we focus in particular on Louis Wirth who offers a way to understand how an urban commons is a form of collectivity, something that is largely ignored by Hardin, whose theory tends to privilege a methodologically individualistic frame of analysis. *Contra* Hardin, Wirth's approach suggests that what is key about a city is not so much the commons as the commoners – and the tragedies that the urban setting may involve for commoning. Among other things, for Wirth, such tragedies may consist of how urban inhabitants are subjected to mass suggestion, with de-individualizing consequences. In the final section we briefly introduce the various chapters that make up this volume and conclude with reflecting on some perhaps novel problematizations resulting from them.[1]

Tracing the commons: Hardin, Ostrom and the question of collective action

The question of governing the commons has been dominated by Garrett Hardin's widely cited 1968 *Science* article 'The Tragedy of the Commons'. That piece owes its popularity to a strong metaphor with which Hardin illustrates his point: he imagined a large number of people feeding their cattle on the shared meadow. This commons represents a scarce resource, constantly threatened by over-grazing. Since each individual is maximizing their own individual benefit, it is only rational for every individual to add one more cow to their herd. While the costs of overgrazing are socialized amongst all, the potential gain of adding yet another cow is privatized. Hardin's own, notorious diagnosis concludes:

> Therein is the tragedy. Each man [*sic*] is locked into a system that compels him to increase his herd without limit – in a world that is limited. Ruin is the destination toward which all men rush, each pursuing his own best interest in a society that believes in the freedom of the commons. [. . .] Freedom in a commons brings ruin to all.
>
> (1968: 1244)

This point has often been taken to suggest that the only way to avoid the tragedy of the commons is to privatize both loses and gains. Property rights will make individuals accountable, and by extension society sustainable.

1 Several chapters in this book are revised versions of papers first presented at an Urban Commons workshop at Copenhagen Business School (CBS), Denmark, in November 2012, jointly organized by the editors and Ester Barinaga. We wish to thank the Public–Private Platform at CBS for funding that event and thereby helping make this book possible. Thanks also to Laura Mortensen for compiling the book's index.

What Hardin's tale seemed to evoke was the troubling conclusion that self-interested, rational individuals who want to maximize their benefit end up destroying the very foundation of their own well-being. Game theory, and especially the prisoner's dilemma, have argued the same point, albeit in a more formalized language: the two prisoners who are interrogated separately from each other will act rationally, confess and blame their co-conspirator in order to receive a mild sentence; yet, because both prisoners deploy the same strategy, their individual best-case scenario develops into a collective worst-case reality.

Yet Hardin offers more than an intervention in discussions about how to avoid overuse of scarce local resources (which also means that the prisoner's dilemma is only an approximation of his real concerns). His entire analysis is conceived as a response to problems that are situated at a far bigger scale, such as pollution, but also and in particular overpopulation (see also Harvey for a useful discussion of scale problems in the commons literature; 2012: 69–70). Taking his starting point in Malthus, Hardin puts forward an ardent critique of unregulated population growth. For example, Hardin states that '[i]f we love the truth we must openly deny the validity' of the 1967 Universal Declaration of Human Rights and how it grants 'that any choice and decision with regard to the size of the family must irrevocably rest with the family itself, and cannot be made by anyone else' (1968: 1246). For Hardin, that situation is unacceptable, and he explicitly states that 'freedom to breed is intolerable' (1968: 1246). Why is this so? The answer is to be found in how overpopulation affects the commons. According to Hardin, 'the commons, if justifiable at all, is justifiable only under conditions of low-population density. As the human population has increased, the commons has had to be abandoned in one aspect after another' (1968: 1248). In other words, the tragedy of the commons is not just a matter of simple incentives to overuse common resources individually; the tragedy is propelled by overpopulation, because a growing population increases the singular family's incentive to overuse in order to secure all its members. Consequently, Hardin ends up rephrasing the above-cited statement that '[f]reedom in a commons brings ruin to all' in biopolitical (perhaps, in fact, eugenic) terms: 'Freedom to breed will bring ruin to all', a statement that is aimed to support his argument for the immediate 'necessity of abandoning the commons in breeding' (1968: 1248).

Hardin's identification of dilemmas of collective action formed the point of departure for Nobel laureate Elinor Ostrom in her seminal book *Governing the Commons* (1990). Although she noted that Hardin was concerned with overpopulation, her interpretation of his work ignored its biopolitical overtones (1990: 3). Key for Ostrom was rather the kind of policy recommendations that Hardin's more prisoner's dilemma-like example of overgrazing implied. Specifically, Ostrom argued, especially in some of his subsequent work, Hardin made clear that two central models presented themselves as solutions to the commons dilemma, namely either a 'private enterprise system' or 'socialism' (Ostrom, 1990: 9). The important point here is not how simple or banal this opposition is, but rather what each solution entails. According to Ostrom:

> The proponents of centralized control want an external government agency to decide the specific herding strategy that the central authority considers best for the situation: The central authority will decide who can use the meadow, when they can use it, and how many animals can be grazed.[2]
>
> (1990: 9)

The privatized system, on the other hand, would, in case of only two herders, 'divide the meadow in half and assign half of the meadow to one herder and the other half to the second herder', with the alleged consequence that 'each herder will be playing a *game against nature* in a smaller terrain, rather than a game against another player in a larger terrain' (1990: 12, italics in the original).

Now, Ostrom's central point is that these two solutions are not the only ones available. She argues that it is possible both empirically and theoretically to conceive of self-organizing forms of collective action that avoid the tragedies predicted by Hardin and others. Her starting point is the observation that the prisoners' dilemma is a dilemma because the prisoners 'cannot change the constraints imposed on them by the district attorney; they are in jail' (1990: 7). But, she adds (not unrealistically), the jail is not the typical institutional setting for most collective action to take shape; in response, Ostrom's work addresses the question of 'how to enhance the capabilities of those involved to change the constraining rules of the game to lead to outcomes other than remorseless tragedies' (1990: 7). On that note, her work develops a theory of collective action in which 'a group of principals can organize themselves voluntarily to retain the residual of their own efforts' (1990: 25). She suggests analyzing the organizational and institutional arrangements (the 'design rules', see 2009: 422) through which Hardin's cattle farmers could communicate with each other and hence avoid their tragic fate. These design rules structure the social interaction of appropriators of the commons and condition their ability to discuss, decide on and monitor self-imposed constraints: 'many groups *can* effectively manage and sustain common resources if they have suitable conditions, such as appropriate rules, good conflict-resolution mechanisms, and well-defined group boundaries' (Hess and Ostrom, 2007a: 11, italics in the original).

---

2 And, Hardin would add, how many children families should be allowed to have.

In effect, therefore, Ostrom suggests a third way of governing collective action: neither state coercion nor private property rights solve the tragedy of the commons; rather, historically grown, institutionalized rules allow for self-governance of the commons (a point Ostrom arrives at not just theoretically, but on the basis of empirical studies of users of common-pool resources). In order to do so, Ostrom's actors have to solve the problem of 'organizing', as she puts it: 'how to change the situation from one in which appropriators act independently to one in which they adopt coordinated strategies to obtain higher joint benefits or reduce their joint harm' (1990: 39). She continues: 'That does not necessarily mean creating an organization. Organizing is a process; an organization is the result of that process' (1990: 39).

The urban commons: rethinking the commons

While the Hardin–Ostrom debate has inspired much of the contemporary writing on the commons, it also takes some problematic assumptions for granted. For instance, both Hardin and Ostrom define the commons as a common-pool resource (CPR), which includes fisheries, groundwater basins, irrigation systems, forests, grazing areas, and other natural resource systems (Ostrom, 2009: 413). These CPRs are characterized by: (1) a difficulty to exclude potential beneficiaries; and (2) by the fact that they are rivalrous, which means that the use of these resources by one person diminishes what is left for others to use (Ostrom labels this second characteristic the subtractability of use, see Hess and Ostrom, 2007a: 7). Dealing with CPRs, the main challenge is how to address free-riding (Ostrom, 1990: 6). Since excluding free-riders from the CPR is difficult, and yet all consumption reduces the value of the CPR, the free-rider is the theoretically and practically unavoidable parasite that sows the seeds of destruction of the commons. Ostrom's CPR commons is a resource that appropriators can use, and whilst doing so, they diminish its value. Each fish caught, each tree cut is consumed for good and not available for anyone else any longer. In these examples the commons is depicted as a self-evident resource (object) that only waits for its appropriator (subject) to exploit it. This objectified notion of the commons has been translated uncritically into urban studies. For example, Foster (2011: 58) applies this notion of the commons to the city, defining the urban commons as collectively shared urban resources that 'are subject to the same rivalry and free-rider problems that Garrett Hardin wrote about in his *Tragedy of the Commons* tale'. This prompts the question about which institutional rules lead to a self-governing system that undermines 'the temptation to free-ride on others' efforts' (Foster, 2011: 64).

However, as we shall argue in the following, the notion of a CPR commons raises more questions than it answers when transposed to the urban level. Before getting to that, though, it should be noted that Ostrom herself was critical of merely understanding the commons in terms of subtractive CPRs. In the book *Understanding Knowledge as a Commons* (2007b), co-edited with Charlotte Hess, Ostrom thus distinguishes between subtractive and nonsubtractive resources. In contrast to subtractive resources, nonsubtractive ones refer to resources where one person's use does not reduce other people's benefits. For example, Hess and Ostrom suggest that knowledge is a nonsubtractive resource since its use does not affect the pool of knowledge negatively when people share it (Hess and Ostrom, 2007a: 5; see also Gudeman, 2001: 27).

Now, what happens if we apply this distinction to the urban domain? Certainly, things start to look a bit messier than Ostrom's own examples suggest. On the one hand, parts of a city – such as roads and traffic systems more generally – might be conceived of as a subtractive resource. Since, for instance, the available space on roads is limited, adding more cars will affect the shared resource in a negative way.[3] On the other hand, however, no city would be a city without the inhabitants actively using its streets. And indeed, both the commercial and subjective value of particular places (such as parks or shopping malls) may increase by being used and shared, meaning that – at least to some extent – they constitute nonsubtractive resources. Put differently: the act of consuming does not detract but rather increases value, a point strongly made in this volume's chapter by Zapata and Campos who demonstrate how waste, one residual of consumption, may constitute a commons for poor people. A related point is, as Bruun argues in her contribution to this volume, that markets and commons may not be as neatly separable as suggested in much Ostromian commons literature: it may indeed be possible to identify commons within market contexts.

Ebenezer Howard's classic *Garden Cities of To-morrow*, published in 1898, illustrates the limitations of understanding the urban commons as mere extension of the natural resource perspective. For Howard (who also figures in Jerram's contribution to this volume), the miserable living conditions in which many poor inhabitants of cities found themselves were the consequence of a mismatch between urban value creation and appropriation. What made property in the city valuable in the first place, he asked. Not bricks and mortar, Howard argued, but the proximity to other buildings and the density of activities unfolding between them. In other words, the value of a property is seen by Howard as essentially relational; it is, to put it in contemporary terminology, a function of the network in which the building is situated. Its value does not result from the landowner's individual activity. Rather, the

---

3 Harvey (2012: 74) makes a similar point, but phrases it in rather nostalgic terms, casting an opposition between the streets of the present which are said to be loaded with cars and the streets of the past where more space was assigned to 'pedestrians and protesters'.

landowner profits from people's activities around his or her property. Howard called the surplus that was created by people's activity but erroneously attributed to the property 'unearned increment' (Howard, 1965). For Howard, the difference between value creation and appropriation was one of the main reasons for the social inequalities and political unrest that characterized the growing industrial cities of the late nineteenth century. Howard's solution to the problem was to entice the poor urban population to leave the city and build their own houses in the countryside, resulting in what he labelled Garden Cities and which were later trivialized as 'suburbia'. The logic of his argument was compelling: because the value of the buildings in existing cities results from people's activities, people could easily reproduce that value if enough urban dwellers decided to relocate – with the decisive difference that this time they would own the buildings whose value they created. In Howard's own words:

> The presence of a considerable population thus giving a greatly additional value to the soil, it is obvious that a migration of population on any considerable scale to any particular area will be certainly attended with a corresponding rise in the value of the land so settled upon, and it is also obvious that such increment of value may, with some foresight and pre-arrangement, become the property of the migrating people. [. . .] It is this arrangement which will be seen to give Garden City much of its magnetic power.
>
> (1965: 59)

In short, Howard argued that the value of the land and buildings is a function of the activity of people: only through their interactions the city becomes a city. Howard's theorizing deviates from Locke's idea of value-creation as a distinctive characteristic of the *homo faber*. Rather, Howard's theory of value is a theory of the urban commons: value is the corollary of proximity and density which are both *relational* concepts (in her contribution to this volume, Löw further develops what a relational perspective might mean for an understanding of urban commons). The building owner is only able to capture the 'unearned increment' through cutting the building off from its surrounding environment and turning it into an isolated, tradable object; its value results from mistakenly attributing network effects to the building itself.

The central observation we take from Howard's work is that, *contra* Ostrom, the notion of a commons as a self-evident and independent object makes little sense when applied to the urban. In the city, the commons is an inherently relational phenomenon. This implies that the urban commons does not necessarily revolve around the problem of free-riding. Rather, usage and consumption practices are a constitutive part of the production of the urban commons: *in fact, consuming the city is nothing but the most subtle form of its production.* This idea is supported by research into knowledge commons in open source software communities: there, free-riders are wanted, as they fulfill several important functions, including setting standards for and testing software (see Weber, 2004; Benkler, 2002, 2006). Under such conditions, the Hardin–Ostrom debate seems problematic, as it focuses on the difference between appropriate use and illegitimate abuse as something that can be policed. Ostrom argues for self-governance based on institutional and organizational arrangements, whereas Hardin's argument points towards privatization and marketization. They both share the assumption that the consumption of the resource diminishes its value. But in the urban commons consumption may be a productive act blurring the line between use and abuse. Are skaters using or abusing car parks? Are bike couriers using or abusing the shared streets? Or do they contribute through their activities to the cultural value, the atmosphere of a city? Again, these questions point towards the ill-defined, more assumed than analyzed notion of 'resource' in Ostrom's work. She assumes resources to be non-problematic, objective and given; yet in reality the urban commons results from people using, consuming, appropriating the city. Hence, an urban resource is fundamentally different form Hardin's and Ostrom's CPRs: the grass on a meadow might be given – but the resources that constitute the commons of the city are contingent on urban actors' ability to use them: whether a wall is an obstacle or central element for a *Parcours* tournament depends on who is standing in front of it. Put simply, resources need framing and formatting before they can be thought of as such and used. The concept of urban atmospheres as outlined in the next section provides an illustration of these reflections.

Urban commons, urban atmospheres

Building on Howard's theory of urban value, density and relationality are key factors in what constitutes the urban commons. And, it may be argued, that which is shared and contested in a city is first of all its atmospheric dimensions. Empirically, the literature on creative industries and urbanism gives testimony to the importance of atmospheres for cultural and economic development. Theoretically, the notion of urban atmospheres can be approached from different angles. We focus on two recent attempts to understand urban atmospheres which share certain phenomenological inspirations, namely the conceptions of atmospheres developed by the German philosophers Gernot Böhme and Peter Sloterdijk.

Sloterdijk puts forward his analysis of atmospheres and cities within the frame of a larger investigation of spheres, published as a trilogy between 1998 and 2004 (Sloterdijk, 1998, 1999, 2004).[4] The central idea being articulated

---

4 For an introduction to and discussion of Sloterdijk's spheres project, see Borch (2008).

in this massive project is that all sociality is situated in particular spatial settings called spheres. Such spheres offer meaning to the people gathered within them as well as protection from the outside world. Both aspects are pertinent to discussions of commons: a sphere in effect constitutes a commons – something is shared, whether in material terms (e.g. the air we breathe) or in immaterial terms (e.g. the ideas we share) – and this is a commons that, like any other collective phenomenon, entails a difference between an 'us' and a 'them', i.e. between those on the inside and those on the outside of the sphere's (material or immaterial) membrane. So what we face here is the question of inclusion and exclusion which is discussed in further detail in Nielsen's and Zapata's and Campos' chapters in this volume (see also Mezzadra and Neilson, 2013).

Sloterdijk particularly makes two points central to the present discussion. The first regards air. In the commons literature, air is often seen as being emblematic of a commons – a resource to be shared by us all (Harvey, 2012: 71; Mattei, 2014). Sloterdijk's take is somewhat different. His key interest lies in how air design of various sorts has been introduced to achieve specific political effects. One of his central examples is how poison gas, first used by the German army against the French forces in 1915, contributed to transforming warfare in a manner where the key target was not necessarily the bodies of enemy soldiers, but rather the air they breathe (Sloterdijk, 2004: 93). Another example, which is parallel to some of the concerns we identify in the work of Louis Wirth below (see next section), is how media propaganda constitutes a kind of air poisoning where people are exposed to uniformly composed and highly politically charged manipulation – with people losing their personality as a consequence, Wirth would add (Sloterdijk, 2004: 182–90). A final, less martial example taken from Sloterdijk's *magnum opus* relates to air conditioning: quite literally, the genealogy of technologies that conditioned air and by extension those who breathe it, is simultaneously a history of instilling order and control over segregated populations. The general points these examples serve to illustrate is that a commons is vulnerable to, for example, political intervention in atmospheres and that the subjectification of commoners may be an integral part of such intervention. That is, similar to the point we made above regarding how resources cannot be taken for granted, the commons is not just something that is shared by pre-existing commoners; rather the commoners may be constituted in the creation or production of a commons.

The second key point we take from Sloterdijk relates more specifically to the urban domain. He argues that a city constitutes a kind of condensed 'macro foam' of singular bubbles, i.e. basic forms of sociality (2004: 655). This image not only entails that relationality and density are crucial features in Sloterdijk's notion of the city. It further suggests that, since each bubble may be seen as a commons, the city is best conceived of not as a macro (or meso) commons, but rather as a 'meta collector' of numerous differentiated commons that only share with one another their physical being-in-the-city (2004: 655). What transpires, in other words, is a notion of a 'polyatmospheric' city, i.e. a city divided into a plethora of minor commons (2004: 659). Importantly, this is not an image of a city devoid of content; Sloterdijk's conception of the city is precisely one of an urban commons (positively defined), yet one where the shared resource lies in making available and bringing into close contact numerous minor commons (2004: 655). And where, as Metzger convincingly demonstrates in his Sloterdijk-inspired contribution to this volume, commoning may take place in more-than-human ways.

Sloterdijk's analysis of atmospheric cities and how urban atmospheres may be subjected to powerful modulation resonates with Böhme's notion of urban atmospheres (e.g. Böhme, 2006, 2014). For Böhme, whose conception is further developed in Löfgren's contribution to this volume, the atmosphere of a city constitutes a commons. As he puts it in Ostromian terms, '[t]he atmosphere of a city is the subjective experience of urban reality that is shared by its people' (Böhme, 2014: 58). This reality or resource, as Ostrom would phrase it, refers to 'the way life goes on' in the city, and is something that must be *sensed* in order to be understood (2014: 48). Yet it is also something that can be produced and is as such intimately linked to power. According to Böhme, '[s]tage design provides the paradigm for this perspective. The general aim of stage design is to create an atmosphere with the help of lights, music, sound, spatial constellations, and the use of characteristic objects' (2014: 50). The point is that the urban commons is, on the one hand, lived and experienced and, on the other hand, strategically produced, in order, for example, to achieve particular commercial or political effects (Böhme's examples of the latter reach from from shopping to Nazi architecture, see 2006).

Some of these ideas reappear in recent commons literature. For instance, Hardt and Negri argue that in a society based on intellectual and linguistic labor, the common 'appears not only at the beginning and end of production but also in the middle, since the production processes themselves are common, collaborative, and communicative' (2004: 148). The common – including language, knowledge, images, etc. – are shared cultural accomplishments that serve as the resources, medium and results of production. As is the case of Böhme, the locus of Hardt's and Negri's commons is the biopolitical metropolis: they conceive of the metropolis as the 'factory for the production of the common' (2009: 250); it is its result and repository. In the words of Hardt and Negri, '[i]n fact, production of the common is becoming nothing but the life of the city itself' (2009: 251). Put metaphorically, the city is for the knowledge economy what the factory was for the industrial production system (Hardt and Negri, 2009).

What these writers (despite significant differences) share is an emphasis on the urban commons as corollary of the encounters the city affords: it constantly brings together, or better: re-shuffles, the well-known and local with the unknown and foreign, the familiar with the strange. Drawing once more on the literature on creative and cultural industries as illustrations of Böhme's and Hardt and Negri's theorizing: it is a 'creative' atmosphere, a 'cool' identity or a 'vibrant' scene that makes a city (or suburb) conducive for creative work. McCullough (2013) for instance, speaks about the 'ambient commons' that makes a city, including tags (from signs to graffiti and web-based augmented realities) that people have left behind and that texture the urban, making it a rich and layered assemblage of multiple meanings.

In sum, the proposed perspective on atmospheres not only challenges central ideas that underpin the Hardin–Ostrom framework as outlined in the previous section but also provides (elements of) an alternative vocabulary to theorize the urban commons. Urban atmosphere is a commons that is not subject to individual overuse and hence prisoner's dilemma problems. Of course, certain atmospheres can be destroyed, e.g. through urban planning (or the lack thereof), but there is nothing inherent to urban atmospheres that makes them vulnerable to overuse. Rather, consumption of the city is a subtle form of producing the urban commons. Moreover, and *contra* Hardin, urban atmospheres tend to benefit from population density. Indeed, density is constitutive of many urban atmospheres. This observation necessitates reflection on a specific form of density – the density of people, or: collectivity.

Urban commons and collectivity in the city

Hess and Ostrom rightly state that, in much commons literature, '[c]ommons is a general term that refers to a resource shared by a group of people' (2007a: 4, italics in the original). Above we questioned the notion of resources underpinning this understanding of the commons and argued that an alternative conception is needed to make sense of urban commons. But this is not the only taken-for-granted part of the usual definition of commons that needs to be addressed. The latter part, i.e. that something is *shared by a group of people*, also necessitates further discussion. It can be argued, for instance, that – more explicitly than Ostrom has done herself – the notion of a 'group of people' poses a series of questions relating in various ways to power. For example, how are the boundaries of a commons defined and governed in an urban context? Who is included and who is excluded from the commons, and by means of what technologies are those boundaries drawn? How is the commons rendered visible and constituted as an object of government or self-government? As we shall argue in the following, such questions pertain to how the notion of commons relates to *urban collectivity*.

Interestingly, whilst not referring to Howard explicitly, many of the early urban theorists, including Louis Wirth (1938), Georg Simmel (1969) and Robert E. Park (1925), defined the unique characteristic of the city and its modes of collectivity in immaterial, relational terms. In his seminal article 'Urbanism as a Way of Life' – an article we shall return to in more detail below – Wirth described the city as engine of difference and diversity:

The city has thus historically been the melting-pot of races, peoples, and cultures, and a most favorable breeding-ground of new biological and cultural hybrids. It has not only tolerated but rewarded individual differences. It has brought together people from the ends of the earth *because* they are different and thus useful to one another, rather than because they are homogenous and like-minded.

(1938: 10, italics in the original)

The resulting 'intensification of nervous stimulation' (Simmel, 1969: 48) is the distinguishing feature of urban life, according to this early literature. Elaborating further Park argued that the city is not the sum of 'congeries of individual men and of social conveniences' such as streets, buildings, etc. but a 'state of mind, a body of customs and traditions, and of the organized attitudes and sentiments that inhere in these customs and are transmitted with these traditions' (1925: 1). As an economic unit the city is a mix of place, people, machinery and 'administrative devices' that are organically related – 'a kind of psychophysical mechanism in and through which private and political interests find not merely a collective but a corporate expression' (1925: 2). The city does not simply provide the stage for its inhabitants to act out their scripts; rather, they are 'characteristic products of the conditions of city life' (1925: 14): the news reporter, the bartender, the stockbroker, the shop girl, the police officer, and a myriad of other roles come into existence as correlate of urban life. This is an important observation: far from being a resource waiting for the appropriator to deploy it, the city constitutes its subjects (for an alternative discussion of urban commons which also establishes links to Chicago sociologists, see Susser and Tonnelat, 2013). Or as Jerram argues in his contribution to this volume, particular urban commons are not simply out there, waiting to be exploited; rather they must first be produced and then constantly reproduced.

Many of the following landmark contributions to urban studies from the twentieth century, including Robert Venturi et al.'s *Learning from Las Vegas* (1972), Reyner Banham's *Los Angeles: The Architecture of Four Ecologies* (1971), Jane Jacobs' *The Death and Life of Great American Cities* (1961), and Richard Sennett's *The Uses of Disorder* (1970), would similarly define the city as a cultural, social, political, and ecological network; like any network it is constituted by the relational linkages between its elements. Restating the important analytical point for this volume from a different perspective: the commons is not a pooled resource; in contrast to water, grass or fresh air, the urban only comes into existence through the encounter of people, things and ideas. Density and proximity are the intangible fibres that are woven into the fabric of the urban commons. Far from being a 'pool', the urban commons is seen here as the corollary of interactions in a dense network.

The notions of interactions and networks take us back to the question of urban collectivity (or, as it would be phrased in network terms, connectivity).

What we want to suggest in the following is that especially Wirth's analysis of the city provides an interesting entry into discussing in more detail how collectivity could be conceived of when speaking of urban commons.[5] Like Howard, Wirth understands cities as dense relational configurations. In the words of Wirth, cities are 'relatively large, dense, and permanent settlements of heterogeneous individuals' (1938: 1). The large number of city-dwellers and the relative scarcity of space that gives rise to density fuel the relational nature of the city and the kinds of collectivity it engenders. Heterogeneity too carries a reference to relationality, as heterogeneity is only relevant to the extent that the heterogeneous inhabitants of a city are brought into some form of relation with one another (and are not neatly divided into distinct, spatially segregated sectors, see 1938: 10). Yet whereas for Howard the relationality of the city is something that constitutes value and can therefore be capitalized on, Wirth takes a more ambivalent stance. On the one hand, Wirth asserts, urban heterogeneity contributes to the alleged 'sophistication and cosmopolitanism of the urbanite', as the latter is constantly exposed to shifting forms of collectivity (or 'group membership', as Wirth calls it; see 1938: 16). On the other hand, he states, this fluctuating nature of the city, with all the differentiation it entails, also has a levelling, depersonalizing effect, where '[i]ndividuals who [due to the fleeting nature of their social relations] are thus detached from the organized bodies which integrate society comprise the fluid masses that make collective behavior in the urban community so unpredictable and hence so problematical' (1938: 17).

Problematic for Wirth is not just the unpredictable nature of collective behaviour, but also, and especially, the kind of de-individualization it entails. Thus, Wirth in effect sees the city as a hotbed of 'mass suggestion', including the 'mass appeals made through modern propaganda techniques' (1938: 17, 18). Linking cities and the theoretical repertoire of crowd and mass psychology (with its emphasis on the de-individualization that allegedly comes with highly suggestible crowds and masses) is not singular to Wirth, but common to a wide range of American observers of modern cities in the late nineteenth and early twentieth centuries, including Ross, Park and others (see Borch, 2012: ch. 4). What is important in this literature is that cities are seen as being particularly prone to forms of collectivity that suppress or at least suspend individuality. Indeed, many scholars at this time would associate collective behavior primarily with destruction and the tearing down of social order. Yet whereas, for instance, Park would also attribute to collective behaviour the ability to liberate individuals from narrowing ties by creating new social forms, Wirth presents a bleaker picture where massification means being subjected to power, something that is only enhanced in an era of mass

5 So, *contra* Harvey (2012) who finds inspiration in Marx, we believe that the Chicago School is a more apt place to begin the discussion of urban commons.

communication. He states, for example, that 'the masses of men in the city are subject to manipulation by symbols and stereotypes managed by individuals working from afar or operating invisibly behind the scenes through their control of the instruments of communication' (1938: 23).

Crowding and massification point to density, and in fact the density Wirth ascribes to the city can be located on two levels. On the one level, the city is characterized by density because large numbers of people are populating a limited space. This is an immediate form of density. Yet, density may also be related to another level, namely the forms of collective (crowd) behaviour, and their depersonalizing effects, which Wirth associates with cities. To see this link it is helpful to turn to the work of Boris Sidis whose 1898 book *The Psychology of Suggestion* was praised by William James because in it, ' "crowd psychology" is discussed, almost for the first time in English' (James, 1898: vii; Sidis, 1898). According to Sidis:

> If anything gives us a strong sense of our individuality, it is surely our voluntary movements. [. . .] Now nowhere else, except perhaps in solitary confinement, are the voluntary movements of men so limited as they are in the crowd; and the larger the crowd is the greater is this limitation, the lower sinks the individual self. *Intensity of personality is in inverse proportion to the number of aggregated men.*
>
> (1898: 299, italics in the original)

What Sidis' analysis suggests is that the crowd is a kind of intensive microcosm of the city. What applies to the city applies even more to the crowd, namely that the dense collective configuration undermines individuality. An important consequence of this for the discussion of urban commons is that both the city and the crowd signify modes of sociality where *commoning* can take place, without this necessarily being a matter of individuals pursuing their singular interests. To put it in Hardin's vocabulary, this part of Wirth's (and Sidis') work implies a focus on the herd rather than the herdsmen. The commons to be examined is the one that is shared by the herd, not the one shared by the herdsmen.

This also means that if, for Wirth, there is any tragedy of the commons in the city it lies not so much in the incentive to overuse limited shared resources, but rather in the above-mentioned ambivalence: the city constitutes a remarkable commons where people are exposed to and actually do share various forms of group membership; however, it is a commons that is vulnerable to fragmentation, since the differentiation of groups is tightly linked to the risk of losing one's personality and unwittingly submitting to de-individualizing forms of collectivity (such as for instance Sloterdijk's notion of atmospheric politics would point to). More precisely, therefore, the tragedy for Wirth is not so much a tragedy of the urban commons as of the *urban commoners*: the city is a place where individuals are at risk of being transformed into dopes not able to pursue their independent individual interests. Importantly, this diagnosis shares Hardin's analytical starting point, namely the individuals (the herdsmen) and their interests. But by taking seriously, such as for example Park does, that crowds constitute a social order that, given its emergent nature, cannot be reduced to a mere aggregation of individuals, and therefore also cannot be adequately analyzed on the basis of any methodological individualism, the notion transpires that the city is also a place for *commoning*,[6] and that commoning as such should not be seen as a tragedy (after all, commoning means assembling socially). This is what the commons of the herds refers to, a commons not locked in Hardin's conceptual (basically individualistic) trap.

One final comment is warranted on Wirth's perspective and its relation to discussions of urban commons. As his ambivalent notion of the city testifies to, Wirth is anything but an urban romantic. The city makes possible new forms of sociality and collectivity as well as a particular urban personality, but the price for this is a series of destructive effects, including '[p]ersonal disorganization, mental breakdown, suicide, delinquency, crime, corruption, and disorder', which are all said to 'be more prevalent in the urban than in the rural community' (1938: 23). Even more important, the fragmentation of social groups in the city means that urban inhabitants can chose from a large pool of social relationships, but these may be neither compatible with nor friendly towards one another. Indeed, Wirth states, the highly differentiated nature of these groups may 'occasionally [give rise to] bitter strife, but always the sharpest contrast', meaning that 'the city as a community resolves itself into a series of tenuous segmental relationships' (1938: 20, 23) – not dissimilar to the 'polyatmospheric' nature of the city that Sloterdijk emphasizes. The corollary of this insight is that the city is not a frictionless agglomeration of commoners, but rather a site for ongoing contestation about what counts as common and who counts as commoners – a point developed in various ways in the contributions to this volume

Overview of the chapters

Three theoretical propositions were put forward in this introduction. The first was to understand the commons not as a resource that is diminished through (over-)use but instead to investigate how the urban commons is entangled in and contingent upon its consumption. The theoretical inspiration for this suggestion stems from Howard and his theory of urban value as a relational

6 Harvey (2012: 73) also defines the commons not as resource or asset but as an 'unstable and malleable social relation' and suggests understanding it as a verb – *commoning* as social practice. Similarly, Linebaugh argues that '[i]t might be better to keep the word [commons] as a verb, an activity, rather than as a noun, a substantive' (2008: 279).

concept. Second, we proposed shifting the analytical focus from the herdsmen to the herd, or less metaphorically, with Wirth: to understand the commons as a product of density and theorize the specific form of population density as a process of commoning that constitutes subjects and new forms of collectivity. Third, and closely related to the two previous points, we argued for downplaying the nostalgia often associated with the commons and for critically scrutinizing some of the powerful processes of commoning, both with respect to how they come into being and how they operate and are maintained. In other words, commons, and urban commons, are not just about *opposing* power and capitalism, such as the commons literature's frequent references to community gardens misleadingly suggest (e.g. Bollier, 2002; Linebaugh, 2008); all sorts of power and politics go into how commons are produced, also in ways that demonstrate that what is common is not equally common to *all*. Or, as Mezzadra and Neilson put it, '[d]ifferent commons can have radically different kinds of legal and political constitution' (2013: 278).

The chapters in this volume continue this work of translating literatures on the commons and the city in order to illustrate the subtleties and intricacies of the urban commons. The contributions to this volume are divided into three matters of concern.

Theorizing the urban commons

'The city is not a Menschenpark: Rethinking the tragedy of the urban commons beyond the human/non-human divide' is what Jonathan Metzger asks for in his contribution to this volume. The argument assembled under this fortifying chapter heading goes to the philosophical heart of the urban commons debate. Metzger points out that most scholars of urban commons take for granted that there are subjects who *use* the commons and objects that *are* the commons. Usually, this divide is deepened by reserving the label of 'human' for the former and a range of others including 'means', 'resources', 'nature', 'environment', etc. for the latter. Based on theoretical resources such as Sloterdijk and actor-network theory, Metzger shows how we can understand the urban commons beyond the taken-for-granted ontological divide between humans and non-humans and how such an understanding can help in realizing the 'deep entanglements' of diverse agents that underpin the construction and deconstruction of urban commons.

Leif Jerram's contribution entitled 'The false promise of the commons: Historical fantasies, sexuality and the 'really-existing' urban common of modernity' investigates the theoretical terrain in which the debates around the commons have been unfolding. From the historian's perspective he argues that despite different definitions of the commons, scholars share a style of arguing – call it an 'academic mood' – when it comes to reflecting on and writing about the commons. The commons as a peaceful, just and hence desirable state of affairs is imagined as a historical artefact – as something that has a past that can be found and perhaps re-connected to. As analytical counter-strategy Jerram offers an analysis of how the modern city was transformed into a specific type of urban commons. He describes the production of urban commons in the form of guides to sites of 'gay' sexuality in London and Berlin. His story that traces the 'practitioners of the appropriation of urban space' is a critique of the market vs. state duopoly underpinning most commons theorizing and offers a more nuanced, ambivalent and (if the word is allowed) truthful account of a concrete practice of commoning.

Practices and processes of commoning

In his chapter 'Sharing an atmosphere: spaces in urban commons' Orvar Löfgren investigates the norms, routines and competences that allow people with no knowledge of each other to create temporary forms of urban commons. Löfgren takes Harvey's notion of commoning as his point of departure which allows him to study the 'unstable and malleable processes' through which different users co-inhabit and regulate a public space. Löfgren uses two most apt empirical contexts for his inquiry: an ethnography of a railway station and an urban beach that illustrate the everyday ways in which modes and moods of use are related in these two forms of urban commons.

Patrik Zapata's and María José Zapata Campos's chapter deals with 'Producing, appropriating and recreating the myth of the urban commons'. Usually, the authors argue, commons is associated with green pastures, fresh water and clean air. But for some urban dwellers, the urban commons is waste. The authors explain how urban waste is transformed into a form of urban commons. By taking the reader on a journey through an open waste dump in Managua, Nicaragua, the everyday practices of commoning are illustrated vividly. The authors show how commoners act as 'informal entrepreneurs' who develop collectively creative and sustainable ways to manage their own urban commons.

Organizing (managing) the commons

How are urban commons rendered visible so that the public, experts and others can argue for, against, or on behalf of them? This question drives Martina Löw's chapter on 'Managing the urban commons: Public interest and the representation of interconnectedness'. In her contribution she explores the conflict arising between public interests associated with the commons and the representation of these interests by experts and professionals. Löw explores two widespread modi of managing this conflict. She identifies one as a consensual approach whereas the other manages the urban commons through creating spheres of relative autonomy which different groups can appropriate. Löw introduces a third governance model which is based on contemporary theories of space. Using a planning process in Frankfurt am Main, Germany, as empirical counter-narrative, she argues that the mapping of multiple and multi-layered connections between social groups could serve as a basis for representation in plural societies and thus help professionals as well as citizens in their understanding and efforts of commoning.

Greg M. Nielsen's chapter 'Mediated exclusions from the urban commons: Journalism and poverty' adds a critical dimension to research on the urban commons. He argues that the commons does not exist as a shared resource but is negotiated and argued over, and that antagonisms, infringements and metaphorical overgrazing against the 'covenant' or regulations have to be called by someone in order to be seen, to be made public – and this is the role that journalists and newspapers play in public life. Nielsen analyzes how journalism produces an 'imagined urban commons' which constructs a notion of the urban poor and how they relate to the urban commons. He concludes that imagined urban commons is a discourse that makes commoners and practices of commoning tangible and hence open for intervention – without giving the subjects concerned with the urban commons a voice in the process. Based on a framing analysis of newspaper articles on poverty in North American cities Nielsen shows how the voices of the poor and homeless find their way into the public dialogue, and how this affects the perceived and real struggles over the urban commons.

In her chapter 'Communities and the commons: Open access and community ownership of the urban commons' Maja Hojer Bruun analyzes Danish housing cooperatives as a form of urban commons. Focusing on the commoners, Bruun argues that members of the cooperatives who own shares in the buildings they live in are not the only legitimate owners. Rather, she argues that cooperative members are 'stewards of a commons', which they inhabit but hold only temporarily. This perspective puts into focus the communities who actually use a specific type of urban commons, and the practices through which they argue for their right to the commons.

Conclusion

We mentioned above that the writings assembled in this volume are translations of the long-standing concepts of the commons and the city. Yet in his essay 'The Task of the Translator', Walter Benjamin reminds us that translation is not repetition but a generative act:

> Just as a tangent touches a circle lightly and at but one point, with this touch rather than with the point setting the law according to which it is to continue on its straight path to infinity, a translation touches the original lightly and only at the infinitely small point of the sense, thereupon pursuing its own course according to the laws of fidelity in the freedom of linguistic flux.
>
> (1982: 80)

This volume touches upon circles in the commons literature (mainly the Hardin–Ostrom debate) and writings on the city in all its polyatmosphericity (to bastardize a Sloterdijkian term), but it touches these circles lightly, at the 'infinitely small point' of the sense they make, in order to illuminate that sense, but also in order to use that sense as a pointer for its own intellectual trajectories.

What we hope to achieve with our collective translations is to move discussions of urban commons some steps forward and to point to timely topics and directions of research not yet explored in the literature. As we have tried to demonstrate in this introduction, debates about cities and commons can certainly inform one another. But uncritically transplanting the notion of the commons to the urban domain is doomed to fail. Rather, translation, to keep it in Benjamin's vocabulary, requires us to substantially rethink what an urban commons is, and how processes of commoning unfold. The present volume invites scholars to do precisely that and to speculate what conception of the city might arise as a result – either through empirical work or, as we have done in this introduction, by enacting the urban commons 'translation' through an engagement with wider debates in philosophy and social theory. Taking up and developing these translations further might well, we hope, be a common project.

References

Banham, R. (1971) *Los Angeles: The Architecture of Four Ecologies*. Berkeley, Los Angeles and London: University of California Press.

Benjamin, W. (1982) 'The Task of the Translator: An Introduction to the Translation of Baudelaire's *Tableaux Parisiens*', in *Illuminations* (pp. 69–82). London: Fontana/Collins.

Benkler, Y. (2002) 'Coase's Penguin, or, Linux and the nature of the firm', *The Yale Law Journal* 112(3): 369–446.

Benkler, Y. (2006) *The Wealth of Networks: How Social Production Transforms Markets and Freedom*. New Haven and London: Yale University Press

Blomley, N. (2008) 'Enclosure, Common Right and the Property of the Poor', *Social Legal Studies* 17(3): 311–31.

Bollier, D. (2002) *Silent Theft: The Private Plunder of Our Common Wealth*. New York and London: Routledge.

Borch, C. (2008) 'Foam architecture: managing co-isolated associations', *Economy and Society* 37(4): 548–71.

Borch, C. (2012) *The Politics of Crowds: An Alternative History of Sociology*. Cambridge: Cambridge University Press.

Böhme, G. (2006) *Architektur und Atmosphäre*. Munich: Wilhelm Fink Verlag.

Böhme, G. (2014) 'Urban Atmospheres: Charting New Directions for Architecture and Urban Planning', in C. Borch (ed.), *Architectural Atmospheres: On the Experience and Politics of Architecture* (pp. 42–59). Basel: Birkhäuser.

Foster, S.R. (2011) 'Collective Action and the Urban Commons', *Notre Dame Law Review* 87(1/2): 57–134.

Gudeman, S. (2001) *The Anthropology of Economy: Community, Market, and Culture*. Oxford: Blackwell.

Hardin, G. (1968) 'The Tragedy of the Commons', *Science* 162(3859): 1243–8.

Hardt, M. and Negri, A. (2004) *Multitude: War and Democracy in the Age of Empire*. New York: The Penguin Press.

Hardt, M. and Negri, A. (2009) *Commonwealth*. Cambridge, MA: The Belknap Press of Harvard University Press.

Harvey, D. (2012) *Rebel Cities: From the Right to the City to the Urban Revolution*. London and New York: Verso.

Hess, C. and Ostrom, E. (2007a) 'Introduction: An Overview of the Knowledge Commons', in C. Hess and E. Ostrom (eds), *Understanding Knowledge as a Commons: From Theory to Practice* (pp. 3–26). Cambridge, MA: The MIT Press.

Hess, C. and Ostrom, E. (eds) (2007b) *Understanding Knowledge as a Commons: From Theory to Practice*. Cambridge, MA: The MIT Press.

Howard, E. (1965) *Garden Cities of To-Morrow*. Cambridge, MA: The MIT Press.

Jacobs, J. (1961) *The Death and Life of Great American Cities*. New York: Random House.

James, W. (1898) 'Introduction', in B. Sidis *The Psychology of Suggestion* (pp. v–vii). New York and London: D. Appleton and Company.

Linebaugh, P. (2008) *The Magna Carta Manifesto: Liberties and Commons for All*. Berkeley, California: University of California Press.

Mattei, U. (2014) 'Eine kurze Phänomenologie der Commons', in S. Helfrich and Heinrich-Böll-Stiftung (eds), *Commons. Für eine neue Politik jenseits von Markt und Staat*. Second edition (pp. 70–8). Bielefeld: Transcript.

McCullough, M. (2013) *Ambient Commons: Attention in the Age of Embodied Information*. Cambridge, MA and London: The MIT Press.

Mezzadra, S. and Neilson, B. (2013) *Border as Method, or, the Multiplication of Labor*. Durham and London: Duke University Press.

Ostrom, E. (1990) *Governing the Commons: The Evolution of Institutions for Collective Action*. Cambridge: Cambridge University Press.

Ostrom, E. (2009) Nobel Prize Lecture: 'Beyond Markets and States: Polycentric Governance of Complex Economic Systems'. Online. Available HTTP: <http://www.nobelprize.org/nobel_prizes/economic-sciences/laureates/2009/ostrom-lecture.html> (accessed 1 August 2014).

Park, R.E. (1925) 'The City: Suggestions for the Investigation of Human Behavior in the Urban Environment', in R.E. Park, E.W. Burgess and R.D. McKenzie (eds), *The City* (pp. 1–46). Chicago and London: University of Chicago Press.

Parker, P. and Johansson, M. (2012) 'Challenges and potentials in collaborative management of urban commons'. Malmö: Unpublished paper.

Parr, A. (2014) 'Urban Debt, Neoliberalism and the Politics of the Commons', *Theory, Culture and Society*: onlineFirst. Online. Available HTTP: <http://tcs.sagepub.com/content/early/2014/06/16/0263276414536234.full.pdf+html> (accessed 1 August 2014).

Sennett, R. (1970) *The Uses of Disorder: Personal Identity and City Life*. New Haven and London: Yale University Press.

Sidis, B. (1898) *The Psychology of Suggestion: A Research into the Subconscious Nature of Man and Society*. New York and London: D. Appleton and Company.

Simmel, G. (1969) 'The Metropolis and Mental Life', in R. Sennet (ed.), *Classic Essays on the Culture of Cites* (pp. 47–60). New York: Appelton-Century-Crofts.

Sloterdijk, P. (1998) *Sphären I. Blasen: Mikrosphärologie*. Frankfurt am Main: Suhrkamp.

Sloterdijk, P. (1999) *Sphären II. Globen: Makrosphärologie*. Frankfurt am Main: Suhrkamp.

Sloterdijk, P. (2004) *Sphären III. Schäume: Plurale Sphärologie*. Frankfurt am Main: Suhrkamp.

Susser, I. and Tonnelat, S. (2013) 'Transformative cities: The three urban commons', *Focaal: Journal of Global and Historical Anthropology* 66: 105–32.

Venturi, R., Brown, D.S. and Izenour, S. (1972) *Learning from Las Vegas*. Cambridge, MA: The MIT Press.

Weber, S. (2004) *The Success of Open Source*. Cambridge and London: Harvard University Press.

Wirth, L. (1938) 'Urbanism as a Way of Life', *American Journal of Sociology* 44(1): 1–24.

Chapter 1

The city is not a Menschenpark

Rethinking the tragedy of the urban commons beyond the human/ non-human divide

Jonathan Metzger

> the possibility of belonging to the order of the city is entirely dependent on a radical exclusion of the 'victim' from the benefits of membership.
>
> Nick Lee and Paul Stenner, *Who Pays?*
> *Can We Pay Them Back?*

> 'we' no longer know *who* we are, nor of course *where* we are, we who had believed we were modern . . . End of modernization. End of story. Time to start over.
>
> Bruno Latour, *An Inquiry into Modes of Existence:*
> *An Anthropology of the Moderns*

Urban commons is a concept that is currently 'trending' in the social sciences. Most of this presently emerging research more or less uncritically builds upon the influential theory of the commons presented by Nobel laureate Elinor Ostrom, and generally focuses upon issues regarding the production, maintenance and access to various forms of urban common goods. One thing that the interlocutors in the expanding academic debate on the urban commons appear to take for all but granted is that the *subjects* of the commons, the commoners, are presumably always 'human', and that the *objects* constituting the commons are presumably always non-human. I want to argue that this taken-for-granted ontological divide between subjects and objects, humans and non-humans, means and ends, resources and extractors, is far too self-assured and remains dangerously unquestioned in this literature. In the light of a dawning understanding of the fundamental ecological entanglements of humanity, we must learn to rethink previously taken-for-granted ontological categories such as culture/nature and human/non-human, destabilizing them to do away with destructive preconceptions that place humans on one side and non-humans on the other. We need, for instance, to recognize that any neat separation of 'commons' on the one hand and 'commoners' on the other involves what philosopher Karen Barad calls an 'agentic cut', and as such bears with it an undisavowable ethico-political burden of responsibility to attend to the effects of any such enactment of ordering categories (Barad, 1998; see further Metzger, 2014).

In this chapter I wrestle with these questions by way of an examination of the historical and contemporary relations between humans and other-than-human animals in European cities, both as concretized/concretizing ideals and as living assemblages. The questions I ask are: how can we understand the urban commons beyond a taken-for-granted ontological divide between humans and non-humans, nature and culture? How can we learn to recognize the deep entanglements in urban areas between those things we normally categorize under these labels in the complex and constantly evolving milieus we describe as 'urban'? Admittedly, this to some degree pertains to a deconstruction of the concept of the urban commons, although not in the form of an undifferentiated critical gesture, but rather proceeding from Karen Barad's (1998: 104) insight that:

> the political potential of deconstructive analysis lies not in the simple recognition of the inevitability of exclusions, but in insisting upon accountability for the particular exclusions that are enacted and in taking up responsibility to perpetually contest and rework the boundaries.

The chapter is structured in the following way: I first present a short empirical vignette that will function as an opening into the wider issues discussed in the text. I then proceed to explicate what I see as some of the trouble with dominant Western historical and contemporary cultural preconceptions regarding 'the urban', which also frame much of the debate on urban commons. In a generally sympathetic but also perhaps somewhat against-the-grain reading of philosopher Peter Sloterdijk's *Rules For The Human Zoo*, I argue that it is precisely as this – an exclusively human zoo – that the city has been conceptualized in much of the Western cultural tradition. In the following section I show how these preconceptions also underpin current and previous debates about 'the commons' in general, and so-called 'urban commons' in particular. I try to destabilize these preconceptions through posing the question if we can ever easily demarcate what constitutes 'commoners' and what constitute 'commons' in complex ecological entanglement, ending up in asking with Bruno Latour: how can we relate to an urban 'we', a collectif of the urban commons, in a responsible way in the Anthropocene?

Wolf in the city

On the night between the 6th and 7th of May 2001 a wolf passed through innermost Stockholm, going south to north along the transport infrastructure originally planned for maximizing human mobility, such as the towering Västerbron bridge across Riddarfjärden. This first recorded wolf passage through Stockholm since the eighteenth century aroused more curiosity than fear and the wolf soon turned out to be but a temporary visitor, a young male on a quest for a soulmate – which we know can carry humans as well as other animals on the most improbable of journeys. The wolf also made his way duly and promptly to greener pastures – quite literally. When tracked down en route through the city, the wolf was given police escort through downtown to get him out as quickly as possible, either by his own will and power or – if necessary – by force. After being tracked down, he was constantly followed at close distance by a zoologist who kept the wolf on mark with a tranquilizer gun in case he showed any aggressive tendencies or any tendencies towards wishing to dwell for a more prolonged period of time in highly populated areas.

Since then, wolf sightings have become quite recurrent in the Stockholm area as a result of the increase in the domestic wolf population during recent decades. In 2012 there were around 100 reported sightings in the greater Stockholm area, a handful of which were also positively confirmed by authorities. Zoologists have argued that this can be seen as evidence of the recent reactivation of a historical wolf's north–south migratory route, as the straits on which the city is located constitutes a natural passage point across the extensive Läke Mälaren, which cuts through a large part of the geographical middle part of Sweden. The increased intensity of wolf sightings, and a few wolf attacks, mostly on dogs, in the close vicinity of Stockholm have started to generate some fears among urban dwellers of the growing national population of the large canine predator, which otherwise has been subject to some romanticization among Swedish urbanites.

The established protocol of close police observation and escort of any wolf that strays into the Stockholm area, to get it out of the city as quickly and smoothly as possible (but preferably without the use of violence) – and the associated feelings that even though wolves are great to have in the countryside, they certainly do not belong in the city – are, although quite understandable reactions in themselves, also clearly indicative of how wildlife – and especially major predators – is seen to be completely anathema to the idea of the city, its mere presence constituting a major disruption or transgression (see also Hiedanpää, 2013). As noted by Philo and Wilbert (2000: 10), many forms of human discourse 'include a strong envisaging of both where animals are placed in the abstract "scheme of things" and where they should be found in the non-discursive spaces and places of the world'. In the so-called Western world, most animals have at least for the past 200 years or so generally been seen as disturbances, threats or hazards by those who have been vested with the power and responsibility to govern urban space – leading to an ever expanded project of evacuating the presence of living animals out of cities.[1]

---

1 To generalize it could be claimed that roughly from the mid-1800s onwards, the presence of animals in urban areas was in Western Europe only accepted in highly demarcated, contained and controlled designated nature-zones such as city parks or botanical/zoological gardens, or in the form of highly domesticated house pets (but see Holmberg, 2013)

But further it could even be argued that also before this, perhaps as far back as antiquity, the Western *idea* of the city has generally been formulated as the ideally exclusive dwelling of humans, standing in direct contrast to the savage nature imagined to exist outside of the city walls. Walls that both physically and symbolically have been seen as generating a protective space in which the unique and supposedly superior traits that have been thought to distinguish humans from animals could be cultivated and fostered.

Ecologizing the urban commons

Relating to the vignette above, it could be argued that there exists a deeply-ingrained Western cultural preconception concerning the otherness of animals to urbanity. An idea that animals simply do not belong in the city – reflecting long-held cultural preconceptions about the 'cultural' achievement of the human-populated city as being the opposite of the 'natural' endowment of animal-infested wilderness, and further positing that these are categories that are ontologically mutually opposed and therefore should be kept apart and purified both conceptually and spatially.[2] As urban historian Christopher Otter has noted, 'civilized society [. . .] was measured by its distance from nature, a distance as much material as moral or spiritual' (Otter, 2004: 46). Nevertheless, the other-than-human animal was never completely successfully expelled from the city – nor from the human for that matter – and in this chapter I argue that it neither can, nor should be.

Rather, in thinking about the city in general, and about urban commons in particular, we need to learn to come to grips with how we can make sense of these phenomena in what we, with Sarah Whatmore, can call a *more-than-human* way (Whatmore, 2002; Hinchliffe and Whatmore, 2006). Such a new handle on 'urban things' could function as a foundation of a new general ecological sensibility that could be argued to constitute a key component in a future survival strategy for our rapidly urbanizing, but also currently highly self-destructive species. In relation to the concept of the urban commons, this is particularly important, seeing that the dominant social scientific theories about commons management that are currently being widely cast as solutions for our unfolding multiple ecological crisis – such as Elinor Ostrom's celebrated theory of common pool resource management – still appear to lean

concerning the strong reactions when such house pets 'step out of place' in the city). Swyngedouw and Kaïka (2008) make the argument that modernist planners tried to infuse 'real nature' into the city, but also from a highly dualistic preconception regarding the *a priori* separation and mutual 'natural' exclusivity of the terms 'nature' and 'culture', i.e. 'wilderness' and 'city'.

2 See e.g. Philo (1995) who argues that many of the expulsions of animals, such as livestock, from the city have in hindsight been argued as rational on hygienic and medical grounds, but were in their time more often motivated by moral arguments rather than medical.

up against a foundational ontology that posits humanity as being primarily not *of* nature but rather *over* and *above* nature, thus imagining humans as superior world-makers and the shepherding crown of creation. In this chapter I try to make the argument that in the approaching impasse facing our species, such an ontological position is deeply problematic in relation to our ideas about commons, urban or otherwise.

I therefore try to do to Ostrom's argument what Michel Serres did to the story of Sisyphus and the rock (Serres, 1987: 301–2). Serres alerts us to how the retelling of this myth always puts the focus on the human character Sisyphus, while barely no attention is paid to thinking about the rock. Just as Serres wants to make the rock count and begin asking such questions as how we can care for the rock, which is so obviously repelled by the designs of men and gods, I want to ask the question about how we can begin to really care for the fate of some of the things, many of which are living, which we imagine as *commons* – and not just those we think of as the *commoners*. With Latour (1998) we may pose this as a project that counteracts the thoroughly modern perspective on the commons offered by Elinor Ostrom with the question: 'how may the commons be ecologized?'

This question is, in our current times, particularly relevant in relation to questions of urbanity and cities. Not only because since 2008, for the first time in history, the majority of the world's human population lives in towns and cities, with a steadily rising pace of global urbanization, but also because cities are global zones of intense exchange or interaction. In the words of historian Fernand Braudel, cities function as 'electric transformers' that 'increase tension, accelerate the rhythm of exchange and ceaselessly stir up men's lives' in relation to not only commerce, but also the circulation of cultural trends and ideas (Braudel, 1973: 373). Or as aptly formulated by Barbara Czarniawska (2002: 1), the city is 'a societal laboratory' and they have 'traditionally been the birthplaces of invention and innovation, but are also sites permitting intense imitation'. Cities are thus places where new things and ideas emerge and may take root. Finally, and in the context of this chapter, importantly: cities have historically also always been sites of cohabitation in the face of intense difference, thus generating philosophies and skills of conviviality among their inhabitants for not only living with and sharing space with – but also in various ways capitalizing on and appreciating – difference as for instance noted in seminal studies by Georg Simmel, Louis Wirth and Jane Jacobs. The city is thus a key space for anyone interested in suggesting new ways of living together across difference, an ambition which this chapter aligns itself with by making an alliance with the growing number of scholars who argue for the necessity of a new more-than-human sensibility as well as the development of political practices for urban multispecies conviviality (Hinchliffe and Whatmore, 2006).

I explicate the above line of argument through a reading of the Ostromian conceptualization of the urban commons that perhaps might to some degree amount to an operation similar to the telling description that philosopher Gilles Deleuze gave as to how he performed his readings of other philosophers: the act of having intellectual intercourse with an author in a way that is banned in many of the states of the US and then giving the author a child that would be its own offspring, yet monstrous to him or her. In this case, the ideosexual abuse is even worse since I am bringing a pack of, perhaps just as unwilling, bed partners with me – and foremost among them are philosophers Donna Haraway and Peter Sloterdijk, as well as a host of (more-than-)human geographers.

The city: a human zoo?

In Western philosophy there has ever since antiquity existed an interest in the role played by the built environment, and in particular the city, for the development of humanity – as evinced by the many pivotal discussions on the *polis* in Greek classical philosophy. In more recent times, many architects today allow themselves to be inspired by contemporary philosophy, and in the 1970s there was a wave of interest in the writings of Martin Heidegger, perhaps particularly the essay 'Building, Dwelling, Thinking' (reproduced in Heidegger, 1975), but many of these readings did not consider that Heidegger most often used the built environment in metaphorical terms, for instance stating that the house of being was language.

A few decades later, as the more superficial reading of Heidegger's work in architecture subsided and the trendy 'starchitects' moved on to appropriate philosophical buzzwords of more contemporary origin, philosopher Peter Sloterdijk embarked on a seminal project to more thoroughly develop a spatial philosophy inspired by, but also partially in response to, Heidegger. This project of 'Being and Space', as complementary and opposed to 'Being and Time', culminated in the great trilogy of *Sphereology* (Sloterdijk, 1998, 1999, 2004). But questions of spatiality, and particularly architecture and the built environment, are also central to the essay 'Rules for the Human Zoo' (Sloterdijk, 2009). The text, originally entitled *Regeln für den Menschenpark*, and also known as the *Elmauer Rede*, was first presented as a commentary at a small international philosophy conference in Elmau in 1999 and later became the focal point of one of those great public intellectual pitched battles that you only get in Germany. This is not the place to get into the details of that *Streit* (but see e.g. Varney Rorty, 2000), but suffice to say that on the back of it I see Sloterdijk as a risky thinker, in the positive Stengersian notion of that term, and the siren song of his work in my ears functions as a navigation mark which helps me calibrate my ethico-political compass, although not always necessarily along the same bearings that he points out. So I will move on and see what possible use can be made in this context of some of the ideas in the paper, keeping in mind that these are potentially explosive ideas that perhaps need to be handled with some care and delicacy.

Proceeding from a discussion of Heidegger's essay *Letter on Humanism*, Sloterdijk unfolds an argument about the technologies of producing humanity, what it is to be a (good) human, and how this is achieved by various means. He particularly highlights education – but also opens the door towards other techniques of cultivation of being-human, such as selective breeding (and genetic engineering as a contemporary powerful variant of this) arguing that these techniques are ancient and ever-present in the history of becoming-human. The question for Sloterdijk thus becomes, not whether we should cultivate – i.e. purposely form a specific version of being human – by way of selection or not, but rather how we can open a public discussion on what traits we should collectively agree on maximizing. Here Sloterdijk comments favorably on Nietzsche, saying that:

> He wants to reveal, by name and function, the people who until now have had a monopoly on the control of breeding – the priests and teachers who pretend to be friends of man – and to initiate a modern, momentous public battle between different breeders and breeding programs.
>
> (Sloterdijk, 2009: 22)

What in the present context is interesting is how Sloterdijk discusses the role played by the built environment in these cultivation programs. He notes that for the classical humanist, as well as for Heidegger, language is the house of being. But Sloterdijk adds to this that:

> as soon as speaking men gather into larger groups and not only connect themselves to linguistic houses but also build physical houses, they enter the arena of domestication. They are now not only sheltered by their language, but also tamed by their accommodations. In the Clearing, as its most obvious marks, appear the houses of men.
>
> (Sloterdijk, 2009: 21)

Based on a reading of Nietzsche, Sloterdijk further argues that the design of the houses contributes to generating specific forms of humanity, that tame and domesticate them in certain ways and in a particular direction, for good and for bad. To Sloterdijk then, the city is a human zoo – quite literally.

The Nietzschean contempt for the domesticated is well-known, and also reproduced by, for instance, Deleuze and Guattari in their discussion on becoming-animal in *A Thousand Plateaus* (Deleuze and Guattari, 1987) – and has been rightfully castigated by Donna Haraway for its overt sexist masculinism (Haraway, 2008: 30). But Sloterdijk is very careful not to fall into this trap when he notes that the question of *anthropotechnics*, techniques for cultivating particular human traits, is not a question of domestication or not, but rather about domestication towards *what ends* and cultivation to further *what traits*. Accordingly, Sloterdijk goes on to note that:

> Where there are houses, there are also decisions about who shall live in them. In fact, and through this fact, it is determined what type of community dwellers will be dominant. In the Clearing, it is revealed which enterprises are worth fighting for, as soon as men emerge as beings who form societies and erect social hierarchies.
>
> (Sloterdijk, 2009: 21)

The Heideggerian Clearing is in Sloterdijk's reading thus by no means a blissful location, but rather a very dangerous place – and the question who and what is made present in the light of the Clearing, or the expanse of the Agora in the Polis, is fundamental to the unfolding fate of humanity. Are there only naked individual and autonomous men present there, or are there always-already equipped and accompanied humans becoming-together with a myriad of others? This becomes a fundamental Cosmopolitical question (cf. Stengers, 2005), a battle of the fate of humanity as a species and her worlds. Further, Sloterdijk notes:

> Only in a few places is the veil of philosophical silence about man, the house and animals as a biopolitical unity lifted. What one would hear on the other side of that veil would be a whirlwind of references to problems that are so far too difficult for men.
>
> (Sloterdijk, 2009: 21)

This is a comment we have reason to keep in mind for the argument that I will attempt to unfold towards the end of this chapter.

The urban commons: background and 'state of the art'

The concept of 'the commons' made its grand entrance into the canon of social theory by way of Garrett Hardin's 1968 paper in *Science*, entitled 'The tragedy of the commons', which has – up until this day – been cited in close to a staggering 20,000 other scholarly publications. Considering how well cited it is, it is surprising to see how superficially it often appears to be read.

Hardin was a trained zoologist and biologist who later took up a professorship in human ecology, and his primary concern in the paper was to point to the insolvability of global ecological challenges under the then (and still) existing global institutional regime based on individual rights and sovereign statehood. In the text he sets forth a lucid and challenging argument, stating that the preservation of collective resources of a commons-type is a 'no technical solution problem', a game that can paradoxically only be won by abandoning the game as intuitively understood, and that successful management of crucial human life-supporting commons can only be achieved by radical institutional rearrangements or, as he puts it, a 'change in human values or ideas of morality' (Hardin, 1968: 1243).

To define the tragedy of the commons, Hardin borrows a definition of 'tragedy' from the philosopher Alfred North Whitehead, the essence of the term here not being unhappiness but rather 'the remorseless working of things' – and that any type of commons will be remorselessly and unavoidably subject to degrading and collapse is the argument eloquently elucidated by Hardin in the paper. Much of the paper is then a plea, not for privatization – as has later been claimed – but for moralization, education and legislation for the protection of fragile commons. It particularly argues that we need to impose strongly restrictive measures to curb human overpopulation of the planet through 'definite social arrangements' in the form of 'mutual coercion mutually agreed upon', finally ending up with the argument that in untenable situations, inaction and wait-and-see options do not amount to doing nothing, but rather to perpetuating and furthering impending disaster.

Considering Hardin's far-right eugenicist political leanings, I am sure I would not want to know the exact onus of the 'mutually agreed upon' coercive policies he particularly had in mind. Nevertheless, he makes a strong case for paying attention to what we today would perhaps call emergent effects in complex ecological systems of action that amount to an unintentional yet globally devastating carelessness generated as unintended consequences of the established political, social and economic mechanisms of Western democracies and the behaviours they produce. Writing in direct response to Hardin and his self-styled disciples, political scientist/institutional economist – and later, Nobel laureate – Elinor Ostrom developed an argument most cogently formulated in *Governing the Commons: The Evolution of Institutions for Collective Action* from 1990. Ostrom studied small and medium-sized ostensibly self-organized, stable collective governance arrangements of natural resource commons such as pastures, fisheries, water resources, etc. She discussed a number of prominent cases of such 'common pool resource management' arrangements and deduced eight so-called 'design principles' when such arrangements would be successful (Ostrom, 1990: 90):

1. clearly defined geographical and social boundaries for the resource, delineating who has the right to draw upon the resources as well as their extension;
2. locally based rules concerning the appropriation and provision of the resources;
3. collective-choice arrangements allowing the participation of the majority of resource appropriators in the definition of the arrangements;
4. ongoing monitoring and auditing performed by or accountable to the appropriators;

5. graduated sanctions that are imposed on those resource appropriators who violate community rules;
6. conflict-resolution mechanisms that are low-cost and local;
7. recognition by higher-level authorities of the community's right to self-organize;
8. more complex and extensive common-pool resource (CPR) arrangements should be institutionalized as multiple layers of nested enterprises, with smaller CPR units as the base.

To those of us who are not fully persuaded by the gospel, Ostrom's solution may actually have a little bit of the flavor of *Leviathan* meets *The Prince* in the formation of collective but very state-like institutions, and it can be more than a little bit difficult to discern how her suggested solution actually radically diverges from Hardin's propagation for 'collectively agreed upon coercion' beyond the focus on small or medium sized ostensibly self-organized human groups in contrast to Hardin's supposed (but – *nota bene* – never stated) focus on more centralized government.

This aspect of the argument – that the successful and stable collective management regimes of commons that she had studied were supposedly self-organized on the scale level of the collective of users, and hence did not involve coercive government imposition – was actually crucial to her line of reasoning, with its point directed towards Hardin. Many of Ostrom's disciples also appear to have extended her argument so as to claim that commons in *all* situations can be successfully managed in this way. But, as pointed out by Notre Dame law professor Nicole Stelle Garnett, Ostrom's optimism is not unbounded. Not only are some of the cases she discussed, such as the special water districts of southern California, actually special purpose local governments – hence making Ostrom's characterization of them as cooperative 'somewhat odd since they developed as a result of litigation spanning more than a decade' (Garnett, 2012: 2003). But, even more comprehensively, Ostrom takes great care to point out all the conditions under which her suggested solutions will by no means have a chance to work – which specifically relates to the types of situations that Hardin is interested in in his original paper, such as global environmental issues (see Ostrom, 1990: 183).

Inspired by the impressive research literature on commons' management that has followed in the wake of Hardin's and Ostrom's work, there today exists an emerging multidisciplinary research front relating specifically to *urban* commons. To give but a few examples:

•   The body of literature that conceptualizes *urban public space* as commons-type collective resources, where liberally inclined planning scholars such as Chris Webster and associates (e.g. Lee and Webster, 2006) have mobilized Hardin's paper in what could be called quite 'traditional' ways to make a strong argument for property rights and privatization of urban public spaces. In response to this type of argument, law scholars such as Garnett (2012) and Foster (e.g. 2006) have developed their own lines of argument that take a more ambivalent or sanguine approach regarding the potential of collective management of urban public space.

- Ecologists such as Johan Colding (e.g. Colding, 2012) and Thomas Elmqvist at Stockholm University (e.g. Borgström et al., 2006), who have built on Ostrom to make a counter-argument about the potential ecological gains of collective management of *urban green spaces* through, for instance, community gardens, allotments and other similar institutional set-ups.
- Activism-inclined radical urban theorists who discuss urban commons in the form of more or less formalized and extensive *cooperative urban communes* produced by active urban communing that generates common resource pools (see e.g. Gibson-Graham, 2011).
- Urban sociologists such as Parker and Johansson (2011), who in an interesting paper also mention some of the more *difficult-to-grasp urban amenities* of a commons-like type – atmospheric properties which to different aspects are often in urban studies somewhat feebly conceptualized as for instance 'social capital', 'attractiveness' and so-called 'Jacobs' externalities' or 'buzz'.

Parker and Johansson further make the interesting observation, worth keeping in mind for later on, that:

> an urban common is always an urban common for someone. An overgrown brownfield could be seen as something worthless – an urban wilderness but it could also be viewed as part of an evolving urban green belt, which could supply ecosystem services and therefore should be treated as an urban common.
>
> (Parker and Johansson, 2011: 7)

Mixed-up urban commons: cities as more-than-human ~~Zoo~~ Ooz

But now it is time to begin mixing things up: apples with oranges, men and beasts, commoners and commons. David Harvey has suggested that we need to reconceptualize the tragedy of the commons if we are not unwittingly to fall captive to most-often unreflectedly taken-for-granted but highly contingent assumptions concerning the *mis-en-scène*, the setup, so convincingly choreographed by Hardin in his seminal paper. For instance, in a recent commentary in *Radical History Review* Harvey (2011) asks why do we not instead of focusing on the untenability in the long term of the pasture as a common, rather focus on the detrimental effect of individual ownership of cattle? Following Harvey's cue to challenge the underlying assumptions of the commons-metaphor, I try to generate a similar move of *détournement* of Hardin's and Ostrom's well-rehearsed stories – but in a somewhat different direction.

In the introduction to her seminal book on commons-management, Ostrom likens CPR management to a type of 'organism', further spelling out that this organism is 'a type of *human* situation' (Ostrom, 1990: 26; italics added) – which may seem a somewhat odd statement when considering the central presence of all sorts of animals, organisms and things in the stories she narrates in her book, which are central to her argument – but in which all these non-humans become lumped together under the passive label of 'resources'. As noted in a paper by Jonas Bylund and Fred Saunders, the operationalization of Ostromian common pool resource theory in the form of community-based natural resource management is also all about '*human* use of *natural* resources' (Saunders and Bylund, 2010: 3). Humans on one side, everything else on the other – a strict ontological divide between human and non-human, commoner and common, agent and structure, extractor and resource, culture and nature, subject and object, active user and passively used. As Chris Philo (1995: 658) has written so cogently in a different context, for instance animals in the urban commons literature generally figure:

> merely as entities to be trapped, counted, mapped, and analysed; as beings whose lives are indelibly shaped by the uses that humans formulate for them, but whose fate resulting from these taken-for-granted uses (along with the human rationales behind these uses) are almost never subjected to critical scrutiny.
>
> (Philo, 1995: 658)

But if we allow ourselves to be inspired by scholars such as Bruno Latour and perhaps, particularly, Donna Haraway to examine these seemingly neat and mutually exclusive categories a little closer, we may begin to see that they are not so neatly separable and that any actual worldly occurrence always consists of complex entanglements of elements, phenomena and tendencies that on paper may seem neatly separated from each other, but which as they occur in the world always turn up as irrevocably entangled and therefore end up messing up all these seemingly neat categories. As Bruno Latour (1993) has observed concerning the 'modern Constitution', the peculiar Western programmatic ontological separation of 'things Natural' and 'things Cultural', this was only ever an ostensive separation, for in practice links between these categories always proliferated covertly, leading him to the conclusion that '[t]here are only natures-cultures, and these offer the only possible basis for comparison' (Latour, 1993: 104).

This even goes to the heart of what it means to be human, the problematic bundle of tangled cultural and biological relations that in various ways have come to be categorized as the essence of mankind. Freud's famous dictum 'the ego is not master in its own house' (Freud, [1917] 1955: 143), does take on entirely new meaning when taking into account the fact that the human genome is found in no more than 10 per cent of the cells constituting a human body, while the remaining 90 per cent are made up of bacteria, fungi, protists, etc. As Haraway says, this implies that humans are 'vastly outnumbered' in relation to their 'tiny companions' (Haraway, 2008: 2). Or perhaps more accurately, 'to be one is always to become with many', leading Anna Tsing to relate that 'human nature is an interspecies relationship' where the human psyche during a short period of time is a guest in, and a result of, the tangle of relations between heterogeneous materials and organisms within and outside of our bodies, forming what we chose to label 'human beings' (Tsing quoted in Haraway, 2008: 19). So not only have we, with Latour, 'never been Modern', we have further 'never been human', if we insist on defining humanity as a mode of being hermetically sealed-off from and standing above other forms of life and existence (Haraway, 2008: 305).

But in what direction would we be heading if we, skirting such a philosophy of human exceptionalism, instead take as foundational the irrevocably intertwined nature of human and non-human, the more-than-humanness of human existence and the fundamental human dependence on things and beings other-than-human both on the tiniest micro-level, the intermediate environmental level as well as the more recognized global macro-level to bear on the study of the city, and specifically, urban commons? Where can we find a handle, a starting point, for such a more-than-human conceptualization of urban areas and urban commons?

For starters, a more empirical and literally down-to-earth approach to 'urbanity' or 'citiness' might be one place to start. Here we can, for instance, home in on and put into focus what can perhaps be called the living *city* as a starting point for such a venture, rather than what could be called the conceptual *City*. What I mean here by the City, capital C, is not only the discursive city-as-concept and related webs of associations, with all the recurring connotations of exclusive humanness, culture, etc., but also all the highly material/izing practices that have as their aim and function to discipline unruly conurbations into something more closely resembling this imagined ideal City (see also Deleuze and Guattari, 1987: 431 ff.).

The ideas and ideals concerning what constitutes a 'proper City' thus, through concrete (in both meanings of that word) practices, reverberate and act upon living cities, constantly in various ways aiming at making cities more 'City-like' through producing and maintaining 'Citiness'. Historically, and to some extent up until this day, such City-making practices have had as their aim to generate the City as the antithesis of countryside and 'nature' – of purging nature from the spaces and materials it works on, thus separating 'nature from the city, both conceptually and materially' (Swyngedouw and Kaïka, 2008: 574). And as further observed by Wolch et al. (1995: 735) '[t]he ideals of urbanization were based on a notion of progress rooted in the conquest of nature by culture', leading to a 'splitting apart of the urban and the rural as distinctive entities conceptually associated with particular human activities and attributes [. . .] the industrial and civilised city, the agricultural and barbarian countryside' (Philo, 1995: 666 – further referencing Williams, 1973).

Specifically in relation to animals in the city, for instance Philo (1995) with regards to Great Britain, and Löfgren (1985) with regards to Sweden, have noted that in Western Europe, much of the programmatic evacuation of animals from cities occurred in the nineteenth century as 'urban and rural worlds were increasingly segregated' (Löfgren, 1985: 199), a process described by Atkins (2012) as 'the Great Separation' of urbanity and rurality that was enforced in nineteenth-century Western Europe.[3] The City, as produced and reproduced by these practices, has thus – through processes of separation and cleansing – been generated as the exclusive home of the human par excellence in dichotomous contrast to, and hence evacuated of, animals and animality through practices that function to produce urbanity in the image of the idealized Greek *polis*, the philosophical image of the ideal dwelling of rational men, and rational men [sic!] alone; truly a *Menschenpark*, an exclusively human zoo, with the purpose of domesticating the human race.

But if we look beyond these practices for producing citiness, for producing cities-imagined-as-City-should-be and projecting images of the ideal City onto material conurbations, and instead turn our attention to the materials these practices work upon – the unruly, sometimes chaotic messes we may perhaps call the 'really-existing' living cities of the world, we will of course see at once that these have always been and still are brim-full of animals, both domesticated, feral and wild, a 'shadow population of nonhumans spanning the phylogenetic scale' (Wolch et al., 1995: 736).

To give but a few haphazard examples:

- As has been noted by ecologist Thomas Elmqvist, 95 per cent of the domestic species of the state of Illinois live within the urban zoned areas of Chicago, which means that when restoration projects are initiated in former prairie areas of the state, the urban population of these species is used as a source population to populate the prairielands (Elmqvist, 2010).

3 See also the papers in Atkins (2012) for nuanced accounts of how this 'Great Separation' was enforced in some parts of Europe. In the context it is also important to keep in mind that in large parts of the world outside Europe the 'Great Separation' in human/animal urban co-habitation has never occurred, with much more generous cultural attitudes towards e.g. urban human–fowl/livestock co-habitation. Nevertheless, the contentiousness – at least in 'Western' eyes – of such habits is well-evinced by the constantly recurring warnings from epidemiologists (e.g. in connection with the recent outbreaks of international viral epidemics such as SARS and H1N1) that such habits may become sources for cross-species viral transmutations that can possibly lead to global pandemics, and therefore must be outlawed.

- In Sweden, 500 of the strictly protected species of flora and fauna on the red list of the Swedish *Artdatabanken*, the Swedish Taxonomy Initiative, can be found in urban areas. As stated by landscape ecologist Bo Eknert (2010), urban areas both in Sweden and internationally have become refuge for many endangered species, and even though urban milieus only comprise a measly few per cent of Sweden's surface, there are just as many red-listed species present there as in more geographically extensive types of milieus such as wetlands.

- Not only that: many of these species are also rapidly becoming specialized by adapting to the urban environment in what ecologists call 'speciation', for instance Hinchliffe and Whatmore (2006) have discussed how urban water voles in Britain may have changed their behaviours and begun to co-habit with rats, which they have not been known to do previously. Further, Urban Emanuelson (2010), professor at the Swedish Agricultural University, has claimed that B vitamin-enriched bread fed to swans by enthusiasts around Stockholm helps the species become more successful in their reproduction, and there even exist qualified reports of urban-dwelling coyotes in the US learning to cross streets with the help of traffic signals (Banks, 1993, quoted in Wolch et al., 1995).

So to recap: practices for disciplining unruly living cities to become more like the ideal City, the (Western) ideal of the perfect exclusively human polis, have never succeeded completely. Living cities, all over the world, have always been and are still full of animals. The production and reproduction practices of the City, even if constantly attempting to 'other' the animal, have repeatedly failed to completely cleanse the living cities of them. So even if 'the animal' is still not recognized as a resident of 'the City' in the conceptual reality of Western philosophy and culture, myriads of other-than-human living things still have cities as their permanent homes. Not yet wolves in Sweden, but foxes in London, deer in Stockholm, boars in Berlin, raccoons all over the US, possums in Australia, peregrine falcons in Birmingham, and rats, rabbits, pigeons, geese, dogs, bats, insects – the list goes on and on – all over the world.

Urban animals: intruders or commoners?

One of the great taken-for-granteds of both Hardin's and Ostrom's conceptualizations of the commons, as well as that of their disciples, is their clear and stable differentiation of commons and commoners, building upon a foundational view of the world in which humans are extractive actors and everyone or everything else is only a resource to be acted upon. Writing in this tradition Johan Colding (Colding, 2012, citing McCay, 2000) has claimed that the commoners of the past may be gainfully reconceptualized as the stakeholders of tomorrow – but then apparently taking it for evident that these are *human* commoners that should rather be thought of as *human* stakeholders. Leaving aside the thorny question of what defines a 'stakeholder' (see Metzger, 2013), we may nevertheless with Tryggestad et al. (2013) question the above assumption by asking: 'what if the stakeholder is a frog?', and with this begin to unsettle the taken-for-granted assumption that the circle of stakeholders to be taken into account in any situation or context is exclusively composed of humans. There are indeed some serious cosmopolitics played out in this question, and I would therefore – with the help of Tryggestad and colleagues – like to rephrase Colding's question and not ask whether the commoners of the past are the stakeholders of tomorrow, but rather if the *commons* of yesterday may be gainfully reconceptualized as the commoners of today, and thus bring the animals of the living cities into the urban *collectif* of the City (cf. Callon and Law, 1995; and also Latour, 2004). But nevertheless, for many, the question probably still remains: *why* would we want to do so?

I have already hinted towards an answer to the above question in the brief discussion of Haraway's concept of becoming-together, but to spell this out ever more clearly: at the current impasse of humanity's development as a species, currently becoming known as the geological epoch of the *Anthropocene* (Crutzen, 2002), the established illusion of humanity as standing outside of and above nature, which is found in its most pronounced form in what Latour (1993) calls 'the modern Constitution', has led up to the currently mounting global multidimensional ecological crisis (see e.g. Rockström et al., 2009; Zalasiewicz et al., 2010), prompting influential ecologists such as James Lovelock to call for humans to literally buy a gun and run for the hills (Lovelock, 2006).

In light of the above, Ostrom's claim that '[m]uch of the world is dependent on resources that are subject to the possibility of a tragedy of the commons' (Ostrom, 1990: 3), really appears as far too modest. For with the recognized advent of the Anthropocene, it is not just 'much of the world' that appears to be subject to the possibility of a tragedy of the commons. Rather, facing radical temperature increases from global warming that would in all probability throw the Earth's whole atmospheric system into a completely new state beyond all Holocenic stability parameters, what appears to be at stake is *the* world as we know it – and with that the fate of humanity as a species. In her book, Ostrom unswervingly and clearly excludes the type of challenge posed by our diminishing life-supporting global atmospheric commons from the range of challenges suitable for amendment through her proposed CPR management solution. She obviously sees no hope in utilizing her generic recipe for institutional design in such hard cases – an intuition that is seemingly repeatedly proven correct by the ongoing paralysis in negotiating an effective global climate protocol between nation-states. With these bleak prospects in mind, we may ask ourselves – is Lovelock's proposed solution of 'sustainable retreat' then the only remaining viable option?

If we return to Hardin's original text on the 'Tragedy of the commons' we see that what he actually most strongly argues for as the necessary basis for any solution to a global tragedy of the commons is not – as is often claimed – the forced mass sterilization of the poor and wretched, and neither is it extensive privatization of collectively owned resources, but rather a call for active effort towards changing fundamental values and related behaviours. So if we are of the vain persuasion that there may still be time, we should perhaps try to heed the call spelled out so clearly in the title of one of Sloterdijk's most recently translated books: *Du Musst dein Leben Ändern* (*You Must Change Your Life*) (Sloterdijk, 2013). But following Isabelle Stengers' (2005) injunction to collectivize the nagging but today generally individually- and internally-asked question 'what am *I* busy doing?' into a collective open question of 'what are *we* busy doing?', this should not be formulated in the form of the individual You, as implied in the title of Sloterdijk's book, but rather as the English, *collective* You (or more sensibly: *we*).

This would, in the current context, amount to attempts towards what Serres (2006) has called the necessary *mastery of mastery* for humanity, a realization that goes well beyond the so-called socio-ecological people of 'ecological literacy', and lying more in line with the fundamental insight of Darwin that all life on earth may well be knitted together in an 'inextricable web of affinities' (Darwin, 1859: 434). As poignantly formulated by the late eco-feminist Val Plumwood:

> If our species does not survive the ecological crisis, it will probably be due to our failure to imagine and work out new ways to live with the earth, to rework ourselves and our high energy, high consumption, and hyper-instrumental societies adaptively [. . .] We will go onwards in a different mode of humanity or not at all.
>
> (Plumwood, 2007: 1)

Such an insight in turn leads us towards what Helga Nowotny has called a politics of the 'expansive present', expanding the range of things and beings we need and can take into account here and now, rather than succumbing to paralyzed fretting about some distant, hazy future climate holocaust (Nowotny quoted in Marres, 2012: 144 ff.).

Towards a politics of conviviality in the urban commons: practical methods and troubling questions

Linking together the above intimations of Darwin, Serres, Plumwood and Nowotny and putting these in relation to the concept of 'the commons' and then also further on to issues of urbanity, will inevitably lead to the setting in motion of a slippage in perspectives. Suddenly, the classic objects of the commons such as fish and sheep do not only appear as dependent upon humans, and their good will and faith, for their continuing existence. 'We' humans, both as a species and as particular groups of humans, both generally and specifically, also appear as dependent on 'them', systematically, for our existence. As a consequence of this insight, there also arises the need to allow a further correlated shift by which we move away from seeing all the creatures and entities peopling the commons as mere passive objects, to instead incorporate them as active fellow subjects in the global commons with their own wishes and interests. Such a perspective would thus proceed from the understanding that '[h]umans are always, and have always been, enmeshed in social relations with animals to the extent that the latter, the animals, are undoubtedly *constitutive* of human societies in all sorts of ways. Humans are ecologically dependent on animals' (Philo and Wilbert, 2000: 2, italics added). Deborah Bird Rose (2012: 109) points out that the scientific term for this foundational ecological *inter*-dependence between species is *symbiotic mutualism*, and is ubiquitous to this planet on every thinkable scale of interaction.

But if we do accept not only the merits, but also the urgency of adopting such a new ecological sensibility which simultaneously takes life-engendering entanglements of local and planetary symbiotic mutualism as its point of departure – how may we reassemble the tragic story of the commons from such an angle, in the direction of a new trajectory towards the future? To begin with: we might come to see that the tragedy of the commons is not an exclusively human affair. It is a trope and/or mechanism that functions just as well in completely non-human situations: the bacteria which infect a body experience a tragedy of the commons. Further, our (here meaning human-induced and humanity-affecting) global atmospheric tragedy of the commons is also a tragedy affecting many others that are not in any way made visible as subjects in the ongoing dispersed deliberations concerning this and related issues. Third, and more specifically related to the particular subject of this chapter and collection, and further linking back to Sloterdijk's remark on our general ignorance of the 'biopolitical unity' of human, house and animal, there are most probably ever ongoing more-than-human urban tragedies of the commons that we humans today, to a large extent, still lack the technical apparatuses to detect, and further lack proper concepts and tools to even begin to sensitize us to them. But as Wolch (2002: 734) has noted, 'once we abandon a strict human-animal boundary with human subjects on one side and animal objects on the other, we seem to be obligated to figure them into our ethical considerations and everyday practice'.

To wrap up this chapter I now focus on this last point and make an attempt to begin to grapple a little bit with the challenge it poses. An interesting opening towards this is Hinchliffe's and Whatmore's (2006) thinking on trans-species urban conviviality, to quote: 'a political project that is concerned with a [. . .] broadly conceived accommodation of difference, better attuned to the comings and goings of the multiplicity of more-than-human inhabitants that make themselves at home in the city than conventional political accounts'. This is not just about learning about how humans and animals cope on their own with 'living in the city' but rather a program with a transformative ambition which purports to reassemble both ecologies as urban and cities as ecological through the conceptualization of urban inhabitants as always-already entangled and 'more-than-human; more-than-animal; more-than-plant [. . .] complex assemblages, mutually affecting and affected by their fields of becoming'. This is about the messy business of living together, across difference, always asymmetrically, but also always irrevocably entwined and also even partially co-dependent in various ways with things we consider other-than-ourselves – and to attune to these conditions.

If we are serious about ideas such as these, we must not shy away from the paramount challenges surrounding the development of methods to begin to tentatively practice this ethos, and we must certainly not fall prey to the idea that this will somehow grow 'naturally' from 'the inside'. Rather we must begin to think how we can technologically, in the broadest sense, begin to produce apparatuses of engagement that can help sensitize us to a more-than-human world of always asymmetric relationships of mutual becoming steeped in difference. It is about generating assemblages of enunciation (Deleuze and Guattari, 1987: 75 ff.) that do not fetishize human modes of subjectivity or the medium of spoken language as the only form of understandable and effective/affective communication. We need to begin to think with material semiotics and to read signals in other ways, not taking for granted that 'we can't know what they want, and neither do they'. For as any dog-owner or parent knows there are signals there to read if we only take the time and go through the pain and effort to attempt time and again to read them. So we should perhaps no longer ask ourselves the question, 'if nature could speak, what would it tell us?' and instead come to realize that myriads of creatures and beings are speaking to us all the time – if we just learn how to listen properly. The name of the game thus seems to be about learning to be affected in new ways, as argued by Émile Hache and Bruno Latour (2010).

Here, we can perhaps find inspiration in the affective innovations of art projects such as the machines for urban trans-species communication and affectation in Natalie Jeremijenko's *Ooz* (Zoo spelt backwards) or Fritz Haeg's *Animal Estates 1.0*, aiming at infusing new ecological sensibilities into the urban environment. In the latter project, Haeg put on display animal dwellings in prominent places in Manhattan, for instance a huge Bald Eagle nest on the roof over the entrance to the Whitney Museum, making strikingly manifest the question of the life currently not in these places, but which could be – and raising the question of how humans can offer affordances to other species in their environment in better ways than at present (cf. also Hinchliffe and Whatmore, 2006). By drawing upon radical ethology and computer science, Natalie Jeremijenko takes her art far beyond anthropocentrism. In the *Ooz* project, Jeremijenko has aimed at promoting and developing urban animal populations through generating sites for human–animal interaction based on mutual interest and curiosity, collective learning and reciprocity across the human/non-human divide, based on questions such as 'what is quality of life for animals? What are their priorities when it comes to lifestyle choices?', and attempting to learn about possible answers to these questions through experimental setups of physical infrastructure for non-humans.[4] These have for instance included robotic geese that enable humans to engage in conversation with geese using known goose signals (both verbal and physical), and further generating affordances for the geese to respond, if they so wish – then storing the biological goose's response in an annotated database so as to enable an infrastructure for learning more about how geese communicate.

In relation to Jeremijenko's reciprocal experimental setups, it is interesting to note that when suggesting ways of tweaking Ostrom's eight design principles for successful common pool resource management design so that they also suit more contentious urban commons, urban sociologists Parker and Johansson (2011: 13) suggest that we add a *zero-principle* before the established eight which reads: 'Appropriators need sufficient knowledge to understand the value of the resource'. This is a case of what Isabelle Stengers has called *Cosmopolitics*: the politics of what exists in the world and how it should be taken into account and cared for, which is never self-evident or straightforward but if not always contested, at least always contestable – and the outcome of which will have radical political or, as Bruno Latour has taught us, even almost meta-political effects (even though they should be brought back into politics on a flat level, as argued by both Stengers, 2005 and Latour, 2004).

Further, and related, learning to be affected entails the engenderment of *response-ability* (Haraway, 2008). Geographer Lennart Tonell (2010) has for instance noted that the regionally endangered *Blåsippa* or *Anemone hepatica* in Sweden has the legal right to a voice in urban development processes according to national legislation – but few listen to it or are swayed by it. So what we need are not only mechanisms to decode but also to take into account, not only to produce 'voice', but to concomitantly also engender 'hearing'. This also includes a sensitization to the voices of things virtual, that which-has-not-yet-arrived or which-might-be, and as Hinchliffe and Whatmore have noted, this further touches upon 'the complex issue of whether the question of something's being present or not is as black and white as it seems', and more boils down to the questions of what could be there, or could arrive – as we do when we demand the pre-emptive installation of equipment to facilitate disability access to various public premises without knowing beforehand if any disabled person at the present time has the need for these particular measures at that particular place. And as has been noted by Feldman (2009: 240) in relation to the work of Fritz Haeg, a highly visible nest or

4 See further http://www.nyu.edu/projects/xdesign/ooz/ooz_intro.html.

even an empty animal dwelling in an urban area can function to 'insinuate nonhuman life' into the everyday existences of the constantly growing global cadre of human urban denizens. There also exist attempts of generating this type of apparatuses of affectation on a grander scale in, for instance, the new constitutions of Ecuador and Bolivia. This is not the place to go into a deeper analysis of these, but I have previously written about Ecuador's granting of constitutional rights to nature which in no way appears to be some kooky banana republic-whim, but rather a well thought-through attempt to seriously place humanity in a wider ecological framing, which has proven to hold up to serious legal testing (Metzger, 2012).

On the urban scale, those trusted with producing urban environments that provide for specific urban amenities of a common-pool resource type, e.g. the public spaces particularly in focus in contemporary normative urban planning ideologies such as New Urbanism, still generally think of these spaces from decidedly narrowly anthropocentric perspectives (Wolch et al., 1995). But there are interesting signs of counter-currents developing against this narrow human focus in urban design and planning, and a greater sensibility towards complex socio-ecological co-dependencies and the need to generate conditions for multispecies life in cities (see e.g. Marcus et al., 2013). Thus, meaningful interventions towards a politics of conviviality need not be grand and constitutional (even though the potentials for such solutions should not be *a priori* dismissed either and for sure make an enormous difference). Instead, there are immense possibilities for here-and-now efforts of a more tinkering type, as sketched by Hinchliffe and Whatmore and also evinced in the writings of urban ecologists such as Elmqvist and Colding, for instance encompassing more mundane interventions such as urban gardening, or the fitting of urban estates and buildings with the necessary equipment to make them hospitable to various urban species. But to *which*? This tricky question I try to touch upon in my final concluding argument.

A carrying idea of this chapter is that 'we', human inhabitants of cities, need to begin to try to make room for the hereto-marginalized residents of cities also into the City – to allow the non-human urban denizens entry into a urban hybrid collectif. So to say: to let the animals of the urban assemblage also enter the urban assembly, to be consulted and have their voices heard (cf. Latour, 2004). Nevertheless, I want as a final note to make clear that what I am arguing for here is in no way a human submission under some mystical illusion of 'deep nature' or its self-appointed spokespersons (see also Latour, 2004). Neither do I advocate a crude vitalist fetishization of bare life at any price – a philosophically cheap stance to take, which may be morally soothing, but which offers very little concrete guidance to ethico-political considerations in complex and conflict ridden situations – and which thus in consequence will soon turn out to be practically much more untenable than a more situated ethics of care, nurturing and killing which rests upon incessant considerations and constantly ongoing negotiations concerning the composition and fate of an always already entangled more-than-human urban collectif. For here, Hardin – the staunchly rightist eugenicist, and Haraway – the radical socialist feminist, appear to come together from their extremely divergent positions in a call for a more situated ethics of becoming-together. As Donna Haraway has so candidly stated: dying as well as killing are ubiquitous ever-presents of the world, and sometimes killing might even be the responsible thing to do. But by whose decision and assumption of responsibility? And in what ways? (Haraway, 2008: 79 ff.).

To make a loop back to the two quotations that opened this chapter, we should here remind ourselves of Lee's and Stenner's insight that any form of order builds upon sacrifice of that which is Othered. As a corollary of this insight we should never stop dwelling in the wicked and ultimately undecidable but nevertheless foundational ethico-political questions: 'Who pays? Can we pay them back?' (Lee and Stenner, 1999; cf. also Watson, 2011) and a commitment to that 'whatever those liens are that you are drawing have to always be taken under erasure, *even as*, pragmatically, those lines have to be drawn and *are* drawn all the time' (Wolfe cited in Broglio, 2013: 181, italics in the original). Further, following Isabelle Stengers, we should demand that whatever existence is temporarily excluded from within those liens, we are always prepared to look into the eyes and stand for our decision without attempting to skirt any responsibility for the consequences of it (cf. Stengers, 2005). And even more challenging, relating to the quote from Latour, we should with our emerging understanding of how our planet is weaved into innumerable layers of scale-less ecological 'webs of affinities' to such a degree that 'we' can no longer know for certain who 'we' are, 'we' must now be cautious and aware that with every act of sacrifice of that which may at a glance seem alien and other to us as humans, we may actually be more or less directly endangering our own future as a species, doing away with it cut by cut.

Thus, what appears to be direly needed by humanity at this specific conjuncture in history is a new type of humility towards the world, perhaps particularly cognizant in relation to Sloterdijk's 'biopolitical unity' of 'man, the house and animals' generally going under the name of 'the City'. So to round off in a Latourian/Sloterdijkian way, we may then perhaps ask ourselves: who gains entrance into the clearing of the urban commons, into the urban collective of things and beings, and who does not – and on what grounds? Who is a worthy urban commoner and who is merely a passive resource or even a pest and a nuisance? And at what costs are these decisions made? Who pays the price, and how are they taken into account in these decisions? These are the daunting questions of nurturing and killing, about enabling and curbing in becoming-together across the human/non-human divide, where the key question, asked by Nietzsche and echoed by Sloterdijk becomes: which are the 'breeding programmes' being enforced here? Or to put this in more agreeable terms from a not-exclusively human perspective, but rather with a view towards complex species interdependence and always asymmetric more-than-human becomings as ubiquitous to humanity and the city: which are the programs for becoming-City-together and becoming-together-in-cities across the human/non-human divide? Who makes the decisions, in whose name, and for the gain of what and whom? Who takes responsibility? In relation to the urban commons – these are truly existential questions.

References

Atkins, P. (ed.) (2012) *Animal Cities: Beastly Urban Histories.* Farnham: Ashgate.

Barad, K. (1998) 'Getting real: technoscientific practices and the materialization of reality', *differences: A Journal of Feminist Cultural Studies* 10(2): 87–126.

Borgström, S. T., Elmqvist, T., Angelstaam, P. and Alfsen-Norodom, C. (2006) 'Scale mismatches in management of urban landscapes', *Ecology and Society* 11(2): 1–30.

Braudel, F. (1973) *Capitalism and Material Life 1400–1800.* London: Weidenfeld and Nicolson.

Broglio, R. (2013) 'After animality, before the law: interview with Cary Wolfe', *Angelaki* 18(1): 181–9.

Callon, M. and Law, J. (1995) 'Agency and the hybrid "Collectif"', *The South Atlantic Quarterly* 94(2): 481–507.

Colding, J. (2012) 'Creating incentives for increased public engagement in ecosystem management through urban commons', in E. Boyd and C. Folke (eds), *Adapting Institutions: Governance, Complexity, and Social-Ecological Resilience.* Cambridge, UK: Cambridge University Press, pp. 101–24.

Crutzen, P. J. (2002) 'Geology of mankind', *Nature* 415(3): 23.

Czarniawska, B. (2002) *A Tale of Three Cities: or The Glocalization of City Management.* Oxford: Oxford University Press.

Darwin, C. R. (1859) *On The Origin of Species by Means of Natural Selection, or The Preservation of Favoured Races in The Struggle for Life.* London: John Murray.

Deleuze, G. and Guattari, F. (1987) *A Thousand Plateaus: Capitalism and Schizophrenia.* Minneapolis: University of Minnesota Press.

Eknert, B. (2010) 'Inledning: varför en konferens om det urbana landskapet?', in E. Lisberg Jensen (ed.), *Det Urbana Landskapet.* Uppsala: CBM, pp. 7–8.

Elmqvist, T. (2010) 'Ekosystemtjänster och resiliens i urbana landskap', in E. Lisberg Jensen (ed.), *Det Urbana Landskapet.* Uppsala: CBM, pp. 20–3.

Emanuelson, U. (2010) 'Den tätortsnära naturens betydelse för biodiversitet', in E. Lisberg Jensen (ed.), *Det Urbana Landskapet.* Uppsala: CBM, pp. 24–8.

Feldman, M. B. (2009) 'Where the wild things aren't': Animals in New York City', *The Minnesota Review* 73(74): 231–42.

Foster, S. (2006) 'The city as an ecological space: social capital and urban land use', *Notre Dame Law Review* 82(2): 527–82.

Freud, S. ([1917]1955). 'A difficulty in the path of psycho-analysis', in J. Strachey and A. Freud (eds), *Complete Works*, Standard Edition, vol. 17.

Garnett, N. S. (2012) 'Managing the urban commons', *University of Pennsylvania Law Review* 160(7): 1995–2027.

Gibson-Graham, J. K. (2011) 'A feminist project of belonging for the Anthropocene', *Gender, Place and Culture* 18(1): 1–21.

Hache, É., and Latour, B. (2010) 'Morality or moralism? An exercise in sensitization', *Common Knowledge* 16(2): 311–30.

Haraway, D. (2008) *When Species Meet.* Minneapolis: University of Minnesota Press.

Hardin, G. (1968) 'The tragedy of the commons', *Science* 162(3859): 1243–8.

Harvey, D. (2011) 'The future of the commons', *Radical History Review* 109(Winter): 101–7.

Heidegger, M. (1975) *Poetry, Language, Thought.* New York: Harper and Row.

Hiedanpää, J. (2013) 'Institutional misfits: law and habits in Finnish wolf policy', *Ecology and Society* 18(1): 24.

Hinchliffe, S. and Whatmore, S. (2006) 'Living cities: Towards a politics of conviviality', *Science as Culture* 15(2): 123–38.

Holmberg, T. (2013) 'Trans-Species urban politics: stories from a beach', *Space and Culture* 16(1): 28–42.

Latour, B. (1993) *We Have Never Been Modern.* Cambridge, MA: Harvard University Press.

Latour, B. (1998) 'To modernize or to ecologize? That's the question', in N. Castree and B. Willems–Braun (eds), *Remaking Reality: Nature at the Millenium.* London: Routledge.

Latour, B. (2004) *Politics of Nature: How to Bring the Sciences Into Democracy.* Cambridge, MA: Harvard University Press.

Latour, B. (2013) *An Inquiry Into Modes of Existence: An Anthropology of the Moderns.* Cambridge, Mass.: Harvard University Press.

Lee, N. and Stenner, P. (1999) 'Who pays? Can we pay them back?', in J. Law and J. Hassard (eds), *Actor Network Theory and After.* Oxford: Blackwell.

Lee, S. and Webster, C. (2006) 'Enclosure of the urban commons', *GeoJournal* 66(1): 27–42.

Lovelock, J. (2006) *The Revenge of Gaia: Why the Earth is Fighting Back – And How We Can Still Save Humanity.* London: Allen Lane.

Löfgren, O. (1985) 'Our friends in Nature: class and animal symbolism', *Ethnos* 50(3–4): 184–213.

Marcus, L., Balfors, B. and Haas, T. (2013) 'A sustainable urban fabric: the development and application of analytical urban design theory', in J. Metzger and A. Rader Olsson (eds), *Sustainable Stockholm: Exploring Urban Sustainability in Europe's Greenest City.* London and New York: Routledge.

Marres, N. (2012) *Material Participation: Technology, the Environment and Everyday Publics.* Basingstoke: Palgrave Macmillan.

McCay, B. J. (2000) 'Property rights, the commons, and natural resource management', in M. D. Kaplowitz (ed.), *Property Rights, Economics, and the Environment.* Stanford, JAI Press Inc, p. 103–19.

Metzger, J. (2012) 'We are not alone in the universe', *Eurozine.* Online. Available HTTP: <http://www.eurozine.com/articles/2012-02-08-metzger-en.html> (accessed 1 February 2012).

Metzger, J. (2013) 'Placing the stakes: the enactment of territorial stakeholders in planning processes', *Environment and Planning A* 45(4): 781–96.

Metzger, J. (2014) 'The subject of place: staying with the trouble', in T. Haas and K. Olsson (eds), *Emergent Urbanism.* Aldershot: Ashgate.

Ostrom, E. (1990) *Governing the Commons: The Evolution of Institutions for Collective Action.* Cambridge, UK: Cambridge University Press.

Otter, C. (2004) 'Cleansing and clarifying: technology and perception in nineteenth-century London', *Journal of British Studies* 43(1): 40–64.

Parker, P. and Johansson, M. (2011) 'The uses and abuses of Elinor Ostrom's concept of commons in urban theorizing', Paper Presented at International Conference of the European Urban Research Association (EURA) 2011, Copenhagen. Online. Available HTTP: <http://dspace.mah.se/dspace/bitstream/handle/2043/12212/EURA%20conf%

20version3.pdf;jsessionid=B3F6A280E3DB378ED0A4F507EB0FA6DB?sequence=2> (accessed 31 December 2012).

Philo, C. (1995) 'Animals, geography, and the city: notes on inclusions and exclusions', *Environment and Planning D* 13: 655–81.

Philo, C. and Wilbert, C. (2000) *Animal Spaces, Beastly Places: New Geographies of Human-Animal Relations*. London: Routledge.

Plumwood, V. (2007) 'Review of Deborah Bird Rose's Report from a Wild Country: ethics of decolonisation', *Australian Humanities Review* 42: 1–4.

Rockström, J., Steffen, W., Noone, K., Persson, Å., Chapin III, F. S., Lambin, E. F., Lenton, T. M., Scheffer, M., Folke, C., Schellnhuber, H. J., et al. (2009) 'A safe operating space for humanity', *Nature* 461(7263): 472–5.

Rose, D. B. (2012) 'Cosmopolitics: the kiss of life', *New Formations* 76(1): 101–13.

Saunders, F. and Bylund, J. (2010) 'On the use of actor-network theory in a common pool resources project', *The Commons Digest* 8: 1–10.

Serres, M. (1987) *Statues: Le Second Livre des Fondations*. Paris: Bourin.

Serres, M. (2006) 'Revisiting the Natural Contract'. Talk given at the Institute for the Humanities at Simon Fraser University on 4 May, 2006. Online. Available HTTP: <http://www.sfu.ca/humanities-institute-old/pdf/Naturalcontract.pdf> (accessed 31 December, 2012).

Sloterdijk, P. (1998) *Sphären: Mikrosphärologie. 1, Blasen*. Frankfurt am Main: Suhrkamp.

Sloterdijk, P. (1999) *Sphären: Mikrosphärologie. 2, Globen*. Frankfurt am Main: Suhrkamp.

Sloterdijk, P. (2004) *Sphären: Plurale Sphärologie. Bd 3, Schäume*. Frankfurt am Main: Suhrkamp.

Sloterdijk, P. (2009) 'Rules for the human zoo: a response to the letter on humanism', *Environment and Planning D* 27(1): 12–28.

Sloterdijk, P. (2013) *You Must Change Your Life: On Anthropotechnics*. Cambridge: Polity Press.

Stengers, I. (2005) 'The cosmopolitical proposal', in B. Latour, and P. Weibel (eds), *Making Things Public: Atmospheres of Democracy*. Karlsruhe: Engelhardt and Bauer, pp. 994–1003.

Swyngedouw, E. and Kaïka, M. (2008) 'The environment of the city. . . or the urbanization of nature', in G. Bridge and S. Watson (eds), *A Companion to the City*. Oxford: Blackwell.

Tonell, L. (2010) 'Naturen i stadsplaneringen – ett historiskt perspektiv', in E. Lisberg Jensen (ed.), *Det Urbana Landskapet*. Uppsala: CBM, pp. 36–42.

Tryggestad, K., Justesen, L. and Mouritsen, J. (2013) 'Project temporalities: how frogs can become stakeholders', *International Journal of Managing Projects in Business* 6(1): 69–87.

Varney Rorty, M. (2000) 'For Love of the Game: Peter Sloterdijk and Public Controversies in Bioethics'. Online. Available HTTP: <http://www.stanford.edu/~mvr2j/for_love.html>.

Watson, M. C. (2011) 'Cosmopolitics and the subaltern: problematizing Latour's idea of the commons', *Theory, Culture and Society* 28(3): 55–79.

Whatmore, S. (2002) *Hybrid Geographies: Natures, Cultures, Spaces*. London: SAGE.

Williams, R. (1973) *The Country and the City*. London: Chatto & Windus.

Wolch, J. (2002) 'Anima urbis', *Progress in Human Geography* 26(6): 721–42.

Wolch, J. R, West, K. and Gaines, T. E. (1995) 'Transspecies urban theory', *Environment and Planning D* 13: 735–60.

Zalasiewicz, J., Williams, M., Steffen, W. and Crutzen, P. (2010) 'The new world of the Anthropocene', *Environmental Science and Technology* 44(7): 2228–31.

Chapter 2

The false promise of the commons: historical fantasies, sexuality and the 'really-existing' urban common of modernity

Leif Jerram

'Commons' are everywhere. The term, in both the singular and the plural, is in widespread usage across a range of disciplines, non-academic discourses and social justice movements. It seems to be liberating, full of potential – but also unthreatening, because of its historical precedence and the way it seems to side-step potentially violent models of socio-political change. However, what the term means or refers to precisely is an issue of much confusion. For Elinor Ostrom, the political scientist most associated with establishing the term in contemporary debate, 'commons' initially meant a natural resource; but by the end of her career, 'commons' could be almost anything – including knowledge and computer code (Ostrom, 1990; Hess and Ostrom, 2006). For planning scholar Jeremy Németh the commons can be thought of as a whole range of things, from libraries, through the internet, sidewalk, light from a streetlamp, to the atmosphere or some food (Németh, 2012: 815). And Hardt and Negri, two giants of the world of contemporary socio-cultural criticism, and advocates of 'common' solutions, define the commons (though they call it 'the common') in yet another way, unconnected to the others: the common is that valuable part of something, the value of which is not determined by its use value, or labor inputs, but created and given freely by potential users, like the trendiness of a bar (Hardt and Negri, 2009: 153–4, 280; Hardt and Negri, 2004: 196–7).

But there are ways in which the multiple popular and academic theorists of the common and the commons are related that strike me, as a historian, as being problematic, both intellectually and for the goals of the wider 'commons project'. While they share diverse definitions of what 'the commons' might be, they often share related moods, or styles of arguing, which can be profoundly – in fact, fantastically – historical. While finding a coherent definition of what is being discussed under the rubric 'common', will tax the scholar indefinitely, finding a coherent *mood* or *attitude* to what is being discussed is a slightly easier task, and I wish to subject this mood to historical criticism, because a critique or policy based on false history will likely prove a poor critique or lousy policy.

The first historical mood that the commons appears in is a *good* mood. 'The commons' almost invariably refers to something from the past which has the character of a solution to something in the present, rather than a problem; and the solution that it offers is almost invariably desirably consensual, peaceful and socially just. When one looks at the use made of the words 'common' and 'commons' in campus campaigns, Occupy movements, and anti-globalization and anti-capitalist protests, commoning is presented as a way of solving that reaches well beyond the concerns of conventional economics or political science. Crucially, commons solutions proactively reject both state and market as primary or preferred ways of contemporary problem solving. Not only are 'commons' good, they are good, in part, because they avoid the Leviathan of the state, and the cruel hand of the market (Ostrom, 1990; Bollier and Helfrich, 2012).

But there is another way that 'the commons' shares a mood: commons theorists and commons advocates often have a profoundly historical tone to their writing, campaigning and theorizing, often detached from disciplined historical methodology. The common is good, but it is also *old*. It is this historical tone which I wish to address in this chapter, because it poses profound problems for the imaginary projects of commons activists. For some commons writers, history is a vague invocation of a moral category, as here with online activist network, On the Commons:

> Here at On the Commons, we believe it is possible to *remember*, imagine, and create a society that goes beyond the constructs and confines of individual ownership. To work on the commons is to work to enliven the *deep and ancient memory we all hold of egalitarian and reciprocal relationship, of belonging, of authentic community, and of love, wonder, and respect for the natural world.*
>
> (On the Commons, 2013; emphasis added)

The role of a vague memory seems important to them, and to others, because collectively they tend to lend some sort of authenticity, intellectual credibility and narrative structure to socio-economic critiques and policy formulation.

For others, like Ostrom (1990), history can be a repository of potentially useful data, though for her it does not have to be approached in its historical context. Whether used as the evocation of paradise lost, or deployed as data out of context, such methodologies of history must lead to unsustainable conclusions, because they start with unreliable foundations or models. History is the cause of the present, not a measurement of it or a theme park in which to escape it. I wish to explore some of the ways that a historian might begin to reflect on the 'urban commons' as a historicizable phenomenon, and in doing so highlight some of the limitations of the ways that commons theories have been composed by foregrounding the problematic historical foundations upon which much activist commons theory has been built.

I will do this, first, by exploring an historical example of the production or appropriation of specific sites within the modern city as a type of common – a resource to be exploited. In major western European cities in the 1930s, men who had sex with men were increasingly forming a resistant identity, while simultaneously becoming more vulnerable to state persecution (Jerram, 2011: 247–316). I will examine two attempts in the 1930s to produce whole cities as sites of resource exploitation for men who had sex with men, in the form of guides to sites of 'gay' sexuality in London and Berlin. But equally important will be the frameworking devices used by these 'urban commons enablers' to explain the city-resource that they sought to exploit, and devise a strategy for exploiting it. This frameworking matters, because it speaks across time to current commons theories, which typically posit both state and market as threats to effective human cooperation at worst, and incompetent obstacles at best. However, these practitioners of the appropriation of urban space in the 1930s presented a more ambivalent, potentially more realist analysis, in which the task was to turn state and market into urban common resources, rather than eliminate them. In short, they embraced the realities of modernity, and worked with them to offer a vigorous arena of political action, one which has helped transform the position of gay men across the West. They offer a powerful practical example, and also an excellent critical perspective on contemporary urban commons thinking.

I will then explore how history has been deployed by more recent commons advocates to produce a critique of the present and plan of action for the future. Many commons advocates' work uses history in a way that historians themselves could not countenance. That is to say, a particularly moral historical common is invoked, a common which was in some way stolen by a collusion of state and market. Even when more recognizably accurate historical data is used, it is not without its problems. I will explore how Ostrom's empirical historical evidence undermines her own conclusions. Both 'romantic' invocations of the past, as well as more empirical deployments of historical evidence, suggest that history is too often used as a moral, rather than analytical, tool in commons thinking.

The third section moves from these two particular varieties of historicizing the commons to offer a wider critique of this habit of (a)historical thinking in commons advocacy more generally. For as long as bourgeois intellectuals have been confronting modernity there have been conversations about how one might imagine a society free from the twin pillars upon which that modernity rests: the modern state, and the modern capitalist system – often called 'the market' in commons discourses. A detailed history of this 'third way' is not possible here, but by historicizing the activity of 'commons' thinking itself, I hope to offer a critique which can move it out of the 'presentist' paradigm, in which the present tends to be described as particularly new, particularly interesting, and particularly important, contrasted with an implicitly more trivial, more static or more moral past, or an exciting, malleable future. I will argue that the realist formulations discussed in section one, and the empirical evidence offered in section two, can be more liberating than radical formulations based on historical fantasies.

Producing an urban common: a practical guide

The 1930s were an important transitional time for the formation of gay identity, and for men who had sex with men. Across Europe, the 1930s marked the end of what literary critic Elaine Showalter has characterized as a period of 'sexual anarchy', and there was a radical upswing in attempts on the part of the state to target men who had sex with men for criminal prosecution across urban Europe (Showalter, 1992; Jerram, 2011). In two European cities in the 1930s, Berlin and London, two unusual guidebooks were produced which were explicitly intended to render the urban fabric and topography more knowable and usable by gay men. The goal of the authors was to take a city that they had not themselves created, and which was not always created with them in mind, and appropriate it, using it for their own purposes of social networking, leisure and sexual gratification; that is to say, to define a common resource and enable its common exploitation. They reveal the city as a very particular sort of common: its common-ness shifts with the time of day, the sexuality of the user, the evolving material artefacts strewn across the city, and the vicissitudes of criminal law and fashion. This is important, because it offers us a contrastive, and particularly *urban*, common to juxtapose with the generally institutional-material common that is invoked in much commons theorizing, and which I discuss later. In this section, I want first to explore the ways the texts reveal the 'production' of very specific urban spaces, locations and places, before going on to highlight underlying assumptions present in the texts which might upset some of the most common tropes of more recent 'commons' discourse.

Punningly-named 'Paul Pry' produced a punningly-titled book entitled *For Your Convenience* in 1937. Effectively, it is a very extensive guide to the locations of transactional sex between men in London. It is a funny read; what is in effect a staggeringly long list of alleys, courtyards, basements, bathhouses, museums, graveyards, churches and above all, public toilets, is made manageable for the reader by setting it as a satirical conversation in a London gentleman's club between a young member (an example of the striving middle classes), and a stuffy older gentleman. Their conversation begins as they both reach for the *Sanitary World and Drainage Observer*, and each marvel at the other's interest in such things. From there, a conversation ensues that produces, amongst other things, a vast guide to locations of sexual encounter in London. Kurt Moreck produced a marginally more conventional guidebook to Berlin in 1931: only marginally so, because its focus was on 'immoral' or 'naughty' Berlin. It was an extensive guide to the sexual geography and timings of the city, and had a chapter on 'places of man-man Eros' and lesbian bars. The heterosexual sections are, in fact, far 'saucier' than the rather staid sections for gay people. Straight bars offered 'snogging booths', S&M bars, bars for cruising (including some with phones on the numbered tables to dial up people customers fancied), strip joints, all-night bathhouses and so on. But the section on gay bars (he calls gay men 'inverts' – I will use gay) is substantial, lasting some 46 pages.

What links the strategies of these two authors is a characterization of what the city is like, and the struggles that the individual may have in converting what looks like a vast, unmanageable and potentially hostile landscape into a resource to enable encounters between like-minded individuals. The city for both has the productive potential of a common, but is, in its raw state, unusable for creating a 'community' of gay men, without suitable training and instruction. They both set up the city as essentially unknowable, but also labile. One of Pry's voices observed:

> In this matter we are discussing I have once or twice found places which I have never been able to find again. I know they were not figments. I know they were solidly there, and as real as Kant allows anything to be. But somehow or other [. . .] my feet have never recaptured the ritual steps that directed me originally. I do not doubt their existence, but I cannot assert it.
>
> (Pry, 1937: 45–6)

For Pry, this might be because such sites were so ephemeral or transitory, or perhaps generated by a fortuitous performance that took place there, but also because of a certain material lability: 'After a lapse of maybe three weeks, one looks for it, and lo, rebuilding operations have begun, the yard is razed, the place is gone, and it is not reborn elsewhere' (Pry, 1937: 26).

The physical form of the city mutated, and as it did, it brought exploitable common spaces into and out of existence. And Moreck, whose account focused on bars and nightclubs, emphasized that many 'gay spaces' were not 'gay' all the time – they were transitory and fleeting. Club nights would open and close, move venue, or may only take place once or twice, and might take place on different days of the week – the 'friendship balls' at Köhlers on Tiekstraße, for example, were only for 'like-minded men' on Thursdays, Saturdays and Sundays (Moreck, 1931: 139). There was a complex temporal map to overlay the physical one, without which the city would be, for gay men, unusable for the purposes which they intended. Unlike an institutional common, like a pasture, forest or common fishery, the urban common is not always there to be exploited. It must be constantly reproduced.

The two 'voices' of Pry's account set the problem of the modern city up first as a paradox of modernization, then as a practical problem. The younger man observes that, by and large, the trend for 'the authorities' has been to strive to make the city more open, more visible, more knowable: they advertise the locations of all sorts of services and encounters, like post offices or fire stations or schools, and they produce technologies, like telephone directories and bus maps, to make the city more knowable still. But 'the authorities' are profoundly shy about identifying any sort of geography of sexual encounter. This is the task that the younger man has set himself: to produce such a geography. As the older interlocutor observes, 'The subject [the sexual geography of London] has not received the attention it deserves, and there is no general clearing-house for information upon it. Even local people I have found deficient in such necessary knowledge' (Pry, 1937: 6–7).

Moreck echoes this urban diagnosis, highlighting that for someone looking for an 'inverted' bar, whether a tourist or a native Berliner who had an awakening desire, they would not know where to go, and information would be difficult to acquire from outside. And further, the more 'notorious' places tended to be 'inauthentic', offering a clichéd performance of what a genuine 'inverts'' bar might look like (Moreck, 1931: 132–3, 148–9). Both authors implied that to open the city up for use by others is their goal; they wished, in short, to take a set of material environments and social spaces, and make them exploitable by a wider public. Moreck argued that the *visible* city was merely a moneymaking device:

> Every city has an official and an unofficial side to it, and it is unnecessary to explain, that the latter is the one that will best help understand a particular city. All those things you find under the street lamps seem to present a face, but they are just a mask. They show a smile designed only to open your wallet. [. . .] He who seeks genuine experiences, demands adventure, hopes for new sensations, he must step into the shadows.
>
> (Moreck, 1931: 7)

The difficulty was, how to get behind the mask? Books like these were attempts to do just that: to offer the city up as a series of moods, experiences, sites, and spaces that would enable gay men to use them to subvert their persecution, and attain an ameliorated sociability in an arena where this was increasingly criminalized.

But there are fundamental (though theoretically complimentary) differences in their analyses too. Pry framed his resource in largely (not solely) terms of the state, for it was generally the state which produced most of the spaces he described – public urinals, yards, back streets, alleyways. Private enterprises like hotels or large office blocks may also produce them, but when thinking about where most of the material environments he was discussing came from, it was 'the authorities' that generated them materially, and he was keen to recognize this over and over. It was also, crucially, 'the authorities' that posed the greatest threat in these spaces: it was important for the individual seeking encounters in these locations that they 'escape the observation of the Dicks' (Pry, 1937: 10). The word 'Dicks' here is a pun, referring to contemporary slang for police detectives, and the enduring slang for penises – the observation of which was precisely what was intended. Repeatedly Pry emphasized that it was the state which produced these spaces, and the state which surveilled them, but that there were so many such sites that they could be appropriated by others to exploit for their own needs. The state giveth, and the state taketh away.

For Pry, the state in its various forms was constantly assigned the role of producing and delimiting this common resource. It did this while both unthinkingly offering a network of sites where some sort of public semi-nudity (at urinals) was required, and some sort of privacy (in cubicles) was assured. In Moreck's analysis, 'Weimar Berlin' was not the tolerant free-for-all that it is often assumed to be, and gay men were becoming increasingly vulnerable around 1931. Moreck was keen to emphasize that many 'gay' bars were the only places that men might escape scorn, mockery and persecution. Further, when meetings were held at the Zauberflöte to organize campaigns against persecution, extra door staff had to be hired, and everyone was forced to use the cloakroom for bags and coats, so weapons could not be brought in. Many were arbitrarily turned away from these meetings (Moreck, 1931: 142–4). But Moreck framed the spaces which gay men might exploit as being both produced by, and threatened by, the market – a threat which he both deplored and facilitated.

For Moreck, the gay world was one of bars, each of which set up by a businessperson – offering that 'smile designed to open up a wallet' mentioned earlier. It was a capitalist world. Some bars were lavish, with decorations to make them look like the Wild West, or a nautical theme for 'Sailors' Night'. Most were 'just' bars, like any other in Berlin. So while the market might produce these spaces for a relatively homogenous purpose (to earn a living for the proprietor), people might (especially with the help of a guide like Moreck's) decide that different uses might be made of them – ones which suited their own (but did not necessarily contradict the owner's) intentions. For example, it would be hard for the owner of a bar like the Café Nordstern to explicitly set out to make it a place where young men who admired older guys might congregate (Moreck, 1931: 138). Bars might have other functions – for example, serving as informal labor exchanges for customers. Some bars attracted workers from specific trades, like building, and functioned as hiring markets for site work (Moreck, 1931: 138).

While these bars might be vulnerable to threats from individuals or the state, the main threat was that same market which had produced them in the first place. Noting the growth of an urban tourist industry, Moreck related how some of the more stylishly decorated or fashionable bars might suddenly become part of Thomas Cook tours, with bus-loads of heterosexual tourists being trundled round Berlin, transforming them from being sites of self-identification and 'like-minded' sociability, into 'cabinets of curiosities and a typical Berlin tourist sight' (Moreck, 1931: 132). Moreck observed that most people 'on the world outside' had an attitude of live-and-let-live indifference towards gay bars, but periodically, one might be singled out as being particularly stylish or fashionable, and then:

> this tolerant outside world is the thing which so often bursts in on the meeting places of inversion, to enjoy the wonderful theatre it offers. Then such a place becomes high fashion, and it becomes a must-see. Then of course a female element also bursts in and they soon wash away, through their superior power (which does not even correspond to their number), the genuine character of the place.
>
> (Moreck, 1931: 149)

Regulars were relegated to the corners, then gave up coming altogether, as their ability to use the resource for their own purposes was eroded. The process of exploitation by either Thomas Cook tourists, or the 'In Crowd', or women, would be all the easier after Moreck's publication. This might be the ruin of the common, for once the fashion moved on, sometimes gay men would be reluctant to return. The market giveth, and the market taketh away.

So one author was keen to take a set of spaces produced by, and threatened by, the state, and turn them into a common resource to be exploited; and the other felt impelled to take a set of spaces produced by, and threatened by, the market and enable their easier common exploitation. Both categories of space were exploitable in ways in which their creators never intended (perhaps the distinctive feature of an urban common), sometimes the consequences being positive for a marginalized set of users, and sometimes negative. They pointed, then, to a particularly pragmatic, flexible, chronologically and spatially dependent specifically urban common. Crucially, these authors and the people reading them, using the knowledge they had of the city, could reasonably hope to adapt *in practice* the city into a commons without searching for a theoretical 'third way'; they did not advocate that rejection of both state and market so dear to many 'commons' thinkers. Such agentic opportunities are not universally available (for a whole host of reasons), but they do hint that *categorical* evasion of state and market are not at all necessary in liberating projects. Pry and Moreck went beyond a de Certeau-ian unconscious use of space, and aimed at resource creation and distribution in a way particularly suited to urban geographies, with their almost infinite range of synchronous multiple locations. They managed to be radical and transformative (for these 'scenes' would be crucial in transforming the status of gay men for the next 70 years), yet still 'render unto Caesar those things which are Caesar's'.

Commons theories and the (ab)uses of history

However, commons theorists tend to emphasize that state and market, two pillars of modern social, political and economic organization, are *categorically* problematic, and they often do alongside appeals to history, both subtle and direct. The number of references to, or invocations of, a historical 'commons' – an institutional pattern of landholding which was dissolved between about 1500 and 1850 in England, but occurred elsewhere – is extensive. Literature across a range of disciplines and campaigns discussing the commons tends not to rely too heavily on any detailed analysis of the past, but invoke institutions from the past with nostalgia or admiration, whilst also bizarrely advocating a quantum separation of themselves from the past, as I will explore in section three.

Even for a sober academic writer like Ostrom, history can serve both as a data set (as I discuss below), and a nostalgic invocation and a moral starting point. She and Hess explain briskly that:

> Historically in Europe, 'commons' were shared agricultural fields, grazing lands and forests that were, over a period of five hundred years, enclosed with communal rights being withdrawn by landowners and the state. The narrative of enclosure is one of privatization, the haves versus the have nots, the elite versus the masses.
>
> (Hess and Ostrom, 2006: 12)

To restore the commons, then, would be to reverse that simple but immoral narrative. Popular social critic Naomi Klein characterized 'commons' thinkers (encompassing anti-capitalists, anti-imperialists, anti-corporates – all those who opposed the 'privatisation of everyday life') as linked by sharing a spirit for the 'radical *re*claiming of the commons', subtly invoking a past in which everyday life was presumably shared (Klein, 2001: 82, emphasis added).

Nor is it just a question of vague, unspecific invocations of a past. Ostrom spends a substantial chunk of her seminal work, *Governing the Commons* (1990), working through the history of the management of the water resources in Los Angeles County, across the first half of the twentieth century. This historical case study was the starting point for her career. She drew from this example a set of ahistorical inferences which led her to conclude that complex, long-lasting, competitive social processes can be managed without state or market, even in the urban West. In this section, I want to tackle these two ways of using the past: one, its invocation as a 'moral mood', and two, the more specific historical narrative which Ostrom uses to make her point.

The quantity of references, often very slight in themselves, contained in the literature in geography, sociology, urban studies, and non-academic campaigns, to a past common is so great that it defies listing. One sees it invoked not only directly, as with Ostrom and Hess above, but also with 're-'-prefixed words like Klein's, and every time the prefix 'neo-' is invoked to mean the return of a particular sort of demon (neo-liberal, neo-fascist, neo-conservative, for example). A quick check online will find hundreds of 'movements' claiming, for example, to '*re*claim' the streets, or some other thing which (the 're' implies) has been lost – the night, media, fields, Bay, future, body, etc. One of the founders of Reclaim the Streets explicitly argues that the streets (and their reclamation) are equivalent to 'the commons' (Jordan, 2013). 'Neo'-liberal politics implies a new type of collusion between capital and state, which had somehow been fended off in the *trente glorieuses* of the 'Fordist consensus'. There may well be new features to recent capitalism (the same river never flows twice), but few critics of neo-liberalism rush to read history books of how corporate interests and the state colluded in the 1950s and 1960s before the 'neo-liberal turn'. British oil interests steered British foreign, defense and intelligence policy in Persia expertly, and British property speculators were highly successful at co-opting local governments to hand over town centers for demolition and speculative redevelopment into shopping centres long before the 'neo-liberal turn'.

Yet both city and streets in modern, Western societies have always been places where the authority of capital and the state have largely taken precedence over the needs of the poor and the marginalized (Engels is magnificent on this), and yet where their exploitation in liberating projects has been possible – as Pry and Moreck sought to demonstrate. It is a commonplace to observe that the Western city and its streets are a product of the collaboration of state and market, as Pry and Moreck so clearly knew (Harvey 1985, 2003; Nead, 2000; Sassen, 1991). One might wish to claim them now; but *re*claiming either city or street assumes that the poor or the marginalized ever owned them in the first place. They did not. That is why Pry and Moreck felt impelled to try to enable people to exploit them, on however small a scale. Presumably, the demand to *take* a street is less palatable than the demand to *retake* it; one sounds like theft, the other restorative justice. 'Re' and 'neo' make implicit historical claims, but with little willingness to be truly disciplined by historical evidence or methodologies.

More specific historical claims about the commons, like Hess's and Ostrom's above, abound. Environmental psychologist Efrat Eizenberg, for example, states first that the urban environment is a 'primary tool of the neo-liberal project'; second that, 'alternatives do exist'; and third that, 'this debate goes back to the commons in England that sustained the livelihood of landless serfs' (Eizenberg, 2012: 764–5). Some of the most sustained evocations of the past mobilized to identify or defend or produce a 'common' can be found in the very influential three volumes of Michael Hardt and Antonio Negri, *Empire, Multitude* and *Commonwealth* (2000, 2004, 2009). Such is the influence of these works in both the academy and wider activist movements, that they merit some attention. In these works, they engage in many substantial historical excursions.

For example, here is their summary of 400 years of European history:

> It all began with a revolution. In Europe, between 1200 and 1600, across
> distances that only merchants and armies could travel and only the

invention of the printing press would later bring together, something extraordinary happened: humans declared themselves masters of their own lives.

(Hardt and Negri, 2000: 79)

History here is a rhetorical gesture, not a data set or a methodology to guide thought. Firstly, many people moved around Europe in the late Middle Ages – pilgrims, monks, fishermen, students, clergy, couriers, Jews, Muslims, tax collectors, bankers, professional navigators, diplomats, jewellers, land owners, refugees, and masons for example (Horden and Purcell, 2000). Secondly, a courier moving 5 miles in present-day Spain might have been moving from Christendom to the Islamic world in 1300, while a monk travelling from York to Rome would have been able to speak Latin in both places to peers, so the evocation of 'distance' looks bizarre. And the idea that 'people declared themselves to be masters of their own lives' is just a nonsense; very few people have *ever* made this declaration about their own lives, least of all at a time of the Black Death, precarious agricultural production, feudal systems of tutelage, chaotic wars attendant on the Reformation and contests over state control, and near-universal faith in an interventionist God.

This is not an isolated instance. It is routine. In Hardt's and Negri's 2004 work, *Multitude*, they even have a section called, 'Back to the Eighteenth Century', which argues:

One good reason to go back to the eighteenth century is that back then the concept of democracy was not corrupted as it is now. The eighteenth-century revolutionaries knew that democracy is a radical, absolute proposition that requires the rule of everyone by everyone.

(Hardt and Negri, 2004: 306)

It is hard to think of which eighteenth-century revolutionaries they could be thinking of. Maybe they mean the ones who excluded slaves, poor white men, all women and all native peoples from the protections of the US constitution, or the people like Jean-Baptiste Carrier, who drowned thousands in the Loire for failing to swear loyalty to the French Revolution. This is historical gibberish.

So, frequently, when a commons is remembered in commons thinking, it is not remembered in detail. It is a shorthand for something nice which was stolen. However, the commons in England were not this. Common land came with labor duty to the landowner which was gradually commuted to a money payment. The class below these commoners (that is, most people) did *not* have right to productive common field, only limited scavenging rights on marginal land. The 'landless poor' had, under the commons system, access to only 4 per cent of cultivated land. The amount of land (called the 'waste') available to the genuinely poor in 1750 (before extensive parliamentary/coercive enclosure) was c. 1m acres, and was used by >2m (by implication, very hungry) people (Clark and Clark, 2001: 1025, 1032). Commoning, then, was a form of bondage and privilege.

The extent of historical fantasy in 'commons thinking' about what commoning was and why it stopped is large, and needs correcting. The first to start enclosing commons were the commoners themselves, on a very small scale. As more livestock were kept, the problem that Hardin (1968) identified (the 'tragedy' of the commons) increasingly occurred, because unconstrained animals in collective fields devastated arable crops. Significantly, around 1700 (so before really widespread enclosure) only about 21 per cent of farmland in England was 'common'; common land farming was *exceptional*, and generally belonged to more prosperous families, and exclusive private property was always extensive (Mingay, 1997; Thompson, 1965: 213–33, 1991: 97–184; Yelling, 1977; Clark and Clark, 2001). As Clark and Clark conclude: 'There was no great expropriation of the rural landless in England by the process of land enclosure in any era after 1600, because [. . .] the landless had access to so little common land' (2001: 1033).

That does not mean we can learn nothing from the transformation – we could learn a lot. The reasons for ending commoning between 1550 and 1850 were powerful and rational, not arbitrary or conspiratorial, and indicate that a greater attention to historical context and interdependence can be instructive because it will teach us to see our present as part of an evolving history, not a moment separate from it (this issue of chronological separation is something I will return to in section three). It is impossible to list them all here (a readily digestible review is Kain et al., 2011: 1–46), but I would like to touch on some of the most important, just to burst the historical bubble.

Firstly, many commoners voluntarily enclosed their lands, either because it delivered an increase in productivity, or because they could not get on with other commoners. For example, Richard Derby of Buckinghamshire in the mid-eighteenth century was entitled to 26 and a half acres of common field. But it was in 24 parcels, some of which were only a quarter of an acre, which is about one-fifth of the size of an American football pitch. These smaller parcels were inefficient, and the number of parcels required too much negotiation to plan easily. Urban commoners often felt that building dwellings on commons was more productive than farming them, as cities mushroomed. Secondly, between 1550–1650 and 1750–1850, the population of England soared; cities grew, requiring more food to be produced with fewer rural hands (Wrigley, 2011). Thirdly, the enclosers of the commons were experiencing severe climate change – the 'mini-ice age' of 1530–1830. Winters were longer (requiring more calories to survive them), summers shorter and less productive (Grove, 2003; Fagan, 2000; Parker, 2013; Brooke, 2014). And finally, during the years 1790–1820, when 50 per cent of parliamentary enclosure happened (and these really were the years of very extensive brutal, non-consensual expropriation), Britain was in close-to-perpetual famine because of rapid urbanization *and* a protean war from Lisbon to Moscow to prevent complete French overlordship of the continent. The productivity rises concurrent with enclosure could not be ignored in a state at war, dependent on its cities for stability (Hawkins, 2011). Commoning failed to offer an adaptable way of farming to commoning farmers, or a sustainable livelihood to millions below the class of commoner. So people changed it – sometimes voluntarily, sometimes by force (of nature, of demography, and sometimes brute force), but the condition of the very poor was miserable before, during and after. There never was a 'golden age'.

Before we imagine that we should 'return' to any time in the past, or even vaguely invoke it, we need to understand that history is a discipline, not a supermarket; disciplines determine what is taken and understood, and are not like a 'pick and mix'. If you pick one thing from 1700 (like commoning), you have to accept that it was situated in a unique set of interdependent circumstances containing *every other thing that was true in 1700*. In the case of the commons, this means servitude, social exclusion, precariousness, warfare, climate change and hunger. Nor is history an unproblematic 'background' of static data to be established before we get on with the real business of dealing with the present, not least because the present is merely a momentary by-product of that history.

Others make better use of history, although draw strange conclusions from it. Here, I want to focus on the substantial historical chunk of Ostrom's major work of 1990, *Governing the Commons* (1990: 103–42). Most of the examples of commons in her work come from the 'Global South' and pastoral situations. There is, though, a substantial chapter which invokes a historical example from the modern urban West. The management of ground waters in Los Angeles County was where Ostrom started her research career. The situation was familiar: industrial, agricultural and municipal users in a rapidly growing city were extracting water from aquifers without regard to each other, or their location in a semi-arid region next to the sea, which would rapidly refill depleted freshwater aquifers with saltwater, destroying them forever. The period covers 1918 to the 1960s. Ostrom does not invoke history as a sort of 'moral mood' this time, but she does make some conclusions that, given the historical evidence that she presents, seem questionable. The over-arching thrust of Ostrom's argument – and the part that charms progressives the world over – is that commons (and in particular, common pool resources) are voluntaristic, and circumvent the need for experts, a strong state or a free market to manage them 'for' the people.

She describes a situation in which actors became aware around 1918 that as Los Angeles grew and industrialized, some sort of collective action to manage the aquifers would be necessary. But what follows in her narrative is not a period of cosy voluntarist consensus formation. What follows is a period of protracted and expensive conflict, in which the state was constantly called upon to force a solution. At every stage of the 50-year contest over water, greed threatened to break the system, leading to the ingress of seawater into the aquifers, degrading them permanently. In order to manage this process, Ostrom details the many state institutions that were required, in a range of roles: forcing compliance; assessing compliance; suppressing opposition; formulating rules; offering expertise; arbitrating disputes; formulating law; devising penalties; negotiating incentives. The eventual outcome relied on the input of the California junior courts; the State of California Supreme Court; the US Geological Survey; the US Supreme Court; the State of California Department of Works; the State of California Watermaster; the State of California legislature; and dozens of very expensive lawyers. This is the state acting, not a self-regulating commons. And it took *50 years*.

The account is peppered with moments when the state acted to force compliance to a set of outcomes. For example, she observes 'it took [. . .] the threat of court action to reach this agreement' (Ostrom, 1990: 119), or 'the judgement continued the role of the Watermaster to enforce the agreement [. . .] The case was appealed to the California Supreme Court and was upheld' (1990: 115). The narrative presented here is not one of Habermasian rational actors coming together in a model public sphere to devise fluid, consensual, democratic solutions. The narrative is actually of many intelligent people recognizing a problem related to urbanization, a greedy few trying to free-ride, and a vigorous, well-organized, expert state resolving the conflict between them with threat of force. But this, strangely, is not the conclusion that Ostrom – or her many admirers – drew from the historical evidence (Ostrom, 1990: 8–20). Despite all this evidence, the state is mocked as 'Leviathan'.

Out of time, out of place: historical fantasies, mythical places and the 'third way' in modernity

This confusing deployment of historical evidence, and this invocation of historical moods independent of historical methodology, require comment. These uses of history are themselves highly typical of much social criticism of the last 200 years. That is to say, commons-type thinking is itself a historical phenomenon typical of modernity. Yet commons advocates tend to argue that commons thinking is separate from historical modernity; a response to it, not part of it. This contrasts with Moreck and Pry's readiness to deal with the world as they found it – and the many other movements that have secured practical and observable increases in rights and dignity for marginal groups by exploiting the common resources of the Western city.

Much of the detailed empirical work that inspires commons thinking focuses on agricultural production in the 'Global South', rather than the types of economies that dominate in the 'Global North' which must, of necessity, be treated in discussions of the 'urban commons'. The many studies of fisheries, forests, mountains, fields and rivers in far away places that are referenced by scholarship in, for example, the *International Journal of the Commons* (www.thecommonsjournal.org) are routinely hedged about with caveats about the uniqueness of the situation. Yet from these unique descriptions of rural life in faraway places, a general 'commons advocacy' has emerged which claims to discuss London, Berlin and New York, not just the High Andes or the Ganges Delta. The co-opting (however vaguely) of pre-modern agricultural settings in the development of intellectual frameworks for handling modern megalopolises, strikes me as a persistent attitude in much modern popular, and some academic, social criticism. Gay men can only be grateful that people like Moreck and Pry did not follow this strategy. The consequences of referring to Nepalese hill farming or Mozambiquan inshore fishing to solve the problems gay men faced in the 1930s hardly bear thinking about.

Periodization is one of the least fashionable, most arcane aspects of historical practice. By and large, historians are gradualists and emphasize continuity, with occasional rows about moments of rupture. But there is a grander scale of periodization which is more stable, and that is in characterizing the last 200–250 years in Europe and North America as 'late modern', sharing some distinctive features. Those features would include (but not be confined to) the significance of state and market for the organization of social, economic and political life (for good or ill); an economy which shifts from agriculture, to industry and services, and from artisanal production to corporations and divided labor; a move from local, personal politics to a massified, imagined-national politics; and the crucial role of expertise and managerialism in allowing state, market, nationalism and corporation to flourish. This is (in caricatured form) the worldsystem that has prevailed in Europe and North America for some time, and while there are variations and oscillations in it (for example, the swing from state to market in Eastern Europe around 1990 was fairly spectacular), they are oscillations within a range which stretches continuously over a substantial period of historical time.

The twin pillars of modernity, then, are market (or capitalism) and state – the basic frameworking devices that dominant social theorists have consistently put at the heart of their analyses, whether Marx, Durkheim, Weber, Gramsci, Althusser, Anderson or whoever. Pry and Moreck saw themselves *in* this system, as did Ostrom's Los Angelinos. Yet influential theorists like Ostrom, Hardt and Negri reject these pillars as both being incompetent or oppressive, and unsuited to solving major contemporary problems, even when nominally democratic (Ostrom, 1990: 8–20; Hardt and Negri throughout, but especially 2004: 191, 231–67; 2009: 263–79). Proposing a world in which liberation might be obtained without reference to the over-weaning state or the cruel market, proposes, even if only implicitly, that the epoch of late modernity can be benignly exited at will. Such post-state, post-market imaginaries suggest that we can exist 'out of time', or after time. Whether 'romantic historical' or 'nostalgic pre-modern', the tradition of rejecting modernity and questing after a non-market, non-state, collaborative, organic method of socio-political organization, has actually been a relatively distinctive strand of what in German is called *Modernitätskritik*: general cultural criticism of modernity.

Such thinking emerged in pre-Marxian critiques of capitalism, in, for example, the Phalanstère in France and the US in the mid- to late-nineteenth century (Beecher, 1990, 2001). One can see it in the attempts to dignify or side-step industrial labor in the British 'Arts and Crafts' movement's early stages (Davey, 1980; Cumming, 2006), and in the convoluted efforts by early town planners like Ebenezer Howard to promote harmony in the idea of the 'garden city' with his 'three magnets' metaphor (Howard, 1898). In National Socialist Germany, there was an attempt to reject both over-weaning state and uncaring market, with the appeal to the *Volksgemeinschaft* as a particularly authentic, organic way of producing consensus (Kurlander, 2011). Similarly, the complex institutions at the heart of Italian Fascist Corporatist economics strove (completely falsely) to imply the 'many-becoming-one' in an organic, conflict-free way (Pellicani, 2012), and many French intellectuals yearned for something similar at the same time (Hawkins, 2002). The non-state, non-market 'third way' dipped out of sight slightly in the 1950s and 1960s, perhaps because both state and market seemed to deliver breath-taking benefits – as any gay man or Los Angelino water-drinker can recognize. But it has seen some traction in scholarship from Anthony Giddens, invoked by the New Labour administration in the UK in the late 1990s and early 2000s, recasting socialism as an ethical category rather than a program of action (Giddens, 1998).

I do not wish to flatten all of these phenomena into one indistinct thing; it is easy to point out many differences between these movements. Nor do I wish to associate 'commons' thinking with any of the moral catastrophes associated with some of these instances of a quest for an organic, consensual world beyond state and market. But there is an interesting historical echo running through them all, up to and including present commons advocates, and that is a faith that beyond market and state there is a particularly authentic, organic and pragmatic way of problem solving that does not destroy or confront market and state, but, by the relaxed fluidity and authenticity of its decision-making, either renders each irrelevant, or neutralizes the poisonous parts of their natures.

Popular and academic social critics tend to deny their positions are merely the most recent iteration of a particular mode of criticism of state and market, however. In part this is to do with academic employment: academics must claim their work is novel for it to be published, and so become adept at developing proofs of novelty. If one sets one's mind to a rigorous historical methodology, one can see that the state and capitalism are in a constant state of flux, but that there was not some diabolical moment when the 'good' state was captured by 'bad' capitalism to form an unholy alliance. We may *wish* that state and market would ebb away, and both as a historian and a citizen,

I can see that there are so many cruel aspects of both. But that is no reason to expect that they will ebb away any time soon.

Commons advocates tend not to think in long historical timeframes, however, despite their keenness to invoke them. Instead, they often assert that we are on the brink of something immediate, a wonderful precipice from which we can see the sunny uplands of the future. For example, the Open Democracy website states boldly:

> State-market relations, and the ideological and political variables that characterised their distinct frameworks of conditionality and dependency, have left a significant mark on the past two centuries. Today we are in a visible process of transition towards a new framework. The new social reality that is configuring itself via technological change has multiple effects and is opening new avenues for social and scientific innovation.
>
> (Subirats, 2012).

They recognize the historical epoch of modernity, and the twin pillars upon which it rests, and promptly propose we are exiting it. Or take the opening of one collection of essays on the commons which states boldly that, 'We are poised between an old world that no longer works and a new one struggling to be born' (Bollier and Helfrich, 2012: Introduction, unnumbered page). Hardt and Negri's works are full of references to how we 'must' recognize the crisis nature of now, and the 'need' to do something as all old certainties dissolve. For the Midnight Notes Collective (2009), capitalism is already in free-fall. This faith might be called 'brinkism': a faith that vast, yet benign, change is just around the corner.

In some senses, that is the nature of being: leaving and becoming. In other senses, that is why people did away with the commons in the first place: they no longer worked for many, and a new world was struggling to be born (if inanimate objects can struggle; if worlds can exist preformed somewhere else awaiting their birth, before they exist here; and if a birth can take 350 years – clearly, ludicrous ways of imagining historical change). There is a certain type of progressive activist academic (or just activist) that always argues that we are at a 'crucial juncture'. From time to time, they will be wholly or partly right; after all, a broken clock is accurate to within an hour one-sixth of the time, and completely right twice a day. Revolutions do happen, though they are generally unpleasant for most people involved. But most of the time, most of us will be at a relatively trivial point in a historical tide of very long duration, although because we are in it, it will seem spectacularly important to us. Facing up to the false history that is present in much commons theory, and the absence of history in the suggestion we can exit the present easily, will enrich the debates around popular social criticism, as well as do justice to real 'practitioners' of liberating urban commons systems like Pry and Moreck.

Conclusion

Commons theorists are not completely hostile to modernity. The empiricists amongst them use modern methods like laboratory experiments in game theory, or detailed field studies of socio-economic systems. Yet it seems that this faith in modernity is only partial, as pre-modern moods are invoked to cloak modern empirical study. The question remains for us: do we follow the strategies of Pry and Moreck, and the Los Angeles water managers, which described the modern world as it is with market and state, and enable its better exploitation by the oppressed and marginalized in however transient a way? Gay men have been particularly successful in developing and exploiting an urban common which has transformed Western thinking about freedom and the body. Or do we advocate a radical exit strategy from the present, based on the reification of the wisdom pre-modern agrarian societies in far-away places, false memories of the past, and an assumption that our epochal position is voluntaristic? Such an exit strategy would also have to assume that any particular present, and any particular history to which it is tied, can be exited at will – and presumably without the catastrophic consequences attendant on historically observable attempts to exit the present on a grand scale.

Some commons theorists are not unaware of the problem of why anything 'commons-like' should happen at all. Political scientist Arun Agrawal sets out 14 interconnected features or institutional criteria that must be met before a commons-type arrangement could even be contemplated (2002), which look highly improbable (in fact, impossible) in modern worldsystems. Ostrom herself highlighted that most real meaningful commons systems exist only on the 'nano' scale, and appealed to an unspecified system of 'nested' or 'polycentric' systems to solve big problems (Keohane and Ostrom, 1995; Ostrom, 2010). Even the more romantic advocates of commons theory sketch out the vast obstacles in the way of it, including most conventional vehicles of protest or change. Most, like Hardt and Negri, will acknowledge that capitalism is in rude health, that New Social Movements are not very effective, observe that development policy is fundamentally flawed, and that labor has become immaterial and decentralized (Hardt and Negri, 2000: 170, 175, 282–300).

Put simply, I would suggest that history shows that cities are too complex, that state and market are too woven into them, that they contain too much that is invisible and ungovernable, to make an 'urban commons' remotely plausible, in the form that activists inside and outside the academy wish for or theorize. Ostrom herself was profoundly aware of this; many of her discussions about nesting and scaling are littered with cautions against 'perverse and extensive uses of policy panaceas in misguided efforts', arguing that, 'we should stop striving for simple answers to solve complex problems' (Ostrom, 2007). But I would also argue that this does not preclude citizens devising methods for turning cities into common resources. It could be that specifically *urban* commons theorists have been looking for the commons in the wrong way, in the wrong form, at the wrong times of day, and in the wrong locations. If we follow Pry and Moreck, and the millions of 'commoning' gay men who have followed them, then in fact, at the heart of many of our most commercial districts, in many of our trendiest bars, amongst some of the most expensive urban real estate, there is our common.

What, then, is to be done? I have no idea. But at least by thinking historically, and accepting that history is a discipline, not a playground, social and academic activists may more convincingly formulate their arguments and strategies. Hardt and Negri attack those who attack people like them for 'making political discussion so obscure that only other academics can understand its intricacies', arguing that, 'such assertions are significant symptoms of defeat, symptoms of the fact that no new ideas have emerged that are adequate to address the crisis' (Hardt and Negri, 2004: 219–20). It is not defeatist to recognize that it is raining, it has been raining for a long time, and the lowering sky implies that it will not stop raining for some time. It helps you remember your umbrella, and suggests you may wish to build a dam. It is not obscure to say that people should really attend to the details of the history from which they argue. And if 'the crisis' in question is the latest iteration of modernity, then from a historical perspective, no, no ideas have emerged that resolve it, 'the common'/'commons' included. In 2011, David Harvey was asked:

> You properly point out that efforts to create socialism in one country, let alone one city, or one small enterprise, have always failed. Why do you think people ignore this overwhelming history and keep trying to make it work anyway?

And his answer was, 'This is one of the most difficult paradoxes embedded in the history of the left (its thinking, its project, and its activities)' (Harvey, 2011). Harvey is speaking both as a leading intellectual of the left, but also one of the few of them who attends extensively to history as it was/is, rather than as it should have been. Substituting 'commons' for 'socialism', as a historian, one cannot help but agree. Further, I wonder if theorists of the urban commons might not benefit enormously from attending rigorously to 'this overwhelming history', and from situating themselves *in* modernity, not at the end of it.

References

Agrawal, A. (2002) 'Common Resources and Institutional Sustainability', in E. Ostrom et al. (eds), *The Drama of the Commons* (pp. 41–85). Washington DC: National Academy Press.

Beecher, J. (1990) *Charles Fourier: The Visionary and His World.* London: University of California Press.

Beecher, J. (2001) *Victor Considerant and the Rise and Fall of French Romantic Socialism.* London: University of California Press.

Bollier, D. (2006) 'The Growth of the Commons Paradigm', in C. Hess and E. Ostrom (eds), *Understanding Knowledge as a Commons: From Theory to Practice* (pp. 27–40). London: MIT Press.

Bollier, D. and Helfrich, S. (2012) *The Wealth of the Commons: A World Beyond Market and State.* Amherst, MA: Levellers Press.

Brooke, J. (2014) *Climate Change and the Course of Global History: A Rough Journey.* Cambridge: Cambridge University Press.

Clark, G. and Clark, A. (2001) 'Common Rights to Land in England, 1475–1839', *Journal of Economic History* 61(4): 1009–36.

Cumming, E. (2006) *Hand, Heart and Soul: The Arts and Craft Movement in Scotland.* Edinburgh: Birlinn.

Davey, P. (1980) *Arts and Crafts Architecture: The Search for an Earthly Paradise.* London: Architectural Press.

Eizenberg, E. (2012) 'Actually Existing Commons: Three Moments of Space of Community Gardens in New York City', *Antipode* 44(3): 764–82.

Fagan, B. (2000) *The Little Ice Age: How Climate Made History, 1300–2000.* Basic Books: New York.

Giddens, A. (1998) *Beyond Left and Right: The Future of Radical Politics.* Cambridge: Polity.

Grove, J. (2003) *Little Ice Ages: Ancient and Modern.* London: Routledge.

Hardin, G. (1968) 'The Tragedy of the Commons', *Science* 162(3859): 1243–8.

Hardt, M. and Negri, A. (2000) *Empire.* Cambridge, MA: Harvard University Press.

Hardt, M. and Negri, A. (2004) *Multitude.* New York: Penguin.

Hardt, M. and Negri, A. (2009) *Commonwealth.* London: Harvard University Press.

Harvey, D. (1985) *The Urbanization of Capital.* Oxford: Blackwell.

Harvey, D. (2003) *Paris, Capital of Modernity.* London: Routledge.

Harvey, D. (2011) 'Geographer David Harvey on the Urban Commons'. Online. Available HTTP: http://www.resilience.org/stories/2012-09-11/geographer-david-harvey-urban-commons (accessed 26 September 2013).

Hawkins, A. (2011) 'The Commons, Enclosure and Radical Histories', in D. Feldman and J. Lawrence (eds), *Structures and Transformations in Modern British History: Essays for Gareth Stedman Jones* (pp. 118–41). Cambridge: Cambridge University Press.

Hawkins, M. (2002) 'Corporatism and Third Way Discourses in Interwar France', *Journal of Political Ideologies* 7(3): 301–14.

Hess, C. and Ostrom, E. (2006) 'Introduction: An Overview of the Knowledge Commons', in C. Hess and E. Ostrom (eds), *Understanding Knowledge as a Commons: From Theory to Practice* (pp. 3–26). London: MIT Press.

Horden, P. and Purcell, N. (2000) *The Corrupting Sea: A Study of Mediterranean History.* Oxford: Blackwell.

Howard, E. (1898) *To-morrow: A Peaceful Path to Social Reform.* London: Sonnenschein.

Jerram, L. (2011) *Streetlife: The Untold History of Europe's Twentieth Century.* Oxford: Oxford University Press.

Jordan, J. (2013) 'Case Study: Reclaim the Streets'. Online. Availabe HTTP: <http://beautifultrouble.org/case/reclaim-the-streets/> (accessed 1 August 2013).

Kain, R. et al. (2011) *The Enclosure Maps of England and Wales, 1595–1918.* Cambridge: Cambridge University Press.

Keohane, R. and Ostrom, E. (1995) 'Introduction', in R. Keohane and E. Ostrom (eds), *Local Commons and Global Interdependence: Heterogeneity and Cooperation in Two Domains* (pp. 1–26). London: Sage.

Klein, N. (2001) 'Reclaiming the Commons', *New Left Review* 9(5/6): 81–9.

Kurlander, E. (2011) '"Between Detroit and Moscow": A Left-Liberal "Third Way" in the Third Reich', *Central European History* 44(2): 279–307.

Midnight Notes Collective (2009) 'Promissory Notes: From Crises to Commons'. Online. Available HTTP: <http://www.midnightnotes.org/Promissory%20Notes.pdf> (accessed 24 August 2013).

Mingay, G. (1997) *Parliamentary Enclosure in England: An Introduction to its Causes, Incidence and Impact*. London: Longman.

Moreck, K. (1931) *Führer Durch das Lasterhafte Berlin*. Leipzig: Verlag Moderner Stadtführer.

Nead, L. (2000) *Victorian Babylon: People, Streets and Images in Nineteenth-Century London*. London: Yale University Press.

Németh, J. (2012) 'Controlling the Commons: How Public is Public Space?', *Urban Affairs Review* 48(6): 811–35.

On the Commons (2013) 'What We Believe'. Online. Available HTTP: <http://www.onthecommons.org/what-we-believe> (accessed 16 July 2013).

Ostrom, E. (1990) *Governing the Commons: The Evolution of Institutions of Collective Action*. Cambridge: Cambridge University Press.

Ostrom, E. (2007) 'A Diagnostic Approach for Going Beyond Panaceas', *Proceedings of the National Academy of Sciences of the USA*, 104(39): 15181–87.

Ostrom, E. (2010) 'Beyond Markets and States: Polycentric Governance of Complex Economic Systems', *American Economic Review* 100(3): 641–72.

Parker, G. (2013) *Global Crisis: War, Climate Change and Catastrophe in the Seventeenth Century*. London: Yale University Press.

Pellicani, L. (2012) 'Fascism, Capitalism, Modernity', *European Journal of Political Theory* 11(4): 394–409.

Pry, P. (1937) *For Your Convenience: A Learned Dialogue, Instructive to All Londoners and London Visitors, Overheard in the Thélème Club and Taken Down Verbatim by Paul Pry*. London: G. Routledge.

Sassen, S. (1991) *The Global City: New York, London, Tokyo*. Princeton: Princeton University Press.

Showalter, E. (1992) *Sexual Anarchy: Gender and Culture at the Fin-de-Siècle*. London: Bloomsbury.

Subirats, J. (2012) 'The Commons: Beyond the State v. Markets Dilemma'. Online. Available HTTP: <http://www.opendemocracy.net/joan-subirats/commons-beyond-market-vs-state-dilemma> (accessed 7 July 2013).

Thompson, E.P. (1965) *The Making of the English Working Class*. London: Gollancz.

Thompson, E.P. (1991) *Customs in Common*. London: Penguin.

Wrigley, E.A. (2011) 'Coping with Rapid Populations Growth: How England Fared in the Century Preceding the Great Exhibition, 1851', in D. Feldman and J. Lawrence (eds), *Structures and Transformations in Modern British History: Essays for Gareth Stedman Jones* (pp. 24–53). Cambridge: Cambridge University Press.

Yelling, J. (1977) *Common Field and Enclosure in England, 1450–1850*. Hamden, Conn.: Archon Books.

Chapter 3

Sharing an atmosphere: spaces in urban commons

Orvar Löfgren

'Is there anyone who has not, at least once, walked into a room and "felt the atmosphere"?', asks Teresa Brennan (2004: 1) in the introduction to her book *The Transmission of Affect*. In recent years there has been a rising interest in the role of atmospheres in social life, not least in urban spaces. How are such collective moods produced, shared or dissolved? I am interested in this chapter in the often invisible norms, routines and competences that make it possible for people with different backgrounds to share the same spaces and create temporary forms of communalities. This dimension becomes important when discussing the making and maintenance of a specific kind of urban commons. Several authors have pointed to the problems of transplanting the concept of traditional commons into urban settings (Parker and Johansson, 2012; Hess, 2008; Bravo and Moor, 2008). The shift is easier when it is a question of pooling or sharing certain kinds of tangible resources, as in the cases of community gardens (Foster, 2011) or co-op housing estates (Rabinowitz, 2012). It becomes more of a challenge when analyzing other kinds of urban communalities, open spaces such as streets, parks and transit places, where people with very different backgrounds mingle (see the discussion in Susser and Tonnelat, 2013).

In discussing the often fleeting and intangible conditions that produce the latter kinds of urban commons, we need to focus on both the unstable and malleable processes of what David Harvey (2012: 73) has termed *commoning*. Processes of commoning may take many shapes, such as defending open access or resisting commodification, but here I am interested in questions of how different users co-inhabit and regulate a public space. The resources in question, then, have more to do with what constitutes social capital in a given urban setting. What is it that is being shared or maintained?

My focus on atmospheres aims to catch such elusive traits of sharing and co-existence. Atmospheres are an important element in many urban commons. They work as a medium through which people read and assess a certain space or social situation. They may be felt as welcoming, alienating, safe or unsafe. First of all, this calls for a focus on the frailty of such a *Gemeinschaft*, that is often upheld less by direct policing or governance but by unwritten rules and agreements about acceptable behavior, attitudes and activities. What kinds of social contracts exist in a given public space? Questions of trust and different forms of sociability are important here. What is OK and what is not – and who decides?

Secondly, many of these urban commons can be seen as *terraine vagues* in the sense that they are not clearly defined or delineated and may change over time, during day and night as well as between seasons. Looking at such kinds of open and fluid spaces is analytically rewarding, because it directs attention to elusive processes of gatekeeping and subtle forms of inclusion and exclusion. (An interesting category are those spaces that hover uneasily between the semi-public and semi-private.)

In the following, I will use the railway station and the urban beach as my two contrasting ethnographic examples. I explore the ways they are transformed or renegotiated in a historical perspective, but before I venture out there I will discuss the concept of atmospheres and some different analytical approaches in the study of them. How is it possible to develop the ethnography of the everyday ways in which modes and moods of use are related in these types of urban commons?

Capturing the mood

The contemporary research interest in urban atmospheres comes from several directions. First of all, from the years of what was called 'The New Economy' around the turn of the millennium, when a cult of creativity and creative industries spawned an interest in how 'creative atmospheres' could be produced and managed. Another dimension of this interest had to do with what came to be called 'The Experience Economy' which meant a focus on marketing good experiences – a pleasant mood or an appetizing event as a potential commodity. How could you produce, package, store or market a good atmosphere (Löfgren, 2015)?

Parallel to this new interest, atmosphere as an analytical concept began to attract attention in the cultural and social sciences. One of the reasons for this was what has been called 'the affective and sensory turns' in many disciplines, an interest in culture not just as text, symbol or discourse but as the understudied non-discursive dimensions of affects, moods and sensibilities (Gregg and Seigworth, 2010; Borch, 2014). Much of this reorientation occurred in urban studies (see, for example, Blom Hansen and Verkaaik, 2009; Calhoun et al., 2013; Saskien, 2013), with questions about how such collective moods were produced, shared or dissolved. The linking of affect and atmosphere has to do with the fact that an atmosphere is often felt and registered in the body, before it is consciously noted or reflected over.

If we want to understand the routes this concept has travelled in academia, we need to look further back. 'Atmosphere' is a term that drifted from physics and meteorology into the description of emotional moods or situations – from its original meaning of a sphere of gas surrounding a body such as a planet, into a 'prevailing psychological climate; pervading tone or mood like the atmosphere of the court', as the *Oxford English Dictionary* puts it. Not surprisingly, this was a metaphorical usage that became common in the early romantic period of the late eighteenth and early nineteenth centuries. Not only planets, but people and settings were surrounded by shifting atmospheres. It was often linked to the concept of mood, not only defined as a personal state of mind but also 'applied to a crowd of people or other collective body' (*Oxford English Dictionary*). It is interesting to note that the original physics of measuring and describing atmospheres also travelled into the description of emotional states. We still find meteorological terms such as air pressure (a heavy or light-hearted atmosphere), or temperature (a chilly or a warm atmosphere). Other common descriptions include words like powerful, stressful or peaceful. People use verbs to describe their reactions, such as being overwhelmed, touched, taken in or moved by a certain atmosphere. Atmospheres are described as energy-reducing, permeated by inertia, boredom, anxiety or stress, while other kinds of atmospheres are described as producing positive energy, using terms like euphoric and energizing atmospheres, or just 'good vibes'. Think, for example, of a statement such as 'the energy that rises from the pavements of Manhattan'.

The pioneer in such studies of mental atmospheres is the German philosopher and architectural theorist Gernot Böhme (1993, 2006, 2014) who has spent years writing books on the study of atmosphere in built environments and private and public spaces. He defines atmosphere as the experience of co-presence. For him atmosphere is the prototypical 'between' phenomenon, linking subject and object. He explores the sensualities of everything from colours and textures to what he calls the 'ecstasies of things'. His approach is shaped by an architectural tradition, searching for ways to understand how good atmospheres can be created in built environments, often with a focus on aesthetics and space. Reading Böhme raises many methodological questions about how to develop an ethnography of these themes. What do we mean when we say that walls are soaked with an atmosphere, and can an atmosphere be stored?

A rather different take is found in Teresa Brennan's book *The Transmission of Affect*. As mentioned earlier, Brennan starts out by asking 'Is there anyone who has not, at least once, walked into a room and "felt the atmosphere"?' (2004: 1). She is interested in processes of *entrainment*, the ways in which people are emotionally affected by others. How do people, for example, unwittingly breathe in the smell of anxiety? Her focus is on how atmosphere is felt on the body, in the body, a communication that dissolves the boundaries between the individual and the environment.

Brennan explores the different roles of the senses; she draws on neurological research on the transmission of hormones (running through the blood) and airborne molecules of pheromones (registered on the skin), the processes called either chemical or electrical entrainment. There is no need to go further into the neurological discussions here; what is important is that the nervous system registers and reacts to the emotional climate of another person, of a group or an environment. Again, there is the tricky question of how people become part of an atmosphere. Think, for example, of a nervous atmosphere, a microclimate that is communicated by body signals and even more by tingling sensations: 'there is a nervousness in the air'.

Ben Anderson (2009) has taken Böhme's and Brennan's work further and his discussion is very much part of both the affective turn and the new approaches of non-representational theory in cultural analysis (Vannini, 2014). He explores the ambiguities of atmosphere, existing in tensions between subjective/objective, material/mental, bounded but also formless, collectively produced but often experienced as intensely personal. He points out that one way in which atmosphere is a good concept to think with, is because it is 'more': 'Atmospheres are a kind of indeterminate affective 'excess' through which intensive space-times can be created' (Anderson, 2009: 80).

The excess, the elusiveness and ephemerality of atmospheres creates an ethnographic challenge. In Heibach (2012) very different approaches are discussed, but still on a rather programmatic level. A more concrete example is found in a study of Jamaican dance halls by Henriques (2010). Like Brennan, Henriques is interested in the transmission of affect, but his focus is on 'feeling the vibes' and trying to find ways of measuring the intensity of atmospheres.

It is striking that researchers often have to resort to metaphors to find ways to describe atmospheres, a strategy which is not unproblematic. I have already mentioned the meteorological metaphors, and Böhme draws on architectural terms such as volume, light effects or surfaces. Henriques borrows from acoustics, not only writing about vibrations, but wavebands, frequencies, amplitudes, rhythms, timbre, tone. These studies complement each other by having different foci, but as Borch (2014) points out there is often a political dimension lacking.

A further development of this field of study needs to pay more attention to actual ethnographies, emphasizing the constant making and un-making of moods (see the discussion in Bissell, 2010). The anthropologists Jennifer Carlson and Kathleen Stewart have used the term 'mood work' to describe such complexities of movement and interplay. They are interested in developing experimental ethnographies of how atmospheres are created, sustained and shared:

Mood is a contact zone for the strange and prolific coexistence of sense and world. An orientation alert to something already set in motion, it is a mundane register of labors to sense out what is actual and potential in an historical moment or a situation. Mood works, in other words, to articulate the labor of living. It marshals bodies, objects, technologies, sensations and flights of fancy into forms of partial coherence. Its legibilities are inchoate and yet pronounced in practices, socialities, scenes, social circles, events, and landscapes.

(Carlson and Stewart, 2014)

It is this perspective of understanding mood work I will take into a discussion of urban commons. The focus is on ethnographies of the intensive interaction between people, spatial properties and materialities; what the cultural geographer Doreen Massey (2005) has called processes of *throwntogetherness*, and the anthropologist Tim Ingold (2011: 115 ff.) has termed *entanglements* in the production and maintenance of atmospheres.

A contested common

I am walking into Copenhagen Central Railway Station through the entrance leading in from the old red light district with its bars, prostitution and drug dealing. Suddenly I hear Mozart playing, rather monotonous and loud. This new orchestration of the passageway was explained in a newspaper article a few days later: 'Verdi and Wagner keep the junkies away'. The journalist stated that 'undesirable elements' – homeless, drunks and junkies – had a tendency to gather here and in the winter of 2002 the station manager began playing loud classical music in an attempt to drive such vagrants out of the passageway. The place was soon abandoned, but the music kept playing for years – and has started again.

Urban railway stations are testing grounds for the borders between private and public, semi-public and semi-private. They represent a special kind of urban commons, a *terraine vague*, neither inside or outside. They are wide open, inviting and centrally located. Although designed as machines for the swift flow of travellers, they are used for other purposes as well. Very different kinds of people co-habit this transit space, long distance travellers, tourists, daily commuters, but also many kinds of non-travellers who for different reasons are attracted to the station: the homeless seeking shelter, bored teenagers looking for action, people out of work trying to pass the day. This mix makes it a special kind of urban commons.

The railway station can be used as a seismographic surface, on which changing tensions of social inclusion and exclusion can be explored. The history of the urban railway station is an ongoing battle between desirable and undesirable visitors. How are the differences between legitimate waiting and illegitimate loitering defined and by whom? To address such questions, a historical perspective is helpful. Using materials from an ongoing study of railway stations (see Löfgren, 2008), I focus on life in transit at the Copenhagen Central station, from its opening back in 1911 to the present. Over a century, different groups and station users have been identified as problems by the station authorities. All kinds of urban vagrants, the down-and-out, the homeless and out-of-work, drug addicts or alcoholics, old age pensioners or teenagers looking for ways to pass the time, groups of immigrants using the station as a meeting place, male and female prostitutes and pimps looking for customers, pickpockets and con-men. The changing social landscape may illustrate the ways in which certain groups are marginalized or seen as a problem in this kind of space. Who belongs here? What kinds of competences do you need in order to be a person who can pose as a 'desirable element' with 'a legitimate errand' in this transit space either in 1911 or a century later? What kind of urban commons is this? Using a historical perspective, we can study changing processes of managing and using a public space, skills and competences evolving, conflicts sharpened or neutralized, but also see how atmospheres are defined as welcoming, safe or forbidding – by whom and for whom.

The making of a new arena

The railway station was a new *zone nerveuse* of the nineteenth century, and the architect who designed the new Copenhagen station that opened in 1911 knew that. He stated that one of his aims in organizing this transit space was to minimize 'travel nervousness', but that was a difficult task. The station should be a place for the quickening pace of modern mobility, assisting travellers as well as the growing masses of suburban commuters, but it should also be a building sending out messages of reassurance and security. There were a number of details, from the layout of the building to many small semiotic details that signalled this. The outer walls are guarded by rows of statues of peasants in folk costumes, symbols of national stability, and on festive occasions and national holidays the entire main hall is still draped in Danish flags (Flindt Larsen, 1994; Ovesen, 1999).

At the opening in 1911, the new setting was described as overwhelming in its grandeur and scale. Modernity was felt in the body as one became part of a journey into the future – with the help of the vast space, the cascades of light from above, the fast crowds, the interaction with newfangled technologies and gadgets, the exciting sounds and sights. The first visitors often described the awe that the monumental building produced, but they also registered feelings of stress or insecurity. Disembarking from the train you were thrown into the chaos of the station and all the senses were alerted. Your body was pushed and jostled in the crowds, the hissing steam and belching smoke; there were the loud and unintelligible noises from the loudspeakers or shouting porters, with strange smells and darting glances from strangers everywhere. Simply too much. Add to this the vastness of the place, a place where one could feel very small and very lost. In Copenhagen, there is a classic saying that labels those who have not yet become streetwise and are identified as unsophisticated country bumpkins: 'Did you arrive on the 4 o'clock train?'

One could tell the newcomers by their clumsy body movements, their gaping gaze and poorly masked amazement.

One was now in the urban danger zone where visitors from the country were thrown to the wolves. Clutching their suitcases, people embarked from the relative safety of the train into this jungle, populated (as they had been reminded back home) by all kinds of shady characters, con-men and tricksters, or as the Danish term runs: *bondefanger* (from the German *Bauernfänger*, literally meaning 'people making a living of trapping peasants'). To newcomers, the station atmosphere signalled a need to be on the lookout, monitoring the sea of strangers surrounding you. Was this a threatening or reassuring atmosphere? A trusting situation or not?

To many early observers, railway stations seemed a condensation of urban modernity, but also a training ground. Here one had to learn the skills of handling crowds, strangers and new challenges.

The history of the railway station can be read as ways of learning to organize and differentiate social classes, as well as developing the skills necessary in a new mass society where people came in close contact with strangers and had to learn to size each other up. The railway supplied different kinds of tools and infrastructures for such a task, developing a formal class system: are you a first, second or third class passenger? In Copenhagen station you can still read the inscriptions *1* and *2 Class Waiting Room* above the entrance to O'Leary's sports bar. In most stations there were attempts at segregating people and providing shelters for upper class travellers who did not want to mingle (see the discussion in Löfgren, 2008). In more recent years, station managers have copied the idea of business class lounges from airports to provide segregated spaces.

Written and unwritten rules

At the entrance to the Copenhagen station there is a long list of do's and don'ts: 'Only persons with legitimate errands are allowed in the transit hall, the waiting rooms and on the platforms'. No biking, skateboarding, littering, scribbling on walls, drinking, begging or offering of merchandise; the list is long and ends with a general warning: 'no behaviour that is noisy or disturbing to other passengers is allowed'.

Public spaces such as stations have often carried these lists of rules and regulations, rarely noticed by travellers. But more important are the unwritten rules of behaviour. How are they formed and learned? I am thinking of the skills required in handling crowds (see Borch, 2012) and strangers and the other competences needed to use the station. In the early days of railway travel, such skills could be discussed as a novelty in travel handbooks. To share a confined space with total strangers should make you prepared for everything: 'In going through a tunnel it is always well to have the hands and arms ready disposed for defence, so that in an event of an attack, the travellers may be instantly beaten back or restrained'. This piece of advice comes from *The Railway Traveller's Handy Book* from 1862, one of many publications trying to teach railway behaviour (quoted in Smullen, 1968: 57). How did one handle the reorganization of time, space and social relations in these novel settings and how should one relate to strangers? (Avoid talking of politics, for example.) A newfangled nineteenth century social institution like the queue is an example of a crowd handling principle people had to learn: 'When a large crowd of people gathers a so called queue should be formed'. This innovation introduced new and often provoking ideas of egality and turn-taking (cf. Ehn and Löfgren, 2010: 40 ff.). In a wider sense, there was the urban competence of judging and classifying strangers, not only by speech and dress but often, more importantly, through body language. People sharpened their observational skills.

During the last hundred years of Copenhagen station's history, there has been an ongoing battle about who belongs here, with different strategies of inclusion and exclusion. Apart from varying forms of policing the territory, there have been constant attempts at reorganizing the infrastructure, trying to prevent people from sleeping on benches or hiding in corners, for example. New forms of governance have, of course, also produced new counter-strategies.

When a policy of 'ticket holders only' was attempted after the Second World War, the vagrants started buying the cheapest ticket available in order to be able to pass as legitimate travellers. When favourite hangouts, hidden corners or comfortable benches were moved, 'the undesirables' regrouped and found new spaces. Vagrants also learned how to keep a low profile and not draw too much attention to themselves.

At different times, various groups of 'undesirables' came into focus. During the Depression in the 1930s, jobless men became a marked element in the station landscape. In the 1960s, Turkish male immigrants began to use the station as an informal meeting place. Or, as one man remembers it, 'I came from Istanbul by train in 1969. The Central station was a special meeting place for us immigrants. We had nowhere else to go, we gathered to meet, talk, get news from home'. Sometimes there could be hundreds of Turkish men gathered in the station, becoming a very visible element, which created complaints of them taking over the place. In a sense they had turned the transit space into a new kind of urban common for informal socializing.

Later, drug dealing and drug users became a growing concern, just as male and female prostitution had been earlier. Lights in the public lavatories could be dimmed in order to make injections more difficult. Boundaries were tested continually, levels of tolerance or forms of policing changing. Processes of inclusion and exclusion may make the hidden norms of urban commons visible, but they also illustrate how different groups of users define an atmosphere as threatening or reassuring, which leads to the question of how atmospheres are produced and experienced.

The station as a sensorium

Teresa Brennan argues that shared atmospheres are created not so much by visual impressions as by the ear, the nose and the skin, three forms of communication which are hard to capture. Smell, sound and touch work much more directly than sight, which, as she points out, is a sense that separates and selects much more than other senses.

When I began to explore the atmospheres at Copenhagen station, the visual dimension was my ethnographic starting point. I went to the station with the camera, looking, staring, glancing – my eyes perhaps open too wide. I returned with scribbled notes and photos that really did not tell me much. The other sensual impressions were just background disturbances. So what would happen if I returned to explore other inputs?

I went back on an August Sunday in the middle of the holiday season. I started to record the soundscape. The first thing that struck me was the diffuseness of the background noise; it was as if all kinds of sounds were blended into a constant murmur. I tried to identify the various ingredients of that mixture. Voices, steps, luggage being dragged along, the faint humming from the escalators. Some sounds broke out of this constant murmur: the clickety-clack of the wheels of bags and suitcases hauled along the stone floor, bits and pieces of conversations drifting past, the sudden ding-a-dong signalling loudspeaker announcements, booming messages into the air, and a returning, rather stressful and angry flow of signals from some kind of invisible machine: beep-beep-beep.

In a discussion of the design of public spaces, Lars Frers (2006: 256 ff.), using railway stations as an example, has pointed to the importance of sound, from stressful noises to attempts to use 'mood music'. He points out that sounds often carry instant messages, drawing people's attention quicker and more forcefully than other senses. It can be the distinct clicks of high heeled shoes against the stone floor, or the sudden impact of raised voices as an alert about a potential conflict.

If sound was difficult to handle, smell was even worse. On the internet I found a cry for help. 'How does a station smell?', someone asked, trying to write an essay. The first answer she got was: 'Do stations smell? I'll have to find out next time'. Terms such as 'smellscapes' have been coined to try to capture olfactory scenes, but smell is one of the least recorded or discussed senses. In this field, the terminology often seems even vaguer or less developed than for sound. Some specialist fields are much more elaborated, as in the poetics of perfume and wine tasting. On the whole, however, it is a fairly limited vocabulary, often focusing on the unpleasant smells: acid, musty, stale, bitter – drifting over into the universe of taste. In this sensory realm, the polarity between pleasant and unpleasant seems more marked than for many other senses. Words like odour, aroma, smelly and bouquet are loaded with positive or negative connotations.

I went back to the station ready to explore smells, lacking an olfactory recorder but relying on paper and pen. Does Copenhagen Central Station smell? My first impression was, no. It seemed hard to capture the smells of the station, although I slowly began to identify some. Maybe I am one of those many persons who have not developed strong olfactory skills, unlike for example a colleague who accompanied me into a station café once. She stopped at the entrance and told me that this place just did not smell good enough to eat in. When I asked her what it smelled of, she took another sniff and answered: 'It feels stale, the air is dense, a strange mix of not so appetizing food flavours, sweating customers, stressed staff. Let's go somewhere else, I don't feel comfortable here. Bad atmosphere, simply'.

At Copenhagen station, I kept wondering about what kinds of smells are present when we describe something as odourless. Does boredom, stress or irritation have an aroma? After sounds and smells, it was time to explore the registers of touch and the haptic. It has been argued that the skin is not only our largest sensory organ, but also as Teresa Brennan has argued, extremely important in the ways we register and are influenced by local atmospheres. Touch works through many registers, from skin reactions to bodily contacts. The haptic dimension is, of course, very present in the ways people handle the material world of the station. When you are in a state of travel nervousness, holding on to objects becomes important. There is a comfort in clutching a handbag, fiddling with the ticket, feeling the warmth of a cup of coffee or taking refuge in your own temporary home on a bench defended by your luggage. In a similar manner there is a constant choreography of strangers in close action, touching or avoiding touch. There are irritated elbows and helping hands, people getting pushed or tripping over luggage, squeezing past others.

All these ethnographic attempts raised more questions than they produced results. The first thing I was reminded of in my attempts to capture sense after sense was that the senses are intensely entangled with each other. Just as scholars have been busy categorizing and labelling emotions, the talk of the five senses can be rather unproductive in ethnography. Returning to Böhme, it is possible to explore the ways in which the materiality of the station building affects all the senses. The gigantic arrival hall makes people smaller. The flow of light from the glass roof, the hard marble floor, the lack of hide-outs and sheltered corners make the scene very public, but as Tim Ingold (2011) reminds us, we do not walk *into* a place or a landscape, our experience is the result of a dense interaction of the senses with the material surroundings. The hardness of the marble floor, the vibrations from the escalator, the weight of the suitcase, the constant presence of other bodies and so on.

Instead of thinking in terms of five senses, it would be more fruitful to think about concepts that bridge them and show how they work together, or block each other. Here, Henriques' analysis is helpful. One of his concepts is *intensity* – on several levels. What are the intensities of the sensual inputs and their effect? Getting a whiff of something or being engulfed by a stench, being surrounded by a din or barely registering a hushed or soft sound (see also McCullough, 2013 on attention in public spaces). In the same way, there is the question of impact; some sensory inputs catch us unaware, unprepared, and make us defenseless. Over time, people learn to overlook an impression, overhear a sound or stop noticing a smell. Another central concept in Henriques' approach is that of rhythm, a concept that spans over many senses and sensations. People get in and out of synch with moving crowds; there are sudden changes between stress and bored waiting. Different rhythms clash both in the body and in the station crowds, from individual heart beats to surging flows.

Changing moods

I took concepts such as intensity and rhythm back to the station with me and used them for another classic ethnographic approach. I began to work with contrasts, in order to get elusive traits to surface and find out how moods change over time and in different social situations. First of all, I moved from space to space in the station complex, registering changes in atmospheres and how the senses worked together. At the main entrance, I had to pass through a dense wall of cigarette smoke. This is where smokers had to stand, their smoke mixing with car exhausts and the different sounds of traffic and slamming doors. In a study of smoking in public places, Qian Hui Tan (2013) has pointed out that over the last years smoke has become a highly contested element. In the heydays of public smoking, it was hardly noticed, but now it evokes angry reactions or moral judgments. Smokers are constantly marginalized, like the people out here outside the station, huddling in the cold, sometimes creating temporary fraternities. As Qian Hui Tan points out, the olfactory politics of smoking reveal much about segregation and stratification in public spaces, but it is also an example of what kinds of sharing are unproblematic or seen as undesirable, or, in this context, unhealthy.

Inside the building, it was noticeably warmer and the smells and sounds became more difficult to pin down. Walking into the crowded ticket office, sounds became much more muted, and here, standing in line, I also sensed the body odours of impatience and irritation. The atmosphere was denser here, space more cramped. The lowered ceiling took away the strong echo effect of the main hall.

On the whole, I found it hard to register and characterize the microclimates of the station area, it was easier to turn to another contrast. I started to observe changes in atmosphere around the clock, by returning at different hours and weekdays. I began late one morning by following a couple of tourists who were hesitantly dragging their luggage around, searching for information. Their body movements gave them away as newcomers to this setting. They are scanning the terrain for all kinds of signs, moving around slowly, often looking lost. All of a sudden, the arrival hall fills up; a late commuter train has arrived and the atmosphere changes drastically. The commuters move swiftly like a military phalanx ploughing its way through the tourist travellers, who try to get out of the way but here and there they are surrounded like islands in the fast flow of commuters striding along the floor, their gazes fixed into the distance. Mentally they may already be at work, they do not observe the station surroundings at all. There is no hesitation in their bodies – just the same old morning routines. They are the station veterans.

In just a few moments the stream ebbs out and the station returns to its atmosphere of lethargy. The tourists are in control again, together with the homeless and others who use the station as their temporary urban refuge or meeting place, surreptitiously checking for the guards or police that circle the station. The homeless are another kind of station veteran, viewing the setting with different eyes.

Moving among the rush hour crowds that are confidently hurrying through the station complex I can feel in my own body what it is to be out of synch. I felt like a country bumpkin; I have lived too long in a small town, just visiting the metropolis, and I realize that I have lost some of the skills of maneuvering in fast crowds. I cannot read the signals, my body movements are indecisive. I frequently find myself about to bump into people, not part of the flow.

Trying to record these rhythms and intensities, I felt the need for more inspiration and turned to a classic site so often depicted in movies: the bustling crowds at New York's Grand Central Station. In a study of space, Tony Hiss watches the crowds here and reflects on the social skills you need to learn to handle this setting. He observes:

> the swirling, living motion of five hundred people walking, two and three abreast, from and toward the fourteen entrances and exits of the concourse. Moving silently, as it seemed, within that sound, I noticed again that no one was bumping into anyone else – that every time I thought I myself might be about to bump into people near me, both I and they were already accelerating slightly, or decelerating, or making a little side step, so that nobody ever collided. On top of this, the weightless sensation in my head gave me the feeling that I could look down on all this movement, in addition to looking out at it. I had a sense that the cooperation I was part of kept repeating itself throughout the vast room around me and the vaster city beyond it.
>
> (Hiss, 1991: 8)

How is this collective choreography made possible, with its coordination of hundreds of different styles of walking and moving? Here is a competence of quick glances, body signals and swift movements. Searching on Youtube for Grand Central scenes I found a flash mob project, where 200 actors at a given signal froze their movements in the commuter crowd. The hidden camera records how the flow all of a sudden stops and amazed fellow passengers look around trying to understand what is happening. It is like the whole arrival hall holds its breath for a moment (www.youtube.com/watch?v=jwMj3PJ Dxuo).

In Copenhagen, the morning rush hour gave the station a very special atmosphere. There was a feeling of expectancy in the air; the start of a fresh working day, a kind of positive stress. Later in the day the tempo slowed down, the sounds and the mood were different, with the echoes of solitary travellers moving along the hall. As the tired commuters returned later in the day to go home, the station had a different feel. Compare this to the festive mood of the station on a Friday or Saturday evening, when groups of people leave or arrive in search of a fun night out. A party feeling begins to pervade the place – and then the mood changes drastically as the place is deserted at night.

Writing about her impressions of the Copenhagen station when waiting for the midnight train back to Sweden, Julia Svensson (2010) has captured the mood of frustration and depression that takes over the station. The train is, as always, late. She is thrown out of McDonald's, the last place to close, and after that there is only the chill of the platforms and the arrival hall.

A Finnish professor of literature remembers the shame of being caught in a police roundup at Copenhagen railway station in the middle of the night while waiting for the first connection in the morning after having missed the evening train. Her husband is off getting the tickets and, pregnant and nauseous, she sits on the benches together with all kinds of people who have been trying to steal a couple of hours sleep. Suddenly two young policemen appear and start ordering everybody out: 'This is no place for sleeping'. On weak legs she hurries towards the door thinking: 'If only you knew who I am, you wouldn't treat me like this'. She concludes, 'My shame had to do with the glances of the policemen: suddenly I could see myself with their eyes, at least for a second I was forced to take in their image of me' (Mazzarella, 2003: 10).

A similar situation is captured by Trude Marstein in her novel *Doing Good* (2006) that traces the lives of the inhabitants in a Norwegian town over a couple of days. It begins and ends at the local railway station, in a mood of morning arrival and midnight departure. A man dragging his heavy suitcase into the station building around midnight feels the forlorn atmosphere and how it seems to penetrate people: 'Sick, sick people, sick, sick place', and he reflects:

> An old lady has gone up and started walking restlessly between the departure screen and the toilets, two points of security [. . .] Here we are, all of us. Where are we all going? Out of here. Anywhere, just out of this place. Everything is closed, the kiosk, the cafeteria, the pub, only

the lavatories are open, I don't think there is a more uninviting place than this.

(Marstein, 2006: 464)

'Everything is closed' – all the closed shutters and locked doors help to produce an atmosphere of being left out. The passengers become a group of losers, marginalized, outside society. What are they doing here, in this godforsaken place? The general mood becomes slightly depressive, gone is all the morning energy. Now even the commuters begin to feel like 'undesired elements' in an unwelcoming atmosphere.

Confrontations

In Warsaw's central station, squatters and the homeless staying in the passages and corridors of the underground sections of the station were called 'trolls' by the police. Some years ago a group of down-and-outs occupied the middle of the main hall in protest against the new regulations which forbade sleeping overnight. They spent several months right there in the center of the building, their blankets creating an island of their own, but were totally ignored by both passengers and authorities. Their new territory just became a non-space that people avoided (Jemielniak and Jemielniak, 2001).

A different kind of attempt to draw attention to the social tensions in the station landscape was carried out by Michael Galanakis (2008) in his study of social inclusion and exclusion in urban public spaces. He carried out fieldwork in the central station in Helsinki, Finland, and noted how the definitions of 'problematic visitors' changed over time. In the early 2000s it was mostly Somali refugees who used the station as a meeting place and an arena for socializing and who were seen by some other visitors as an unwelcome element. Galanakis decided to carry out an experiment. One day in 2005 surprised travellers encountered a new setting in the middle of the station's main hall. There were a couple of sofas and chairs, and tables with neat tablecloths and burning incense; a bookcase and a couple of lamps with a warm and inviting light. A cozy living room oasis in the middle of this anonymous transit space. Galanakis was out to create a certain cultural confusion, turning a private home-setting into a public arena, with the help of thrift store furniture and all kinds of knick-knacks – a new kind of urban common. The project stayed for a week and the message was communicated on posters:

For the living room of the city
Private in public or public in private?
What is private and what is public space?
Does public space belong to all of us equally? Who is all and how equally? [. . .] may I sit next to you?

His project evoked strong emotional reactions. In the beginning, Galanakis was nervous of his living room being vandalized or taken over by certain groups, but there was something about the openness of this space that made all kinds of people sit down and start talking to strangers. Galanakis had quite consciously included a number of Somalian objects in the setting, Somalian incense, Somalian books. His main point was, however, that this was a mixed space. In his book he reflects on the reactions his project created, using them to discuss what kinds of processes make urban spaces open or closed, welcoming, hostile or indifferent. In places such as Copenhagen's Central Station, an ongoing battle developed to define who belongs and who does not and what kinds of behaviour or uses of the station are wanted or unwanted.

During the many hours I have spent observing life at the Copenhagen station, I have become extremely self-conscious of my own body language and loitering as I roam around the building, seemingly without any purpose. I feel the glances from others as they try to work out what kind of person I am, not a regular traveller surely, nor an 'illegitimate visitor'.

Today urban railway stations are often highly monitored territories. Fears of terrorist attacks have led to the establishment of sophisticated electronic surveillance systems in many places. Waiting for a train at a London station I keep encountering messages asking me and other travellers to report 'any suspicious behavior' and I know that the surveillance cameras around me are programmed to detect activities and movements that are suspiciously different. Suddenly I become obsessed with 'behaving normally', again being conscious of the body language of myself and fellow travellers.

What is a normal station behaviour at any given time and in any given setting? British travellers visiting colonial Indian railway stations remarked that the peasants often came a day early in order not to miss the train and settled down with their families in the station area. What they did not know was that for many squatters this was a permanent arrangement. They were not waiting for any train but had turned the station into their home (Richards and MacKenzie, 1986: 139).

Waterfront commons

Another way to confront that special character of stations is to turn to a very different kind of urban common: the beach. Across the bridge from Copenhagen is the city of Malmö, a rather segregated urban setting. A long beach area in the middle of the city is perhaps the most striking of urban commons here. During the summer months it is heavily used by city dwellers who walk, bike or drive to the beaches. It becomes a densely populated territory, with a mix of groups that is very striking, from teenagers to senior citizens. Women from Middle Eastern backgrounds play football or go into the water properly dressed, while in the shade of the trees there are men with water pipes, families gathered around the barbecue. Next to them,

'Swedish' middle class families bask in the sun, working on their tan or swimming in the sea.

The Malmö city beaches were created in the 1930s by ferrying sand to build up coastal beaches. Back then modern beach life was developing and just as with the railway station, the beach was seen as a training ground for modern life (Ristilammi, 2003). People learned to handle their bodies and leisure life in new ways, but also to co-exist with strangers on a packed beach (see Löfgren, 2000: 227 ff.). Many urban beaches started out as different kinds of commons, a free space used by fishermen and other local groups, but as beaches became the focus of urban leisure, such users were often driven out and the beachscape 'cleaned up', as the historian John Gillis has shown (Gillis, 2012: 147 ff.). Old fishermen's huts could be torn down in order to improve the sea view.

Unlike many other arenas, beaches have brought classes together, sometimes in an uneasy coexistence, sometimes in strikingly unproblematic ways. There has been the chance to observe, very close at hand, 'those other people' at play. In the history of British tourism this role of the beach as one of the few 'neutral grounds' is very marked. Here the working class entered the scene much earlier than in many other nations, or as the historian John K. Walton describes the situation in the late nineteenth century: 'At the seaside rich and poor, respectable and ungodly, staid and rowdy, quiet and noisy not only rubbed shoulders [. . .] they also had to compete for access to, and use of, recreational space' (1983: 190). This may be overstating the classlessness of the beach. There were endless debates about beach morals and beach rules as different lifestyles were confronted, but on the whole there was rather little official intervention. On some British beaches an informal zoning took place and people sorted themselves out.

Compared with many other urban shared spaces, the beach appears less conflict-ridden. The geographer Yi-Fu Tan argues that the beach offers simultaneously refuge and escape, security and openness (quoted in Gillis, 2012: 155), and these dimensions are very visible in the classic study Robert Edgerton (1979) made of a Los Angeles beach which could attract as many as 400,000 visitors on a busy day. He called it 'Southland'.

Most tourist beaches tend to be crowded, which has led to all sorts of tactics for creating private space. When Edgerton interviewed Los Angeles beach goers, the vast majority argued that the first thing they did was to carve out space on arrival by rolling out their towel and arranging their private belongings: 'I pick out my little plot of sand and set down my towel. For the next few hours that is my own little world; it belongs to me'. To cross over this private territory or to sit down next to it was considered a provocation, and rarely happened. Beach etiquette thus starts with the micro-rituals of making yourself at home and at the same time marking a physical and mental distance from others. Some visitors complained of beach life being too private, with people going to great lengths not to communicate with those close by.

'It's like being in an elevator where nobody talks', one woman told Edgerton. Those who consistently broke these rules of privacy and non-communication were small kids and dogs, but there were often clashes between different lifestyles and ideas of propriety as well. In Los Angeles, many white middle class visitors complained about Chicano families: they did not understand the need to keep your distance. Scandinavian visitors were also seen as provoking, as they used to change into swimwear right on the beach. Other kinds of irritations were, for example, overly loud music being played (Edgerton, 1979: 150 ff.).

On the whole, however, the Southland visitors stressed how easy it was to be on the beach. 'The sand is like a sanctuary to me', a young woman told Edgerton. 'Once I'm there I relax and mellow out' (Edgerton, 1979: 153). Other beach studies underline some of the basics of this easygoing attitude. It is hard to envisage a territory with a more pronounced mix of people. The Malmö beaches are a good example of this. Here, different ages and classes, as well as ethnic groups, mingle; inner city people mix with tourists new to the city. There is hardly any other place where groups like this would sit down next to each other; it is a mass confrontation which in many other settings would be volatile. On the other hand, as Michele Lobo (2014) has pointed out in her study of 'affective energies' at an Australian beach, there are subtle forms of exclusion communicated. Aborigines and black immigrants feel less welcome here.

The beach is supposed to be an arena of relaxation, of minding your own business, of doing what you want. But behind such notions of anarchy or individualism, there is a heavily regimented behavior. The French sociologist Jean-Claude Kaufmann's study of beach behaviour on French beaches illustrates this very clearly. Many of his beach informants stated strongly that, 'Here on the beach everybody does what they want', but behind such declarations a world of unwritten rules and regulations was revealed. People knew exactly where the borders were drawn, how to look, how to dress and undress, how to move the body (Kaufmann, 1995).

One of Kaufmann's main arguments is that the beach is a laboratory for the sophistication of that sense which has come most into focus during the twentieth century: the gaze. People he interviewed often said, 'I don't spend any time looking around, I am in my own world'. There is, of course, no way you cannot look. People on the beach are constantly testing different ocular techniques, consciously or unconsciously switching between different ways of seeing: watching, staring, glancing, scanning, looking from the corner of your eye, pretending not to look, making brief eye contact, looking away. There is a constant observation of how other people handle these techniques and very quick registration of those who break the rules. 'When bodies are naked glances are clothed', the sociologist Erving Goffman once put it (quoted in Edgerton, 1979: 152). As the French beach sociologist Jean-Didier Urbain (1994: 83 ff.) points out, the ways in which people observe at the beach have changed over time. The colonizing gaze of the Victorians would today be considered most provoking and unsophisticated. The degree of learning ocular competence also becomes obvious when kids constantly have to be told, 'Don't stare'. You have to learn to discipline the ways you look at others in a suitably disinterested way: glancing but never staring.

A beach is, as we have seen, a very special commons, often with clear boundaries. The kind of behaviour that is OK down by the water is not OK in the parking lot or on the other side of the beach road. Beach life may seem banal, but these banalities express very basic conceptions about private and public, decent and indecent, individuality and collectivity. Most of the rules regulating beach behavior have never been written down, many of them can hardly be verbalized, and yet – down at the beach – people know.

There is a constant tension between the beach as an individual experience and the beach as a cultural arena, impregnated with rules, routines, rituals. When Jean-Claude Kaufmann (1995) tried to sum up his beach observations, he found himself saying things like: the beach does this or that, the beach thinks, the beach prefers and so on. There was an unconscious cultural collectivity of beach life to be set against the fact that for the individual the beach is often experienced as a liberating space, where habits are broken, not made. This ambiguity rather nicely catches the cultural complexities of beach life. The holiday beach is built up around the polarity of city life and work, but however distant the beach is located from city life, it is still impregnated by urban culture. It is the city competence of handling privacy and communication in crowds of strangers that makes the beach as a global project possible.

The production of shared atmospheres

Using the concept of atmosphere in exploring urban commons is helpful in several ways. First of all it addresses issues of how such moods are produced, anchored or changed. Secondly, it opens up the question of how people come to share an atmosphere or are taken in by it, and how an atmosphere may dissolve boundaries not only between people but between the body and the material surroundings. Thirdly, it is a concept that focuses on the totality of an emotional mood, the ways in which many different sensual elements are combined. The strikingly different materialities of the station and the beach underline the importance of how material structures, props, people, activities and mindsets work together to produce an atmosphere.

I have described some of the processes of *throwntogetherness* that produce beach and station atmospheres. The station may seem like a very stable bricks-and-mortar monument, but it is really built by all the comings and goings, as well as the very diverse tasks, motives and mental luggage dragged into it. It is helpful to see it rather like an *entanglement*, a messiness created by the constant interweaving of the flows and ebbs of people, heavy luggage or malfunctioning ticket machines, shining hard floors, the unintelligible loudspeaker calls, the damp cold wind from outside, the trash in the corners, the vastness of the light from above or the smell of hamburger fat. The ethnographic task is to explore how this mess works together – reinforcing, blocking, uniting, separating.

The throwntogetherness of the beach atmosphere carries very different ingredients. There are the beach basics: water, horizon, sky and sand. The languid water movements, the rhythm of the surf has a calming, soothing effect, and the endless horizon proves to be a perfect medium for daydreaming. Its vastness opens up a wide space for wandering thoughts and fantasies. The horizon is both empty and full of secrets, as people gaze over-seas. Out there, past a distant ship on its way to an exotic destination, there are other worlds. The French philosopher Gaston Bachelard (1994: 205 ff.) sees a connection between the immensity of the seashore landscape and the depth of 'inner space'. The horizon produces a slightly glazed look, which seems to be looking at nothing and at a hidden world at the same time. All such elements combine to produce what Southland visitors called 'a mellow atmosphere'.

In both cases we should remember Tim Ingold's point that people do not walk into the beach or the station, but create these territories by their movements and senses interacting with everything else. 'We are not in it, we are with it', as he puts it. It is this constant mingling of activities and impressions that makes it misleading to talk about delineated sensual 'scapes' (from soundscapes to smellscapes). In perceptual practices, these sensual registers cooperate so closely and with such overlap of function that their respective contributions are impossible to tease apart (Ingold, 2011: 136).

Weather is one such integrating dimension, often missing from studies of social atmospheres, as Ingold points out. This dimension is, of course, most striking on the beach where even small weather changes affect the local atmosphere. A rising wind, a clouded sun all of a sudden makes the beach seem less welcoming. Waves, wind, sun and sky are present as an all-enveloping experience of sound, light and feeling – an atmosphere. 'To feel the air and walk on the ground is not to make external, tactile contact with our surroundings, but to mingle with them' (Ingold, 2011: 115). In the midnight hours of the station, both mental and meteorological atmospheres are chilly, reinforcing each other.

Both these two kinds of commons share the problem of accommodating changing flows of strangers within a restricted space. It may seem a mystery how you can mix so many strangers on the same strip of flat sand, in full exposure, with very little protective clothing and in close proximity to each other, and yet the beach works. Unlike the station, this is a totally open territory, with no hiding places, but the beach is also a place for leisure and relaxation, people are united by a mindset of having fun or of being childish, playful or meditative.

The passengers in the station exist in a more complex structure of feelings, with a tension between active and inactive, restfulness and restlessness, gravity and levity (Adey et al., 2012: 172 ff.). Very different activities co-exist or clash. Most visitors are just passing through, while others turn the station into a temporary living room. Travellers' movements also change from stressed running to bored waiting. What is it to be part of a crowd, a waiting line, a packed train? What kinds of comforts and conflicts emerge, what skills are put into action? The structure of feeling among a group of passengers waiting for a train can produce quick changes in atmosphere. People may start to share jokes and complaints. The stranger next to you becomes a fellow passenger and a fellow sufferer. The crowd can sink into a meditative state of waiting, with exchanges of sighs and shrugs, but the passenger collective can also be highly combustible as irritation and anger erupts. Bodies begin to fidget, people become less tolerant of others trying to make way in the crowd, all of a sudden the mood changes.

Both commons share a specific rhythm that creates changing moods. Stations have a lifecycle; they are reborn every morning and die a little bit late at night. The atmosphere of a newborn freshness in the cleaned-up Copenhagen station was strengthened by the morning smells of commuters, whiffs of deodorants and shampoos drifted by, tie knots and mascara lines were still perfect.

In the same way, the rhythm of urban beaches changes; an empty space re-invented every day after the morning crew has removed all traces of the previous day's visitors. In the early mornings, senior citizens search for coins or jewelry in the sand with their metal detectors; alongside them are the morning joggers. Later, families take over and at night the teenagers may dominate this urban common.

Concluding remarks

'The area is put under the protection of the public', runs a signpost at a Copenhagen waterfront setting. In analyzing urban commons, we need to know what is being protected and by whom. I have argued for a closer look at the kinds of urban commons that represent open meeting places, where people with very different backgrounds might mingle. These kinds of commons are often seen as crucial but vulnerable resources for a vibrant city life, but also as a form of democratic arenas, in the sense of Hannah Arendt's concept of 'spaces of appearances' (Arendt, 1958: 190 ff.). She stresses the ways in which such fleeting meeting places are constructed by people's movements and interactions, a discussion that can be linked to Ostrom's (2000) interests in commons and citizenship, a specific dimension of commoning, to return to Harvey's term (2012: 12).

As Susser and Tonnelat (2013) have pointed out, in situations of increased social segregation and marginalization of certain groups open urban spaces become even more important as arenas where people with very different backgrounds meet and have to negotiate some common understandings. For urban social movements claiming 'the right to the city', such territories become crucial testing grounds.

In the discourse on urban life, there is always a risk of a constant emphasis on *loss* – the open and colourful city life in public spaces being privatized, commodified or segregated in new ways. Urban commons are always under threat, but with the help of a historical perspective it is possible to see how some arenas and meeting places are enclosed or disappear while others are born. In a constantly changing cityscape, there are restrictions imposed but also new emerging potentials for claiming collective space.

The two kinds of urban commons I have discussed are very different but they share being transient spaces with a high turnover of users. They are also policed and governed in different ways, but they have a common characteristic: the coexistence of very different groups within a limited space.

There is a rising interest in the problems and potentials of urban commons as open spaces. My approach has centered on three themes. First of all, I have argued for an analysis of the social competences behind the making, un-making or maintenance of such kinds of urban commons. There is an informal learning process here, often with a long history, from handling unwritten norms to the skills of moving your body or interacting with strangers. This kind of knowledge is increasingly globalized. As a new visitor to a station or the beach, people already know many of the unwritten rules. How is a specific beach habitus (Caletrio, 2009: 119) created and maintained, how has passenger behaviour evolved over time at the station? Secondly, the politics of governance may be studied in the often subtle processes of inclusion and exclusion. There will be official rules of behaviour in such urban spaces and different forms of monitoring, from security guards to surveillance cameras, but perhaps the most important monitoring comes from the gaze of other users or feelings of being welcome or not. There is a strong and sometimes indirect governance by sociability here which makes it important to study who is allowed to make (or break) rules of behavior and the often indirect ways in which normative behavior is communicated or challenged. The beach and the station is governed by written and unwritten rules about proper behavior, and the boundaries between public and private which constantly are being negotiated and contested. Both these two commons demonstrate different kinds of governance, from direct monitoring or 'pacification by design' (Frers, 2006) to the more subtle forms of governance by sociality (which groups set the rules for behaviour?).

Forms of exclusion and inclusion vary as I have shown. The exposure of bodies at the beach makes some people whose bodies do not live up to ideal standards feel less welcome. On some holiday beaches, the locals are no longer welcome (Löfgren, 2000: 230) or visitors with the wrong skin colour (Lobo, 2014). The railway station, designed as it is for swift passenger mobility, can make not-so-mobile persons feel out of place.

Gender is another dimension. Who feels exposed or vulnerable and in what situations? At Copenhagen station back in the 1950s, young country girls were warned that the station was a dangerous territory and a YWCA mission took on the task of assisting them. Observing stations at night Frers (2006: 257) noticed how many women took to a brisk pace and avoided eye contact at a time when there are few persons around. At the beach, however, women told Edgerton: 'I feel so safe here, people are mellow, the environment makes people behave [. . .] It may be one of the places a woman can go alone and yet feel safe' (Edgerton, 1979: 153). When Kaufmann (1995) interviewed women on the beach, they made it clear that they had no problem in discerning what they felt was pleasurable attention from an intimidating male gaze.

Feeling safe or at home is a crucial condition of inclusion in the urban commons, and in any given setting or situation there will be people who feel misplaced, unwanted or under critical scrutiny, as we have seen in the discussion of the railway station.

Finally, in both cases discussed, atmosphere becomes an interesting issue and I have argued here for an experimentation of different kinds of ethnographies in order to capture the ways in which modes and moods of use interact in shaping urban commons. Such ethnographies are needed to understand how different actors live the same setting. The beach and the station arenas will look very different according to the social position and mind frame through which you are experiencing it.

References

Adey, P., Bissell, D., McCormack, D. and Merriman, P. (2012) 'Profiling the passenger: mobilities, identities and embodiments', *Cultural Geographies* 19(2): 169–93.

Anderson, B. (2009) 'Affective atmospheres' *Emotion, Space and Society*, 2(2): 77–81.

Arendt, H. (1958) *The Human Condition*, Chicago: Chicago UP.

Bachelard, G. (1958/1994) *The Poetics of Space*. Trans. by M. Jolas. Boston: Beacon Press.

Bissell, D. (2010) 'Passenger mobilities: affective atmospheres and sociality of public transport', *Environment and Planning D: Society and Space* 28(1): 270–89.

Blom Hansen, T. and Verkaaik, O. (2009) 'Introduction – urban charisma. On everyday mythologies in the city', *Critique of Anthropology* 29(1): 5–26.

Böhme, G. (1993) 'Atmosphere as the fundamental concept of a new aesthetics', *Thesis Eleven* 36(1): 113–26.

Böhme, G. (2006) *Architektur und Atmosphäre*. Munich: Wilhelm Fink Verlag.

Böhme, G. (2014) 'Urban atmospheres: Charting new directions for architecture and urban planning', in C. Borch (ed.), *Architectural Atmospheres: On the Experience and Politics of Architecture* (pp. 42–59). Basel: Birkhäuser.

Borch, C. (2012) *The Politics of Crowds: An Alternative History of Sociology*. Cambridge: Cambridge University Press.

Borch, C. (ed.) (2014) *Architectural Atmospheres: On the Experience and Politics of Architecture*. Basel: Birkhäuser.

Bravo, G. and Moor, T.D. (2008) 'The commons in Europe: from past to future', *International Journal of the Commons* 2(2): 155–61.

Brennan, T. (2004) *The Transmission of Affect*. New York: Cornell University Press.

Caletrio, J. (2009) ' "De veraneo en la playa": belonging and the familiar in Mediterranean mass tourism', in P. Obrador Pons et al. (eds.), *Cultures of Mass Tourism. Doing the Mediterranean in the Age of Banal Mobilities* (pp. 111–28). Farnham: Ashgate.

Carlson, J. and Stewart, K.D. (2014) 'The legibilities of mood work', *New Formations* 82: 144–33.

Calhoun, C., Sennet, R. and Shapira, H. (2013) 'Poiesis means making', *Public Culture* 25(22): 195–200.

Edgerton, R.B. (1979) *Alone Together: Social Order on an Urban Beach*. Berkeley, Cal.: University of California Press.

Ehn, B. and Löfgren, O. (2010) *The Secret World of Doing Nothing*. Berkeley, Cal.: University of California Press.

Flindt Larsen, M. (1994) *Vi Mødes Under Uret. . . Glimt Af Livet På Københavns Hovedbangård Gennem Tiden*. Copenhagen: Banebøger.

Foster, S. (2011) 'Collective action and the urban commons', *Notre Dame Law Review* 87(1): 1–63.

Frers, L. (2006) 'Pacification by design: an ethnography of normalization techniques', in H. Berking et al. (eds), *Negotiating Urban Conflicts. Interaction, Space and Control* (pp. 249–62). Bielefeld: Transcript.

Galanakis, M. (2008) *Space Unjust: Socio-Spatial Discrimination in Urban Public Space. Cases from Helsinki and Athens*. Helsinki: Publication Series of the University of Art and Design Helsinki A 82.

Gillis, J. (2012) *The Human Shore: Seacoasts in History*. Chicago: Chicago University Press.

Gregg, M. and Seigworth, G. (2010) *The Affective Theory Reader*. Durham: Duke University Press.

Harvey, D. (2012) *Rebel Cities: From the Right to the City to the Urban Revolution*. London: Verso.

Heibach, C. (ed.) (2012) *Atmosphären. Dimensionen eines Diffusen Phänomens*. Munic: Wilhelm Fink.

Henriques, J. (2010) 'The vibrations of affect and their propagation on a night out on Kingston's dancehall scene', *Body and Society* 16(1): 57–89.

Hess, C. (2008) 'Mapping the New Commons', Paper presented the 12th Biennial Conference of the International Association for the Study of the Commons, University of Gloucestershire, Cheltenham, England, 14–18 July, 2008.

Hiss, T. (1991) *The Experience of Place: A Completely New Way of Looking at and Dealing with Our Radically Changing Cities and Countryside*. New York: Alfred A Knopf.

Ingold, T. (2011) *Being Alive: Essays on Movement, Knowledge and Description*. London: Routledge.

Jemielniak, D. and Jemielniak, J. (2001) 'Public and private space. The final frontier', in B. Czarniawska and R. Stolli (eds), *Organizing Metropolitan Space and Discourse* (pp. 67–88). Malmö: Liber.

Kaufmann, J.-C. (1995) *Corps de Femmes. Regards d'Hommes*. Paris: Nathan.

Lobo, M. (2014) 'Affective energies: Sensory bodies on the beach in Darwin, Australia', *Emotion, Space and Society* 12(August): 101–9.

Löfgren, O. (2000) *On Holiday: A History of Vacationing*. Berkeley, Cal.: University of California Press.

Löfgren, O. (2008) 'Motion and emotion: Learning to be a railway traveller', *Mobilities* 3(3): 313–30.

Löfgren, O. (2015) 'Urban atmospheres as brandscapes and lived experiences', *Place Branding and Public Diplomacy* 10(4): 255–66.

Marstein, T. (2006) *Gjøre Godt*. Oslo: Gyldendal.

Massey, D. (2005) *For Space*. London: SAGE publications.

Mazzarella, M. (2003) *Linjer Mellan Stjärnor. Om Identitet*. Helsingfors: Forum.

McCullough, M. (2013) *Ambient Commons: Attention in the Age of Embodied Information*. Cambridge, Mass.: MIT Press

Ostrom, E. (2000) 'Crowding out citizenship', *Scandinavian Political Studies* 23(1): 3–16.

Ovesen, H. (1999) *I Mellemtiden – En Arkitektonisk Analyse af Københavns Banegårdsplads*. Copenhagen: Center for tværfaglige urbane studier.

Parker, P. and Johansson, M. (2012) 'Challenges and potentials in collaborative management of urban commons'. Online. Available HTTP: <http://dspace.mah.se/bitstream/handle/2043/14619/PARKER%20and%20JOHANSSON.pdf?> (accessed 29 August 2014).

Rabinowitz, D. (2012) 'Residual residential space as commons', *International Journal of the Commons* 6(2): 302–18.

Richards, J. and MacKenzie, J.M. (1986) *The Railway Station: A Social History*. Oxford: Oxford University Press.

Ristilammi, P.-M. (2003) *Mim och Verklighet: En Studie av Stadens Gränser*. Eslöv: Symposion.

Saskien, S. (2013) 'Does the city have a speech?', *Public Culture* 25(2): 209–22.

Smullen, S.I. (1968) *Taken for a Ride: A Distressing Account of the Misfortunes and Misbehaviour of the Early British Railway Traveller*. London: Herbert Jenkins.

Susser, I. and Tonnelat, S. (2013) 'Transformative Cities: the urban commons', *Focaal. Journal of Global and Historical Anthropology* 66(Summer): 105–32.

Svensson, J. (2010) 'Spår med snår', *Sydsvenska Dagbladet*, 4 February: B4.

Tan, H.Q. (2013) 'Smell in the city: smoking and olfactory politics', *Urban Studies* 50(1): 1–17.

Urbain, J.-D. (1994) *Sur La Plage. Moeurs et Coutumes Balnéaires*. Paris: Éditions Payot and Rivages.

Vannini, P. (2014). *Non-Representational Theory and Methodologies: Re-envisioning Research*. London: Routledge.

Walton, J.K. (1983) *The English Seaside Resort: A Social History 1750–1914*. New York: St Martin's Press.

Chapter 4

Producing, appropriating and recreating the myth of the urban commons

Patrik Zapata and María José Zapata Campos

Managua, Nicaragua, November 2013. Conversation with Víctor Arias, former waste picker at La Chureca, the city's dump:

Víctor: I am from Chinandega. She [pointing towards his wife, María] is from Villa del Carmen. We met in Chinandega [. . .] and we started making a family. Look, at that time I used to work on the sugarcane fields, harvesting sugarcane for many years.

María: All the children were so small, and he sometimes had to leave at eleven in the evening to start working. He got a ride with a truck that drove far, far away [. . .] and he sometimes got back, like, at one in the morning the day after [i.e. 26 hours later].

Víctor: I ended up with sugarcane field sickness – the sugarcane causes that [sickness] creatine [. . .] I left with that diagnosis, I got 'retired'.

Our arrival [in La Chureca] was because I wanted to change jobs. Her brothers [pointing at his wife again] advised her to come to Managua. They said 'It is true, it's La Chureca [i.e. Managua's open city dump], but there you can make a good living'. And here [i.e. in La Chureca] her brothers lived and worked! One of the boys was a *suelero* [i.e. collector of shoe soles], and he still searches for the few soles that are left, which he buys and sells.

María Now, there are very few people here in La Chureca. Just an hour ago there were, like, 20. There are very few left now.

Víctor: And I told my wife, 'I can't find a way to work with rubbish'. And we asked the boys [in a tone of surprise], 'But, can you sell this? And this?'

María: The first month we moved here we learnt what shoe soles, aluminium, plastic were. But there was a lot more to learn, what was worth collecting or not. When we moved here we started collecting glass, for three months.

Víctor: For me it was terrible – the stink, the smoke, the sun [. . .] I mean, in my life I have always worked hard under the sun, but [. . .] If you could have seen [. . .] But, look, we started to learn. And we could earn 600, 700 pesos a day, and look, we got home at one or two in the afternoon.

And, hey, once I noticed a truck that was bringing fish and they were throwing it out [. . .] Yes, yes, frozen fish! Healthy fish! And a big fish head fell in front of me [. . .] And I couldn't stop staring at the fish head. And people took as much as they could and they left, and I still stood staring at the big head in front of me. But you know, I know about fish, I lived by the sea. It was a *bomero*'s head, but the size of a pig's head! I grabbed it with my hook and touched it – frozen, frozen, all ice. I said. Look, we are going to take this head with us.

María: I'll tell you the truth. It was so disgusting to see the animal [. . .] and since we had been living by the sea, I thought, 'Where have we ended up?' But thank God, here at La Chureca we've got a place to work and live, as we have all these children, nine children, can you imagine? As they were so small . . .

Víctor: So, we grabbed the head and she made a soup. It was so good, a big pot of soup. What can I say? It gave such a big pot, and so good [. . .] that we even gave some to the neighbors. And since then we started eating these kinds of things. Until one day I said 'No, man, this is a job, I am not stealing, I am working'. It was like two months

Figure 4.1 Waste pickers collecting recyclables at La Chureca.
Photo by Patrik Zapata and María José Zapata Campos.

after we moved here. After that we became masters. Who could imagine that at La Chureca there are *reales* [i.e. money], there is food!

Waste is an urban commons

The putrid and nauseating rubbish that Víctor Arias used to collect – although radically different from the pristine waters, green forests, and abundant fisheries that were Ostrom's (1990) focus – constituted an urban commons for the 2000 waste pickers who worked daily at La Chureca, and similar rubbish serves the same purpose for millions of urban poor in the world (Gutberlet, 2010). Cities are factories for the production of these commons, as Hardt and Negri (2009) have argued. In this chapter, informed by the work of Ostrom (1990) and Harvey (2012), we claim that urban waste constitutes a commons, and examine the process by which this commons is produced, appropriated and recreated as a myth by waste picker communities that continually struggle to defend their rights.

In an increasingly urbanized world, a third of the global urban population will soon live in informal settlements (UN-Habitat, 2003) unconnected to most public services, such as roads, paved roads, water supply, sewage disposal, adequate housing, street cleaning, and waste collection. The formal city is often reduced to an island in an ocean of slums (Abbott, 2004). Urbanization represents the perpetual production of urban commons but also the perpetual appropriation of these commons by specific groups and interests (Harvey, 2012). In this context, whereas the formal city provides access to exclusionary commons – which in their more extreme forms are delivered in gated communities to affluent citizens – most informal settlements remain poorly connected to the production, protection, and use of public goods (Hardoy, Mitlin and Satterthwaite, 2001).

Yet low-income residents do not remain passive. Citizens and informal entrepreneurs often devise creative and sustainable collective ways to manage common resources and produce their own urban commons for both individual and collective benefit, as Ostrom has demonstrated (1990). For example, an extensive informal sector of waste pickers, such as Víctor and his family, is involved in collecting and sorting household solid waste (Katusiimeh, Burger and Mol, 2013; Oteng-Ababio et al., 2013; Zapata Campos and Hall, 2013; Zapata Campos and Zapata, 2012, 2013a, b, 2014) in millions of informal settlements in cities around the world and in open dumps such as La Chureca used to be. Waste pickers' collectives make a significant but hidden contribution to improving low-income residents' health, recovering materials, creating jobs and income among the poor, and even reducing the carbon footprints of cities (da Silva Carvalho et al., 2012; Mitlin, 2008; Wilson et al., 2008).

But under what conditions is a resource such as waste transformed into a commons? Or, expressed differently, what practices govern the production of urban commons? The story of Víctor Arias and La Chureca, the dump where thousands of waste pickers like Víctor have been working for years, illustrates the process of urban commons production.[1]

Producing the urban commons

At La Chureca, urban waste was a resource accessible to dispossessed and displaced poor such as Víctor. However, La Chureca and its waste were far from a taken-for-granted commons to those alien to the place and to whom the value of the waste was unknown. Many waste pickers, when they first heard that they could make a living from waste, exclaimed 'Can you really sell this?' and 'They make a living at La Chureca?' Waste as a resource is hidden and only rendered visible by those familiar with waste and with its socio-materiality (Corvellec and Hultman, 2012) and diverse values (Hultman and Corvellec, 2012). It was through the practice of waste picking that Víctor and his family, to their own surprise, learned to discern, disassemble, and transform the valuable materials discarded at La Chureca.

As the saying goes, one man's trash is another man's treasure. Star (1999) has argued, in relation to the study of infrastructures, that users acquire 'a naturalized familiarity with the infrastructure and its objects, as they become members' (1999: 381). When Víctor and his family moved to La Chureca and became members of the Churequeros community – as these waste pickers call themselves – they developed the often tacit knowledge and competences necessary to work with waste.

The process of transforming waste into a commons involves, first, rendering visible waste and its value. It is in the process of seeing value in waste that

1 The chapter is based on our field work conducted since 2009 up to 2014 at La Chureca, which used to be the open rubbish dump and slum of Managua, Nicaragua, and its renewal programme, the Barrio Acahualinca Integrated Development Programme. During these years we have conducted over one hundred fifty personal interviews with waste pickers, slum residents, community leaders, NGO workers, development aid organization officers, city managers, public officers, politicians, ambassadors, development aid organization managers and directors, municipal waste operators, waste collection cooperative members, trade union representatives, waste handling and recycling corporations, NGO volunteers, engineers and architects. Many of which have been interviewed yearly. We have also conducted press coverage about La Chureca and its renewal programme from 1990 up to 2014 in the largest Nicaraguan and Spanish newspapers. Using Google, a number of blogs, social networks, and video-sharing websites on YouTube were identified, capturing photos, films and texts. We also took part in non-participant observation at meetings and events during project implementation. These included environmental campaigns involving cleaning brigades, social events organized by the municipality at the slum and the dump, waste picker cooperative meetings, meetings of development aid organizations and city managers, conferences, or workshops to evaluate development projects with residents and community leaders. Since 2009 we have documented these events by taking photographs, filming videos and keeping a field diary of our observations in a historical data archive which allows us to retrospectively dive into the data to explore new theoretical stances, such as is the case of this chapter based on the urban commons.

Figure 4.2 Intermediaries, sellers and buyers.
Photo by Patrik Zapata and María José Zapata Campos.

the commons is created by these poor communities. Waste is there to see for all of us, but where affluent citizens can only see trash, waste pickers can see reusable and recyclable materials, food, construction materials for housing, and toys.

This is how dispossessed communities create their own commons: by creating and appropriating their own resources. On top of that, in the process they help reduce the environmental footprint of cities and support the public health of billions of low-income slum dwellers.

Although waste in Managua was free for the taking by all kinds of urban poor, in practice, waste picking was relatively exclusive to a particular social group, i.e. the thousands of waste pickers working at La Chureca. They had worked at the dump for decades and woven networks through longstanding collective action (Lindberg and Czarniawska, 2006) – such as picking, cleaning, disassembling, storing and transporting – based on family and market relationships with intermediaries, sellers, and buyers throughout the city. Like Víctor, many waste pickers learned about La Chureca and its waste through relatives with whom they also developed employee and employer relationships. However, the precise spatial boundaries of La Chureca and its waste picker community aside, La Chureca's social boundaries were more fluid, fuzzy, and porous than Ostrom's (1990) studies and principles of common pool resource management would suggest. Although family ties could provide newcomers with access to the Churequeros community, they were not the only entrée. Sporadic waste picking was typical of waste pickers with addictions and of students who needed money at the beginning of the school year to buy books and clothes. Another divergence was how, despite existing mechanisms for excluding outsiders to some extent, the waste did belong to local society and was appropriated by the waste picker community. The

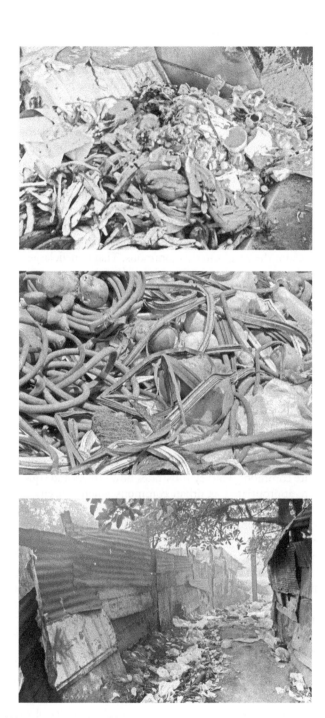

Figure 4.3 Waste as a common: food, toys, material constructions.
Photos by Patrik Zapata and María José Zapata Campos.

inflow of new waste to this common resource pool was decoupled from the needs of the local community. A reservoir used for irrigation in southeast Spain depends on the rain to be refilled, and if too much water is used or too little rain falls it may dry out, or an alpine meadow can be overgrazed, but waste keeps flowing into a city dump every day regardless of the needs of its denizens. This commons does not need regulation in the same way as do reservoirs, meadows, or fisheries: despite waste also being limited, it continues to grow in volume with urbanization, a process of which, paradoxically, these new Churequeros members were also part.

Regardless of the environmental contribution of the work of waste pickers in the context of rapid urbanization and waste generation, waste – as food, construction materials, and other services and assets exchangeable for money – provides both individual and collective benefits to the Churequeros community, who claim their right to this commons. That beneficiaries are claiming their right to the waste is a characteristic shared by other common pool resources that Ostrom (1990) examines, such as land, water, or fish stocks. The Churequeros also claimed that they earned their right to this commons because many had been born there or lived there for years, enduring the contamination and other health risks (e.g. high mercury levels and respiratory problems) that their waste picking work entailed: 'I was born here, I have been swallowing the smoke here, my children have been swallowing the smoke' (interview, La Chureca resident). This claim of the right to use and benefit from this commons recalls Harvey's (2012) concept of the right to the city of the laborers who participate in producing the commons, enabling the city to function.

Harvey (2012) argues, however, that public goods such as water, public space, and sanitation services cannot automatically be equaled to commons. They first must be re-appropriated by citizens through political action before they constitute commons. Harvey illustrates how streets and squares as public goods were re-appropriated as urban commons when citizens used them in networked social protests, as occurred in public spaces such as Taksim Square in Istanbul, Plaza del Sol in Madrid, and Wall Street in New York City (Álvarez de Andrés et al., 2014).

According to Harvey, urban resources and commons are socially defined, meaning that commons are not a particular kind of asset or resource. Rather, they are defined in terms of socio-material assemblages involving, beyond their materiality, social practices, institutional arrangements, organizational processes, and socio-cultural meanings. Therefore, urban commons are not static but instead entail a social practice of *commoning*: 'an unstable and malleable social relation between a particular self-defined social group and those aspects of its actually existing or yet-to-be-created social and/or physical environment deemed crucial to its life and livelihood' (Harvey, 2012: 73).

By this means, the waste at La Chureca is transformed from an asset into a commons, as the social groups participating in the practice of waste picking try to defend the free production, accessibility, and appropriation of waste; and in so doing, they engage in political action through the articulation of cooperatives, a trade union, and other social networks, as we find in following the story of Víctor Arias.

Appropriating the urban commons through political action

A few years after Víctor Arias and his family had moved to La Chureca, the waste picker community went on strike. Jorge Larios, Víctor Arias' brother-in-law, is a representative of the La Chureca Trade Union and he tells us how the waste picker community was mobilized:

> Our protest started because of the very few opportunities we had for political and social recognition. In society they looked at us in the same way [. . .] because we lived among the rubbish, they considered us rubbish. And that's also how they treated us. But then we discovered, first, that recyclable material was something that could be reused. And we could say that we were the pioneers of recycling in Nicaragua. Then, from that moment, the municipal operators that collected the waste in trucks started to set aside all the valuable material that we call the *prepa*. Then we started thinking about how we could start fighting, and asked the waste collectors employed by Managua City not to take the *prepa*, which is what we needed to survive, with our families. And we decided to close the dump, because it was the only way for us to reach the Managua City administration.
>
> On strike, during the day there used to be all of us. And at night we were in shifts. We used to leave 15, 20, 30, 40 volunteers. [. . .] Then, to compensate, to be able to eat something and stuff like that, we already knew about the trucks that brought food from, like, the supermarkets or McDonald's. Or 'look! The Mercedes Hotel truck'. And we allowed those trucks to come in, as we were the bosses here. We, ourselves, were the bosses. 'This one can go over there'. There was a group of women and men. Women cooked and served the food, and in a very organized and ordered manner! Everybody was in a queue. We cut off a piece of plastic and the food was served there. Another piece of plastic for coffee, or pinolillo [a local drink made of cacao and corn]. Whatever there was, it was shared . . .
>
> We managed to stay on strike for 35 days because of, first, a thirst for justice, second, the big necessity to get food for our families. So, that was the moment of truth when we had to tighten our belts, as we Nicaraguans say, be strong even if we were weak. [. . .] And we won, we won even though the waste operators still continued to take part of the *prepa*. [. . .] We not only learned to mobilize and organize ourselves. We also learned and made others understand that the fact that we are Churequeros doesn't mean that they can run over us without our saying 'ay' at least. Now things are very different. Now we are organized. We have a city

Figure 4.4 Protests at the dump.

Photos reproduced with courtesy of AECID (The Spanish Agency for International Development Cooperation).

administration that knows that there is a trade union here, that people are organized, that 85 percent of the workers are organized.

(Interview, Jorge Larios, FNT-Chureca representative)

In May 2008 the waste pickers at La Chureca went on strike, and for 35 days they succeeded in stopping the entrance of municipal waste trucks into the dump. Víctor Arias was one of the hundreds of waste pickers who participated in the protests. They protested against the practice of municipal waste operators' skimming the *prepa* off the waste before entering La Chureca – that is, separating the most valuable of the recyclable material, lowering the quality of the materials disposed at the dump and reducing the income of La Chureca waste pickers. Marisa Salgado, a waste picker and resident of the La Chureca slum, was the representative of the Movimiento Comunal (Communal Movement) labor organization at La Chureca who started the mobilization that led to the strike. Like other waste pickers, she had noticed how her income decreased because of the pre-selection of recyclables by the municipal operators. She decided to act and asked the Movimiento Comunal's representative for help. She asked her son, also a waste picker, for help in calling for a protest among other waste pickers:

> I could see that we were fed up [i.e. with earning so little due to the pre-selection by municipal operators]. And I said, no more! Then I spoke to my oldest son and I told him, 'Francisco [. . .] look, we have the idea of closing the dump because we cannot find a way to make a living any more'. And he answered, 'OK mother, I and the people will support you', because he was a Churequero. My other son Javier was also a Churequero. Then I said, 'I want you to support us because this is going to be good for us in the future'. He said it was all right and that he would support me by telling the people. Even her son [pointing towards a neighbor] supported us as well. It was through family, relatives, and neighbors that they informed people, told them. And an assembly was held, a few of them. And in these meetings we discussed how it was important to meet the municipal officers and politicians. But there was no way to negotiate, and this is why we had no choice but to close the dump.
>
> (Interview, Marisa Salgado, Movimiento Comunal Chureca)

The call to strike spread quickly. Several assemblies were held at an old playing field, one of the few public spaces in the slum where a large number of people could meet. Meetings were later held twice a week. The strike leadership positions were periodically rotated to guarantee representativeness. The strikers organized themselves into groups to secure water, wood, and food, to cook, and to guard the entrance to the dump. According to one of the waste picker movement's representatives, the residents evolved 'from individualism to collective action' (Interview, Movimiento Comunal representative), which is the essence of the Movimiento Comunal labor movement in Nicaragua. For a community in which individualism and physical force were predominant, the mobilization experience was transformative: 'Tomorrow at 9.00 am there is a meeting to discuss the strike. We have to go on strike. Everybody was at the meetings. We were certain that we were going to change this' (Interview, Jorge Larios, FNT-Chureca representative).

These mobilizations constituted exclusionary mechanisms established by the community of commons users to control access to their resource. Unlike Ostrom's principle of the presence of well-defined boundaries around a community of users and their resource system, the waste picker community claimed their right to access waste that was beyond the geographical boundaries of La Chureca. They claimed their right to access all the waste collected by the municipal trucks, as there was no full congruence between the appropriation and provision rules and the local conditions (principle 2, Ostrom, 1990: 90). Waste is an accessible commons, for better or worse.

As a result of the protests, the community increased its ability to mobilize and organize, and its members gained self-confidence and awareness of their resources:

> Yes, yes because at least as a result of this [i.e. the strike] we were, like, more confident about what we could do. If I say that we will have a meeting and I ask everybody to attend and I say, look we are going to have a meeting for this purpose or that one [. . .] I know that people here [. . .] I invite all these people and they will come.
>
> (Interview, Marisa Salgado, Movimiento Comunal, Chureca)

Self-recognition emerged among the waste pickers concerning their right to produce and use waste as an urban commons. The meanings associated with waste and with those working with it were also reconstructed by this community. The process of appropriating waste as commons implied redefining the self-identity of those working with waste. In retrospect, they could understand that they had been struggling with the double stigma of being poor and working with waste: 'Because we lived among the rubbish, they considered us rubbish. And that's also how they treated us' (Interview, Jorge Larios, FNT-Chureca representative). Víctor Arias stood up to this stigma: 'No, man, this is a job, I am not stealing, I am working!'

Through these mobilizations, many waste pickers acknowledged this stigma and contested it by recreating the meanings associated with waste, waste picking as a profession, and their own identity. Since the strike, they have regarded waste as something valuable, not only economically but also socially and environmentally. The Churequeros reconstructed their identity as pioneers of recycling in Nicaragua, as the words of Jorge Larios show. By transforming waste into an urban commons and defending their right to produce, use, and appropriate it, the Churequeros redefined their own identity and their contribution to city making. Through these protests user and resource boundaries (Ostrom's design principle 1) were re-established, new conflict-resolution mechanisms (Ostrom's design principle 6) were set in place and further recognition rights from the authorities (Ostrom's design principle 7) were gained. But beyond any of Ostrom's design principles, the La Chureca community illustrates how the mechanisms that kept this community a common pool resource institution also involved socio-cultural mechanisms such as identity construction; which role as an institutional regularity has not been explicitly developed in Ostrom's work.

In a more political perspective, La Chureca's waste picker trade union was created as a result of the 2008 protests. The creation of the local chapter of Frente Nacional de Trabajadores (FNT, i.e. National Workers Front) at La Chureca was supported by the Communal Movement. The La Chureca chapter was named in honor of Ramón García, a Churequero who died during the strike, 'of sadness, alone in the middle of the dump'. The strength of the FNT trade union is entrenched in the Sandinista political party, which relies on the mobilizing ability of the trade union movement for national and local politics:

> We tried all kinds of administrative solutions, until we couldn't any more. But when they don't want to see us anymore – it is not that they do not

see us, it is that they don't want to see us – then, we go to the streets. This is why the National Workers Front is the right hand of the government.

(FNT trade union representative)

We have been fighting so that nobody is left outside. I have always said, as general secretary of the trade union, that unfortunately the only losers will be the *zopilotes* [i.e. vultures], because they have no trade union that can save them.

(FNT Trade Union Chureca)

Similarly, Red Nicaraguense de Emprendedores del Reciclaje (REDNICA, i.e. Nicaraguan Network for Recycler Entrepreneurs) was created as a result of the protests. REDNICA has worked to mobilize waste pickers throughout the country and is now part of national and international waste picker networks that have emerged in Latin America in recent decades, such as the Latin American and Caribbean Network of Waste Pickers (Red Lacre) and the Global Alliance of Waste Pickers (globalrec.org).

Since 2008, waste picker cooperatives have emerged in Managua, and later in other cities in Nicaragua, to support the work of individual waste pickers and negotiate with authorities, corporations, and non-governmental organizations (NGOs). One of them is the cooperative Cooperativa La Chureca Guardabarranco of which Víctor Arias is a member. In Managua's informal settlements, new cooperatives such as Manos Unidas (Joined Hands) or Limpiando Fuerte (Cleaning Hard) emerged simultaneously as citizen-based initiatives supported by NGOs and aid development agencies. Using horse carts, bicycles, and motorbikes, these waste pickers collect household solid waste from informal settlements where there was previously no regular and official waste collection system (Zapata Campos and Zapata, 2013a).

For common pool resources, such as waste, that are 'parts of larger systems', Ostrom formulated the principle that 'governance activities are organized in multiple layers of nested enterprises' (1990: 90). The process of appropriating the urban commons at La Chureca illustrates how the community creates connections and knits networks of power both between waste picker groups and between multiple governance levels, involving public authorities, NGOs, markets, and international organizations. The connections created between waste picker communities – among the poorest and most stigmatized social groups – around the world via global networks such as the Global Alliance of Waste Pickers exemplifies how the management of commons at the local level can be extended to encompass larger communities through these networked social movements.

In light of Ostrom's (1990, 1996) insights, the work enacted by waste picker communities – organized in cooperatives, networks, and trade unions – encourages us to rethink how the 'tragedy of the commons' may not be as prevalent or as difficult to solve as the word 'tragedy' implies (Hardin, 1968).

Rather than merely being the 'end of the pipe' of the waste management system, the waste picker community claimed ownership of La Chureca and its waste, as producers and users of this commons, and were ready to fight for it at any cost. In this process, the forgotten waste pickers were transformed into policy actors and – perhaps unexpectedly – became city constructors by self-organizing their settlements, producing, using, and appropriating the urban commons.

This process of co-production (Ostrom, 1996) constitutes an urban social movement that not only bridges the divides between state, market, and civil society but unintentionally challenges the nature of the state and civil society (Mitlin, 2008). While in cities in affluent societies, participatory democracy and citizenship are undergoing a crisis in which citizens are being reduced to mere recipients of services, in many cities of the Global South, residents produce their own commons, constructing the city, brick by brick. The story of La Chureca illustrates how, from the process of producing the urban commons, power emerges through organizing (Czarniawska and Hernes, 2005). Citizenship is something one must fight for and win through the practice of commoning.

The enclosure of the urban commons, obdurate communing, and the myth of the commons

The story of Víctor Arias does not end here. Since 2013, Víctor, together with 500 other former waste pickers, has been working at the municipal waste recycling station at the La Chureca dump site. As a result of a development program funded by the Spanish Aid Development Agency, the open dump has been closed, a new sanitary landfill has been built at the same place, and a new waste recycling station has been constructed at the entrance to La Chureca. At the recycling station, waste is now sorted by former waste pickers, now employees of a municipal corporation. A wall has been constructed enclosing La Chureca and unregulated waste picking at the landfill is now prosecuted by the police. Waste has been transformed into a public good, as the municipality has enclosed and re-appropriated the commons that is no longer freely accessible – at least legally. Although 500 of the 2,000 former Churequeros are now employed at the municipal recycling plant, many other waste pickers have been excluded from the dump and their livelihoods. Many have moved to the city to collect recyclables directly from households and companies; many others, however, still continue waste picking at the dump, albeit illegally.

The process of transforming La Chureca mirrors the transformation of waste from an open urban commons – accessible to the urban poor – to a public good only legally accessible to the municipality. The enclosure of urban waste in Managua illustrates how the public goods stemming from one commons, such as residents' health and the individual income of 500 waste pickers, may be protected at the expense of another, i.e. free access to waste.

Figure 4.5 Obdurate waste picking at La Chureca.
Photo by Patrik Zapata and María José Zapata Campos.

As Harvey (2012) argues, questions of commons and their enclosure are contradictory and always contested, since conflicting social and political interests underlie who can access a given commons, and therefore who benefits.

By making a public good of waste and changing the rules governing La Chureca, as a commons institution, Managua City subverted the Churequeros' recognition of their right to waste. Yet, the story of La Chureca as a commons institution did not end here, as Ostrom would suggest, when it no longer fulfilled the commons design principle of providing minimal external recognition of the right to organize. The process of municipal re-appropriation is being contested by the La Chureca community. In fact, on our latest visit to La Chureca, we could see that waste as an urban commons has turned out to be more enduring than municipal authorities anticipated. Some of the old waste pickers together with new waste pickers have continued to work illegally in the landfill, claiming their right to the commons. This illustrates how the practice of commoning is enduring, persistent, as the communities of urban poor perpetually reappear to claim their right to the city.

In many other cities of the world waste is being transformed from a common to a private good. For example, in Cairo, the Zabaleen community, which has owned the right to waste collection for decades, is struggling with the privatization of waste collection and the entrance of a multinational corporation to handle waste disposal (Fahmi and Sutton, 2013). This loss of urban communalities reflects the global and sustained wave of privatizations that have occurred during the last decades (Harvey, 2012). And how a common pool resource institution, such as waste picking communities, can be threatened when multinationals with the power to wrest control of a commons from a user community, show interest in the commons, as with waste and its increasing market value.

Víctor Arias and his new colleagues at the waste recycling plant have not forgotten their former colleagues at La Chureca. Even those who got jobs at the plant have relatives, neighbors and friends who need to continue picking waste. Several strikes, mobilized by the FNT trade union, have been held at the recycling station in solidarity with waste pickers who were arrested by the police at the dump.

Just one year after they started working at the recycling station, the waste pickers, when asked about their new life away from the risks of the dump, share with us – to our surprise – their nostalgia: 'Oh, La Chureca [. . .] yes we used to earn our good *reales*'; 'There was lots of money there'; 'It was very good'; 'I got in, earned and got out'.

The old La Chureca has been reimagined by the former waste pickers as an 'El Dorado', a paradisiacal city of riches where waste was a common

Figure 4.6 Waste picking in Gothenburg.

Photo by Patrik Zapata and María José Zapata Campos.

resource available to the urban poor, where anyone could enter at any time and, by commoning, freely procure food and income for their families.

Waste as an urban commons is not confined to poor communities in Global South cities. Just as we were writing what should have been the last sentences of this chapter, on a sunny early summer day in Gothenburg, we headed for Slottsskogen, the largest urban park and most emblematic commons in the city of Gothenburg. In the park, we noticed waste pickers, from southern and eastern European countries, collecting abandoned recyclables while we continued enjoying the sun (a rare common resource at these latitudes), fresh air, park atmosphere, and urban nature. Unlike most commons, the excessive consumption and overflow (Czarniawska and Löfgren, 2013) of stuff connected with our lifestyle as good as guarantees the size of the resource for the foreseeable future. There is no such thing as too much waste picking. Urban waste is a commons, everywhere, for now and for times to come.

References

Abbott, J. (2004) 'Upgrading an informal settlement in Cape Town, South Africa', in K. Tranberg Hansen and M. Vaa (eds), *Reconsidering Informality: Perspectives from Urban Africa* (pp. 193–209). Uppsala, Sweden: Nordiska Afrikainstitutet.

Álvaréz de Andres, E., Zapata Campos, M.J. and Zapata, P. (2014) 'Stop the evictions! The diffusion of networked social movements and the emergence of a new hybrid space: the case of the Spanish Mortgage Victims Group', *Habitat International*, http://dx.doi.org/10.1016/j.habitatant.2014.10.002

Corvellec, H. and Hultman, J. (2012) 'From "less landfilling" to "wasting less": societal narratives, socio-materiality, and organizations', *Journal of Organizational Change Management* 25(2): 297–314.

Czarniawska, B. and Hernes, T. (eds) (2005) *Actor–Network Theory and Organizing*. Copenhagen: Liber and Copenhagen Business School Press.

Czarniawska, B. and Löfgren, O. (eds) (2013) *Coping with Excess: How Organizations, Communities and Individuals Manage Overflows*. Cheltenham, UK: Edward Elgar.

da Silva Carvalho, M., Pinguelli Rosa, L., Luiz Bufoni, A. and Basto Oliveira, L. (2012) 'Putting solid household waste to sustainable use: A case study in the city of Rio de Janeiro, Brazil', *Waste Management and Research* 30(12): 1312–19.

Fahmi, W. and Sutton, K. (2013) 'Cairo's contested waste: the Zabaleen's local practices and privatisation policies', in M.J. Zapata Campos and M. Hall (eds), *Organising Waste in the City: International Perspectives on Narratives and Practices*. Bristol, UK: The Policy Press.

Global Alliance of Waste Pickers (n.d.) History. Online. Available HTTP: <http://globalrec.org/history/> (accessed 1 September 2014).

Gutberlet, J. (2010) 'Waste, poverty and recycling', *Waste Management* 30(2): 171–3.

Hardin, G. (1968) 'The tragedy of the commons', *Science* 162(3859): 1243–8.

Hardoy, J.E., Mitlin, D. and Satterthwaite, D. (2001) *Environmental Problems in an Urbanizing World: Finding Solutions for Cities in Africa, Asia and Latin America*. London: Earthscan Publications.

Hardt, M. and Negri, A. (2009) *Commonwealth*. Cambridge, MA: Harvard University Press.

Harvey, D. (2012) *Rebel Cities: From the Right to the City to the Urban Revolution*. London: Verso.

Hultman, J. and Corvellec, H. (2012) 'The European waste hierarchy: from the sociomateriality of waste to a politics of consumption', *Environment and Planning A* 44(10): 2413–27.

Katusiimeh, M.W., Burger, K. and Mol, A.P.J. (2013) 'Informal waste collection and its co-existence with the formal waste sector: the case of Kampala, Uganda', *Habitat International* 38(C): 1–9.

Lindberg, K. and Czarniawska, B. (2006) 'Knotting the action net or organizing between organizations', *Scandinavian Journal of Management* 22(4): 292–306.

Mitlin, D. (2008) 'With and beyond the state: co-production as a route to political influence, power and transformation for grassroots organizations', *Environment and Urbanization* 20(2): 339–60.

Ostrom, E. (1990) *Governing the Commons: The Evolution of Institutions for Collective Action*. Cambridge: Cambridge University Press.

Ostrom, E. (1996) 'Crossing the great divide: co-production, synergy and development', *World Development* 24(6): 1073–87.

Oteng-Ababio, M., Arguello, J.E.M. and Gabbay, O. (2013) 'Solid waste management in African cities: sorting the facts from the fads in Accra, Ghana', *Habitat International* 39(C): 96–104.

Star, S. (1999) 'The ethnography of infrastructure', *American Behavioral Scientist* 43(3): 377–91.

UN-Habitat (2003) *The Challenge of Slums*. London: UN-Habitat.

Wilson, D.C., Araba, A.O., Chinwah, K. and Cheeseman, C.R. (2008) 'Building recycling rates through the informal sector', *Waste Management* 29(2): 629–35.

Zapata Campos, M.J. and Hall, M. (eds) (2013) *Organising Waste in the City: International Perspectives on Narratives and Practices*. Bristol, UK: The Policy Press.

Zapata Campos, M.J. and Zapata, P. (2012) 'Changing La Chureca: organizing city resilience through action nets', *Journal of Change Management* 12(3): 323–38.

Zapata Campos, M.J. and Zapata, P. (2013a) 'Switching Managua on! Connecting informal settlements to the formal city through household waste collection', *Environment and Urbanization* 25(1): 1–18.

Zapata Campos, M.J. and Zapata, P. (2013b) 'Translating aid development into city management practice', *Public Administration and Development* 33(2): 101–12.

Zapata Campos, M.J. and Zapata, P. (2014) 'The travel of global ideas of waste management: the case of Managua and its informal settlements', *Habitat International* 41 (January 2014): 41–9.

Chapter 5

Managing the urban commons[1]

Public interest and the representation of interconnectedness

Martina Löw

Are we facing a crisis in the field of designing the urban commons? Some would even say we are already in the midst of it. According to the organizers of the International Building Exhibition (IBA Hamburg, 2012), public planning is suffering from a lack of legitimacy, as its goals and objectives are no longer grounded in what is usually called 'public interest'. Pluralization and individualization – the hallmarks of modern societies – have resulted in a large variety of divergent interests and circumstances of life, which makes it difficult for urban planners to define shared values and common goals needed to provide guidelines for the design of urban commons.

That conflicting interests and diversified social contexts might make a community ungovernable is not an entirely new idea, of course. Jürgen Habermas (1973) has discussed the 'legitimation crisis' of advanced capitalist societies; Fritz W. Scharpf has raised concern about 'the agency of the state at the end of the 20th century' (1992: 93), and Armin Nassehi has put forward the proposition that modern societies are 'ultimately ungovernable' (2012: 40).

What is new in recent debates is the assumption that the crisis is not limited to the legal system and the state alone. Various other groups who, in the name of public interest, administer common resources or design the public commons (yet are neither elected representatives nor lawmakers) seem to be equally affected by this crisis. This is especially true for those working in the field of urban collectivity. Here, practitioners are experiencing a dramatic loss of agency due to what is perceived as 'overwhelming' diversity. That includes architects and urban planners designing public spaces; conservators trying to determine what qualifies as cultural heritage; artists and intellectuals tending to social and cultural memory; social workers providing community organization; teachers who must make choices between what is worth knowing and what is irrelevant, and so on.

In what follows I will explore the conflict arising between public interests associated with the commons and the representation of these interests by

1 The article was translated by Bettina Mathes and Bettina Seifried.

experts and professionals. I aim to show that under conditions of structural diversity the idea that different parts will finally integrate into a whole is no longer viable in the search for new modes of urban collectivity. In order to explore new possibilities in dealing with and managing common resources it is necessary to first of all ask whether diversity is in fact increasing. I argue that diversity – a defining characteristic of modern societies – continues to be a challenge for experts, precisely because diversity and the specific issues it presents are never the same. The main difficulty for planners acting on behalf of the public (interest) is not so much an increase in diversity but the fact that previously agreed upon standards and processes of normalization are no longer perceived as unproblematic by the public. I will outline the pros and cons of two models of public interest representation: the first one implies seeking consensual agreement among heterogeneous groups as a basis for managing the public commons; the second relies on managing the commons by granting each social group the right to create and administer their own social space. In a further step, I shall propose a different conception based on contemporary theories of space, offering a notion of public interest grounded in interconnectedness, interrelations and networks of overlapping interests. It is my contention that the mapping of multiple and multi-layered connections between social groups can serve as a new basis for representation in plural societies and thus help to guide professional action. In the absence of a successful case of urban planning focused on interconnectedness, I will use the negative example of Frankfurt am Main, Germany, to finally illustrate how in the face of general helplessness planners get stuck in the dead end of homogenizing historical constructions, and how previously visible and manifest structures of reference between very divergent architectural forms and historical narratives are being obliterated rather than further emphasized and developed.

Urban commons, public interest and the representation through experts

According to Hardt and Negri (2011), the commons is defined as 'first of all, the common wealth of the material world' (2011: viii), yet also, and 'more significantly [as] those results of social production that are necessary for social interaction and further production, such as knowledges, languages, codes, information, affects, and so forth' (2011: viii). '*Urban* commons', a notion associated with the work of David Harvey (2012), allows focusing more closely on public spaces and their design, including the use of public space as places of commemoration.

Elinor Ostrom (1990) examined strategies for how commons could be equitably created and governed. Her answer can be briefly summarized as follows (see also the introductory chapter and Metzger's contribution in chapter 1): managing the commons requires diverse institutional arrangements and organizations to ensure equitable treatment of the parties involved. In many cases, direct negotiations between the individuals concerned are made impossible because there are too many actors involved in the process, and not all parties have the same capacity to articulate their interests.

Modern societies tend to rely on the competence of experts, who, on the basis of their being aware of the complexity of the subject matter to be negotiated, take over the role of mediators between different groups, and who – in the service of public interest – often establish institutional forms, sometimes whole organizations, for the intended purpose. In the field of the *urban* commons, the expert groups are clearly specified: they comprise planners, architects, urban designers, conservators and social workers. As citizens' participation and governance are a matter of growing importance in societies, the role of these experts is changing. They no longer represent merely abstract technical expertise but become real mediators of conflicting interests. It is their task to strike a balance between professional expertise and diverging citizens' interests, with a view to facilitating collective designing and management of the commons. From the point of view of citizens, this process inevitably gives rise to ambivalence between the struggle for self-administration and the recognition of the need for professional expertise. On the experts' side there is the challenge to take into consideration various particular interests and yet remain loyal to their mandate, i.e. to act on behalf of and in the public interest. 'Questions of the commons', writes Harvey (2012: 71), 'are contradictory and therefore always contested. Behind these contestations lie conflicting social and political interests'. What defines the relationship between authorities, professional citizens' representatives and participation and the degree of organization in the process of designing the public space through authorities, private investors, political representatives, independent experts and citizens' initiatives varies from country to country. In the case of Germany (and many other countries) it does not seem to make much sense to distinguish between public spaces as a 'matter of state power and public administration' on the one part, and public spaces as urban commons appropriated by means of political action on the other, as Harvey does (2012: 72). If Syntagma Square in Athens, Tahrir Square in Cairo, and the Plaza de Catalunya in Barcelona are urban commons in this definition, it is nevertheless still true that public spaces like Frankfurt's Römerberg (see analysis below), whose new design was achieved in active negotiation with the citizens, also qualify as 'urban commons'. A narrow definition of urban commons focusing on results (here: their being collectively occupied in political protest) would be to romanticize the concept, as Raman (2011) rightly argues. Even if one group enforces their interests better than others, even if the appropriation of space takes place 'only' in talks and through negotiations, even if the citizens are not in protest but in favor of the decisions of authorities and experts regarding design and redevelopment of a public space – even then this public space is both a social product and a prerequisite for social interaction, hence an urban commons. However, citizens' interests are usually very different in nature, which is why experts who are supposed to represent (and mediate) these interests are facing a huge challenge if they are to act simultaneously in the public interest as part of their mandate.

A rather undetermined legal concept such as 'public interest' acquires meaning only in relation to the ever-changing definitions of what counts as commons, which are co-created by the professionals in the groups mentioned above (Böckenförde, 2002: 63). Legal scholars agree that in a constitutional democratic state the process of defining what constitutes a public responsibility 'is largely assigned to society' (Böckenförde, 2002: 24). In other words, while in democratic states (as opposed to fascist regimes or monarchy) the legal system normatively refers and relates to the notion of public interest, it is nevertheless true that any 'essentialist, a priori definition of what constitutes the common wealth is not compatible with the principles of liberal democracy' (Münkler and Fischer, 2002: 10).

The term 'public interest' is closely linked (if not equated with) the question of the commons. Acting 'in the public interest' is essential if forms of collective action are the desired way of society formation and resources are to be governed collectively. Reference to the public sphere, however, evokes a *pluralistic* structure on which this interest is founded – a type of structure that precisely challenges acting in *the one and unified* public interest (Vobruba, 1994: 171 ff.). Both public interest and the commons are regarded as bedrocks of the 'constitutional foundation' (Häberle, 1970: 204) of the legal system, and public interest is attributed a key role as integrating communicative force (Brugger, 2000: 68) generating social cohesion in communities. Moreover, public interest is not only subject to interpretation but also without doubt is used as an appellative or argumentative tool in the process of justifying political actions and decisions.

Professionals representing public interests have increasingly raised concerns that due to expanding social diversification, their mandate is becoming uncertain. The problem is obviously how to design public places in a 'city [meant] for all' (a formula nowadays used by NGOs and international architecture firms such as Albert Speer alike). Different motion patterns of children and adults, diverging expectations of women and men regarding public spaces, as well as dissimilar aesthetic preferences depending on social milieus are putting pressure on urban planners, for whom these interests all too often appear to be mutually exclusive.

Even priorities are a matter of controversy: should the focus primarily lie on designing public space for as many different interests groups as possible in one single space, or is aesthetics the key factor (and whose aesthetics)? Is it more important to promote local businesses or to counterbalance social inequality? And in what relation does the design of the public place stand to the overall structure of the housing market?

The complexity of the concept of public interest is also reflected in another political task: There is hardly any doubt that it is in the public interest to promote a society's cohesion and sustainability through collective memory and commemoration. In the field of urban commons, however, new projects have always been highly controversial. In Germany, for instance, memory politics referring to the crimes of National Socialism is a striking (but by no means unique) case in point. Here, the task of designing and building major memorials has been mostly delegated to foreign architects and artists (often of Jewish origin): Micha Ullman, Richard Serra, Daniel Libeskind and Peter Eisenman. That means: 'Germans have delegated the task of giving expression to the memory of Nazism and the Holocaust to those who were once targets of Germany's genocidal politics' (Mathes, 2012: 165). Controversial projects include, for instance, the (demolition of the) Palace of the Republic in Berlin, the memorial for Marwa El-Sherbini (a Muslim resident of Dresden who was stabbed to death during a court hearing by a German male against whom she testified), and the planned construction of the imperial coronation path (*Krönungsweg*) in the city of Frankfurt am Main. The difficult question is always: Is it possible at all to build memorials 'in the public interest' in modern plural societies? Which and whose speech-act is capable of expressing the public interest to account for the many different, conflicting values, lifestyles and world-views we encounter in contemporary life? Similar issues apply for other areas, such as social work, art, education and the media. The problem is how to manage the commons so that the cohesion of a society finds its expression if the experience of shared interests and common symbolic forms is fading away.

Diversity today

A closer look at diversity touches upon the question whether it is diversity itself, or merely the perception of diversity, which has increased. In most European countries there are no longer strong correlations between social class and electoral behavior, trade union membership or churchgoing (Schnell and Köhler, 1998). Interests have diversified and are less predictable. Nonetheless, most people's educational opportunities are still largely determined by family background. In a recent study comparing 18 European countries, Fabrizio Bernardi comes to the conclusion that the probability of earning a college degree depends heavily on the social class a person was born into (Bernardi, 2009; also Lörz and Schindler, 2011).

On the other hand, leisure activities are now much less self-segregated than they used to be. One's taste in music (Otte, 2010) or films (Rössel and Bromberger, 2009) does not seem to be determined by age, ethnicity or social standing anymore. While expensive leisure activities continue to be open to only a few, it is also true that the wealthy and the well-educated are interested in a wide variety of activities and aesthetics, something which tends to subvert the traditional link between class and how people spend their leisure time (Chan and Goldthorpe, 2007). What has not changed however is that people continue to assign class membership to themselves and to others. Although it has become harder to infer social position from looks or appearances (Pape et al., 2008), it is not clear how much difference there really is and whether diversity has indeed increased. In some areas we can observe an escalation of social inequality, for instance due to soaring rents in urban centers. In other areas there is convergence – shared leisure-time interests across classes and ethnicities are but one example. Yet if we look at traditional ties to parties, trade unions and other interests groups, there seems to be a new wave of diversification. Still another scenario opens up if we look at immigration. Within the last 50 years the number of immigrants living in Germany has risen by 400 per cent (Pries, 2012). As a consequence (and not only due to immigration) life in urban centers is now shaped by a multitude of religious communities and cultural traditions.

While paid work still seems the central reference point for agency in all social groups (Blossfeld et al., 2008), forms of employment are more flexible and fluid, and there has been an increase in precarious work. Planning for the future proves to be more unpredictable for all milieus (Dörre, 2010) but it is experienced as especially threatening by the middle class. Yet a broad middle class is considered a powerful integrative core of society. If the middle classes diminish, we would expect an increase in social inequality and a polarization of society that jeopardizes social cohesion. However, if we look at the middle range of incomes – by which the middle class is generally defined – the decrease in income is, in reality, rather insignificant (Institut für Sozialforschung und Gesellschaftspolitik, 2011). While there is no denying that there is downward mobility, there is always also upward mobility. Some experience social insecurity as a burden, while others interpret it as the price to be paid for an increase in freedom and choice. Moreover, there is no clear evidence that among the middle class feelings of insecurity have indeed increased or are felt more strongly than by other social groups (Burzan and Kohrs, 2012).

Diversity is thus a social fact, and cities are the hallmark of diversity. From a sociological perspective one may safely say that there is no city without plurality. In terms of languages, religions, nationalities and citizenship, Europe is certainly more diverse today than 50 years ago. In that sense we may indeed speak of progressing pluralization. However, from a historical point of view 'religious diversity in Europe has rather been the norm than the exception' (Nagel, 2012: 158). This raises the question of how we might distinguish between a mostly media-induced perception of social disintegration and the inevitably ambivalent processes of social change, biographical re-orientation, alienation and newly-won familiarity.

To sum up briefly, diversity is here to stay. The difficulties in managing the commons collectively cannot be put down to processes of diversification but are a sign of the pervasive uncertainty regarding the legitimacy of actions. Moreover, diversity is 'a consumer good with a short half-life' (Bukow, 2011: 213), precisely because what we perceive as foreign today has become familiar by tomorrow. It is often difficult to say whether a new social trend evidences an increase in heterogeneity or homogeneity. For instance, is the fact that same-sex unions are now legally recognized a sign of a new tolerance for difference or quite the reverse – an act of assimilating into the mainstream a way of life that once used to be a marker of difference? Diversification is an ambiguous process. Any new type of diversity and every new wave of experienced difference will inevitably provoke debate. One obvious example is the growth of religious communities in Europe. What poses a challenge to defining public interest is not the fact that there *is* diversity but rather the *kind* of diversity there is. It is the specific content that seems to be causing discomfort.

A further issue is that the self-conception of experts is changing. Promoting diversity and struggling with the challenges it poses does not necessarily mean that everyone is affected by or relates to diversity in the same way. Some are always more diverse and different than others. As Erving Goffman argued for the US in the 1950s there were seekers and consumers of diversity who themselves were never perceived as different, who would not experience the social stigma and shame that comes with being labeled as different: 'in an important sense there is only one complete unblushing male in America: a young, married, white, urban, northern, heterosexual Protestant father of college education, fully employed, of good complexion, weight and height, and a recent record in sports' (Goffman, 1963: 128).

The perceived increase in social diversity and related doubts as to whether anyone might still be in a position to identify, represent and balance divergent public interests in a plural society, suggest the loss of a symbolic center such as Goffman's 'unblushing male'. Returning to urban commons at this point, there is no denying that for decades planners have imagined adult, white, married and well-employed males as their central target group. Only at the margins special zones for kids – playgrounds – were established, while the formula 'bedroom community' erased the daily lives of women from public discourse. After the battle of the sexes in the 1970s and 1980s, after the shock of shrinking white populations at the end of the millennium, Europeans are forced to finally recognize that immigration and an aging society are social realities, and none of us is exempt from 'blushing' any longer. The core group, the imaginary center around which European societies revolved, has ceased to exist. Today we cannot help but acknowledge that we are all interconnected and continually engage in a multitude of interactions and relationships, that we are in fact *constituted* by relationships in which gender, age, class, ethnicity, sexuality and nationality function as crucial markers that define that relation.

Forms of representation

The insight that diversity is a necessary feature of modern societies is as old as modern societies themselves (Durkheim, 1893). We know that without the division of labor there would be no daily routine, just as there would be no change without immigration, and no choice without diverse and differing ways of life. We need difference to form attachments and be in relationships. Interdependency and interrelatedness are part of our collective experience (Elias, 1970). What seems to have been lost is the central figure in the web of differences, a figure that blinds out all differences. That symbolic figure used to be a man: white, Christian, hard-working. He embodied the norm – an island in a sea of plurality, the part that stood for the whole; man represented humanity; he used to be the Self that encountered the Other; much like heterosexuality quintessentially represented sexuality. Nowadays we can no longer be sure.

Confronted with our uncertainty and the fact that we can all be shamed, we are forced to acknowledge that unifying processes have lost credibility, and, more importantly, that the 'traditional scheme of integrating the parts into a whole is no longer valid' (Koschorke, 2010: 12–13). We can infer from debates on legitimacy that seeking agreement by common consent does not seem to make much sense anymore. The idea that public interest could be represented politically built on the assumption that, under conditions of plurality, reason and reasonable discourse facilitated consensus and agreement rooted in shared values, which in turn would provide guidelines for future action – along the lines of 'where there is a center, there is a way'. It is hardly surprising that Hannah Arendt's idea of a pluralistic and agonal sphere of agency (what she calls *Öffentlichkeit*, i.e. public sphere), in which individual audacity, resistance and equality of opportunity rather than consent promote social change, has received little attention in such a context (Arendt, 1994; Thaa, 2009). Perhaps because Arendt, who remained skeptical about the possibility of political representation, focused primarily on the individual who is courageous enough to step into the limelight of the public sphere. Yet governance of and concern for the commons necessarily transcend the individual and particular interests. Hence, consensual decision-making and the formation of will by broad consent seemed to be the obvious solution (also for Elinor Ostrom, see 1990, 1999, 2011). If consent was not an option, group representation would be the alternative. As Iris Marion Young (1997) suggests, minority rights are best ensured in a minority representation model, since forms of direct democracy tend to silence the voices of minorities. Young is of course aware that group representation is a dialectical process, in which identities are at once re-presented and created. To give one example: in Berlin, the monument for the homosexual victims of National Socialism contributed to the homogenization of German gay and lesbian identities. It is nevertheless Young's contention that minorities fare better when represented as a group.

What Young and others (e.g. Rem Kohlhaas for urban planning) object to is the widespread belief in the synthesizing power of consent. Koolhaas (1997) argues that the figure of common consent found its home in comprehensive planning, especially in the notorious master plan. Offering solutions for different problems in an integrated way, the master plan promised harmonization and the achievement of unity and uniformity. Through regulated procedures and measures it was possible for all to delegate interests and design to a group of experts. But now it seems the plan has lost its master. What we see today is that synthesizing and integrational efforts do not necessarily produce consent and agreement. The public confidence in comprehensive urban planning is shattered. New images are emerging: images of multiple interconnected spaces; of multiple worlds co-existing in a shared space in search of representation yet; images of spaces, in which the parts no longer *add up* to a whole. In this new world integration seems impossible. This is, however, not to say that there are no overlaps, yet the different social environments do not converge and cannot be subsumed under one another. Public interest thus requires that each social group gets its own separate voice.

Interconnectedness and relatedness

Modern societies are characterized by a high degree of diversity. For urban planning (and other professions) this means that diversity is an ongoing challenge and by no means a new phenomenon. Diversity is always different, variable in its manifestations, yet it is a hard social fact. As for the political representation of diversity, there seems to be only two options: one model rooted in well-established, reliable, reason- and discourse-driven mechanism of achieving common consent on the one hand, and minority group representation on the other. However, serious criticism of the outcomes has diminished public confidence in consensual procedures; and group representation entails a division of the public space according to particular and sectional interests of a society's minority groups – their separate spaces and historical narratives, their specific patterns of relevance.

I am, however, not entirely convinced that there should be no other alternative than between broad consensus and group representation. The loss of a society's symbolic center also opens up a third way, an opportunity for creating new forms of cohesiveness based on the recognition of the crucial importance of social relations and interdependencies (Schütz and Luckmann, 1975: 97–8). Rather than expecting common consent or group representation to be the ultimate solution, a shift in focus to the relational aspects of social interaction and interconnectedness seems more promising. If it is true that we become the person we are by being in relationship(s); if there is no Self without an Other; if our identifications change as we grow (see Benjamin, 1998) and adapt to changing environments, these processes must be examined and described more closely also from a sociological perspective.

The sociology of space seems to offer a useful starting point for a *relational* approach to promoting and managing urban commons. Building on Lefèbvre (1991, 2004), there are numerous scientific studies redefining and specifying the concept of space to provide a new theoretical basis for urban theory. A now widely shared sociological understanding of space proposes a duality of structural phenomena (Bourdieu, 1977; Giddens, 1984: 263 ff.). Based on double structuring, it is assumed that structures are not only constituted by action but also act as mediators in the process of the constitution of space. Spatial (and temporal) structures are hence tied to social action, just as action is embedded in spaces (and temporal structures). Space is thus understood as a complex set of relations between possible object fields, not as a fixed setting or absolute factor (e.g. a 'container'). Spatial relations and their institutionalization are analyzed as a result of action and interaction (de Certeau, 1989; Löw, 2001, 2008; Cresswell, 2004; Semi et al., 2009) which – building on processes of synthesis and placing – in turn strongly prestructure action. Every constitution of space is thus based on objects/people being connected and interrelated in such a way that boundaries emerge and become discernible, and spatial contexts develop out of individual objects. This process is called synthesis. It develops through processes of perception, ideation, and memory (Löw, 2008). If space is created through perception and thought, it is also simultaneously constituted by situating social goods and people and/or positioning primarily symbolic markings in order to render ensembles of goods and people identifiable and distinguishable. Yet the processes of placing and synthesizing are embedded in routines, which is why there is little or no cognitive awareness of the spatial dimension of action in everyday life.

Rather than seeking to analyze absolute space (itself divided into numerous sub-spaces), it is my contention that much is to be gained by embracing a spatial framework focusing on pathways, intersections and nodal points. For all too long sociologists and urban planners have described average values and meticulously discriminated between groups (victims, perpetrators, a quota for every minority, and so on). It is important now to take greater account of the multiple, complex patterns of connections, interdependencies, frictions, disjunctures and mutual attachments in a highly diverse society.

What I am suggesting is that it is *in the public interest* to establish a new language capable of describing the intricate web of social relations, group formations, and their interdependencies. Contemporary modes of urban collectivity are much better understood and captured by acknowledging the ever-shifting relationships between inconsistent social groups and by identifying nodal points, hubs and overlaps in this complex structure. The networks we live in and which shape our society do not represent rigid structures but could be described as responsive embeddings. That means there are various identification processes simultaneously at play, there are loyalties, preferences, relationships, energies, and overlaps at any given moment. The Others are not merely silent actors in the background, on the contrary, they generate resonances and reverberations, create momentum and produce resistances.

In our modern age, which is prone to fundamentalisms of all sorts, it would be all the more inspiring to avoid amalgamation and razor-sharp differentiations for once. Regardless of what we are dealing with, be it the design of public spaces, the organization of public education, the management of neighborhoods, or the preservation of historic monuments and collective memory, the use of experts to protect the interests of the population in the field of urban commons can fulfill the function of *re-presenting* the public interest not by seeking common consent or complying with the particular interests of a single social (sub)group, but only by bringing to light the relatedness and interconnectedness of groups (which implies both opposition and attachment) that exist in time and space. Only then that which has been invisible and discursively latent will come to the surface to show its presence – the complex patterns of mutual involvement and interconnectedness. Hence, governing the commons must be based on the premise and the shared experience that coherence is a result of interdependency and interrelations.

Frankfurt am Main: managing the urban commons

Good examples for architectural projects reflecting and expressing interconnectedness in reciprocal dependency are still hard to find. Arguably there are a few exemplary buildings like, for instance, Jean Nouvel's Musée du Quai Branly in Paris, but the new perspective has not yet been used strategically in planning processes across larger city areas. Therefore I will refer to an example (the reconstruction of Frankfurt's historic center) that points to a failure in this respect. In Frankfurt am Main a polyphonic, rather disharmoniously assembled inner-city building ensemble, which developed during the post-Second World War crisis era, is currently being modified and redeveloped into a homogenized, Disneyfied quarter of half-timbered re-builds of historic houses – out of sheer helplessness on the side of the planners faced with the impossibility to achieve a broad, city-wide consensus, so it seems. In practice, this 'planning crisis' has resulted in strategies that will at least have considerable impact on tourism development. However, a great opportunity has been lost to use physical space to give *material and visual* expression to a society based on difference.

Inner-city redevelopments tend to be highly controversial and may take decades to complete. Frankfurt am Main is no exception to this trend. Like other European cities in the nineteenth century, Frankfurt attempted to fight poverty and darkness in the old city center with the construction of large apartment buildings and wide boulevards that cut through and replaced narrow alleys. Allied air raids in the Second World War almost completely destroyed Frankfurt's historic center. Since the 1970s Frankfurt has been involved in an ongoing controversy about the right approach to rebuilding the 'Römerberg', an area which for most locals represents the heart of the city. Not surprisingly, this process has not been going easily and smoothly. After the war the area between the Dom (Frankfurt's medieval cathedral) and the reconstructed Paulskirche (St Paul's Church) was initially used as a parking lot. The final choice was then for a mix of simulated 'historic' timber-framed buildings contrasted with modern architecture. Built by Bartsch Thürwächter and Weber, the Technische Rathaus (home of the city's building and planning authorities), an oversized city hall in typical 1970s brutalist concrete style, was designed to represent the hallmark of a modern Frankfurt. The building's size as well as its material integrity corresponded with the city's emerging skyline, symbolizing modernity and an orientation toward the future. Right across from the Technische Rathaus, the Schirn gallery – a playful, postmodern art exhibition hall – was erected. The entire ensemble consisting of Technisches Rathaus, Schirn and the medieval cathedral brought together different architectural styles ('material authenticity meets postmodern bricolage') and temporalities ('modernist architecture meets the Middle Ages', with the cathedral itself being an assemblage from the thirteenth, sixteenth and nineteenth centuries). At the same time, the city decided to redevelop the area adjacent to Technische Rathaus and Schirn Gallery in its prewar form. This 'traditional site' was to feature copies of historic buildings dating back to the Middle Ages, and promised 'the possibility of recreating a lost Frankfurt. Reconstructive architecture was employed in an attempt to heal the wounds torn by the war' (Vinken, 2013: 121).

It is a moot point if the building projects of the 1970s and 1980s in Frankfurt's old city center were a success: The architectural sophistication of the Technische Rathaus – a compromise between the city's and the architects' visions – seems mediocre at best. The attempt to beautify the Römerberg square with fake historic facades appears awkward and begs the question whether modern architecture couldn't have offered different solutions to address the desire for identity. There is, however, no denying that the ensemble was always well received by both locals and visitors to the city.

The aggregation of buildings designed in different styles using different kinds of material, represented differing, if not opposing, ways of coming to terms with the disaster of the Second World War and National Socialism: blunt, technical, with a strong emphasis on material on the one hand; playful, pluralistic, eclectic; metaphorical, emulating, in search of identity on the other. In this, the Römerberg symbolically stood for the impossibility of agreeing on the one right way of reconstructing a city and move on after the war and the Holocaust. The buildings never formed a harmonious unit and left passersby puzzled and slightly amazed – which does not mean that the buildings were perceived as isolated, solitary structures. On the contrary, they entered into a dialogue and actually communicated with each other, it was just that they could not easily agree on anything, perhaps not even on the common topic of their conversation. Nonetheless, many local residents and tourists experienced this amazing assemblage as an instance of constructive memory politics.

In 2007 the city decided to tear down the Technische Rathaus on the grounds of technical, functional and aesthetic deficits. The future use of the void created by the wrecking ball was discussed in action groups especially set up for this purpose, on the web and in the media. While some favored an approach that would advance Frankfurt's cosmopolitan character and give modern architecture a second chance, others supported the historic reconstruction of the old buildings destroyed in the war with old photographs of the prewar marketplace serving as blueprints for the preferred historic look.

In the end the city decided to green-light a plan that proposed historic reconstruction. In the space formerly occupied by the Technische Rathaus, a row of 40 reconstructed prewar houses (copies of those on the old postcards) was to be erected. 'Raising the profile of the cityscape is of fundamental importance to Frankfurt', the head of the city's planning department justified the decision. Redevelopments were based on prewar street lines and construction volumes. Of the 40 new buildings, eight are copies of destroyed houses; the remaining 32 structures are designed to convey a nostalgic 'old-town atmosphere'. To top it all, the city has decided to have the largely unknown and historically irrelevant 'Imperial Coronation Path' (Krönungsweg) reconstructed (*staged* would probably be a more appropriate term). This is how conservators describe the project: 'In Frankfurt, the old town will consist of a homogenous, homey and likely profitable ensemble of newly constructed buildings; a ubiquitous architectural pattern designed to reproduce and evoke a certain kind of schmaltzy sentiment' (Vinken, 2013: 136).

What has been lost is the productive tension that used to characterize the public space. Neither officials nor locals realized that this site-specific tension – the result of differing post-Second World War opinions on architecture and urban planning after the Holocaust and the role of the city – would have been an excellent starting point for modern Frankfurt's architecture and contemporary forms of multiculturalism and diversity to interconnect. Instead, the newspaper Frankfurter Rundschau cites a local innkeeper: 'It must be ensured that the new quarter is run by folks who intimately know Frankfurt, who get the traditional *feel* of the city'. And local journalists have been checking the family trees of future shop owners in the area: one is distantly related to Goethe's family, another runs a business founded in the old city in 1732, and a third one has owned a traditional restaurant in nearby Sachsenhausen since times immemorial. In brief, the city focuses its efforts on unifying and harmonizing strategies recurring to an imaginary 'essence' and 'historic character' of Frankfurt. Nowhere is this character conceptualized or envisioned as a *relational* and multi-layered fabric of differing elements – on the contrary, all facades must look the same in the name of local tradition, unity and continuity.

That the demolition of a signature building like the Technische Rathaus would trigger a major debate on how to fill the void was hardly surprising. Yet the city's administration shied away from controversies over planning policies. Rather than guiding the process with the bright eyes of curiosity looking for innovative ways of addressing folks' desire for identity and continuity, rather than promoting a new architectural language and taking the modern approach of the 1970s and 1980s one step further, rather than prioritizing ambiguity and contradiction to sound out the intertwining and interconnectedness of different social perspectives and periods in time – the city council has readily opted for the comprehensive homogenization of the cityscape.

Conclusion

This article has taken up the current debate among urban planning experts and other professionals in the fields of education, social work, and culture, who have raised the question of whether under increasing diversity, difference and individualization acting in the public interest is still possible with respect to the management of the commons. Urban commons, and the design of public spaces in particular, are subject to social negotiation processes between social groups. In modern knowledge societies these negotiations and their technical and creative implementation require the support of experts. Their increasing uncertainty about their role and possibility for action refers to fundamental problems in dealing with the urban commons. To open up an alternative approach to designing the urban commons, it was noted that the term 'public interest' is generally understood as an underdetermined legal concept that can only be assigned meaning by social processes of public negotiation rather than being defined in normative terms. In a next step, the hypothesis that European societies are actually facing an *increase* in diversity was rejected. Pluralization, it was argued, is an ongoing process in modern societies, which continually leads to new forms of differentiation, while existing differences lose importance. Taking into account the perception that ongoing diversification is a social fact, the thesis was put forward that the idea of a central (male, white) figure of reference has been lost in the wake of global migration, demographic developments and feminist movements. Along with this central figure the confidence in consensual decision-making and great master plans has evaporated, especially when it comes to matters of public interest. My key argument is that the crisis of representation (and related awkward attempts to design urban commons, as in Frankfurt, for instance) can only be overcome by a fundamental change in perspective. With reference to spatial theory, I have argued that dividing public space into sub-areas of partialized spaces to represent minorities structurally continues to focus on the idea of one single unified (public) space. Spatial theory's recent change in perspective toward a *relational* understanding of space was therefore applied to the current debate on public interest and representation, and proposed as a future rationale for projects within the larger field of public interests. My point is that public interest can no longer be premised on consensus building or separate decision-making processes for particular interest groups. Under conditions of diversity, acting in the public interest and managing urban commons must include the task to make visible and clearly profile the interrelations and interconnectedness between different groups and periods, and to symbolically and materially represent the social fabric as a multi-layered, heterogeneous ensemble composed of a multitude of differences. For Frankfurt's inner-city reconstruction project it would have been a bold and truly contemporary statement to visibly expose and emphasize the interconnectedness of the city's socially and ethnically highly diverse population through different forms of architecture instead of opting for the replication of an imaginary past and 'imperial coronation path'.

References

Arendt, H. (ed.) (1994) 'Kultur und Politik', *Zwischen Vergangenheit und Zukunft: Übungen im Politischen Denken I* (pp. 277–304). Munich: Piper Taschenbuch.

Benjamin, J. (1998) *Shadow of the Other: Intersubjectivity and Gender in Psychoanalysis.* New York: Routledge.

Bernardi, F. (2009) 'Globalizzazione, individualizzazione e morte delle classi sociali: uno studio empirico su 18 paesi Europei', *Polis* 2: 195–220.

Blossfeld, H.P., Hofäcker, D., Hofmeister, H. and Kurz, K. (2008) 'Globalisierung, Flexibilisierung und der Wandel von Lebensläufen in modernen Gesellschaften', in M. Szydlik, Marc (ed.), *Flexibilisierung: Folgen für Arbeit und Familie* (pp. 23–46). Wiesbaden: VS Verlag.

Böckenförde, E.W. (2002) 'Gemeinwohlvorstellungen bei Klassikern der Rechts- und Staatsphilosophie', in H. Münkler and K. Fischer (eds), *Gemeinwohl und Gemeinsinn im Recht: Konkretisierung und Realisierung öffentlicher Interessen* (pp. 43–65). Berlin: Akademie Verlag.

Bourdieu, P. (1977) *Outline of a Theory of Practice.* Cambridge: Cambridge University Press.

Brugger, W. (2000) 'Gemeinwohl als Ziel von Staat und Recht', in D. Murswiek and H. Quaritsch (eds), *Staat – Souveränität – Verfassung: Festschrift für Helmut Quaritsch zum 70 Geburtstag* (pp. 54–71). Berlin: Duncker and Humblot.

Bukow, W.D. (2011) 'Vielfalt in der postmodernen Stadtgesellschaft – Eine Ortsbestimmung', in W.D. Bukow et al. (eds), *Neue Vielfalt in der urbanen Stadtgesellschaft* (pp. 207–31). Wiesbaden: VS Verlag.

Burzan, N. and Kohrs, S. (2012) 'Vielfältige Verunsicherung in der Mittelschicht – eine Herausforderung für sozialen Zusammenhalt?', in L. Pries (ed.), *Zusammenhalt durch Vielfalt?: Bindungskräfte der Vergesellschaftung im 21. Jahrhundert* (pp. 101–22). Wiesbaden: Springer VS.

Certeau, M. de (1989) *Kunst des Handelns.* Berlin: Merve.

Chan, T.W. and Goldthorpe, J.H. (2007) 'Social stratification and cultural consumption: music in England', *European Sociological Review* 23(1): 1–19.

Cresswell, T. (2004) *Place: A Short Introduction*. Malden, MA: Blackwell Publishing.

Dörre, K. (2010) 'Die Selbstmanager. Biographien und Lebensentwürfe in Unsicheren Zeiten', in A. Bolder et al. (eds), *Neue Lebenslaufregimes – neue Konzepte der Bildung Erwachsener?* (pp. 139–49). Wiesbaden: VS Verlag.

Durkheim, E. (1893) *De la Division du Travail Social: Étude Sur L'Organisation Des Sociétés Supérieures*. Paris: Félix Alcan.

Elias, N. (1970) *Was ist Soziologie?* Munich: Juventa.

Giddens, A. (1984) *The Constitution of Society: Outline of the Theory of Structuration*. Berkeley, Cal.: University of California Press.

Goffman, E. (1963) *Stigma: Notes on the Management of Spoiled Identity*. Englewood Cliffs: Prentice-Hall.

Häberle, P. (1970) *Öffentliches Interesse als Juristisches Problem. Eine Analyse von Gesetzgebung und Rechtsprechung*. Bad Homburg: Athenäum Verlag.

Habermas, J. (1973) *Legitimationsprobleme im Spätkapitalismus*. Frankfurt am Main: Suhrkamp Verlag.

Hardt, M. and Negri, A. (2011) *Commonwealth*. Harvard: Harvard University Press.

Harvey, D. (2012) *Rebel Cities. From the Right to the City to the Urban Revolution*. London, New York: Verso.

IBA Hamburg (2012) *IBA Hamburg Schriftenreihe. Band 6. Metropole: Zivilgesellschaft*. Berlin: Jovis.

Institut für Sozialforschung und Gesellschaftspolitik (2011) *Überprüfung der These einer 'Schrumpfenden Mittelschicht' in Deutschland*. Cologne: Bundesministerium für Arbeit und Soziales.

Kaltenbrunner, R. (2012) 'Die kirche im dorf lassen. Kein falscher alarm! Ein stadtteil wie Berlin – Kreuzberg kann gar nicht vollständig', *Frankfurter Rundschau* 24 April: 32–3.

Koolhaas, R. (1997) *Delirious New York: A Retroactive Manifesto for Manhattan*. New York: Monacelli.

Koppetsch, C. (2010) 'Jenseits der Individualisierten Mittelstandsgesellschaft? Zur Ambivalenz Subjektiver Lebensführung in Unsicheren Zeiten', in P.A. Berger and R. Hitzler (eds), *Individualisierungen: Ein Vierteljahrhundert 'jenseits von Stand und Klasse'?* (pp. 225–43). Wiesbaden: VS Verlag.

Koschorke, A. (2010) 'Ein neues Paradigma der Kulturwissenschaften', in E. Eßlinger et al. (eds), *Die Figur des Dritten: Ein Kulturwissenschaftliches Paradigma* (pp. 9–31). Frankfurt am Main: Suhrkamp Verlag.

Lefèbvre, H. (1991) *The Production of Space*. Oxford: Blackwell

Lefèbvre, H. (2004) *Rhythmanalysis: Space, Time and Everyday Live*. London: Continuum.

Lörz, M. and Schindler, S. (2011) 'Bildungsexpansion und soziale ungleichheit: Zunahme, abnahme oder persistenz ungleicher chancenverhältnisse – eine frage der perspektive?', *Zeitschrift für Soziologie* 40(6): 458–77.

Löw, M. (2001) *Raumsoziologie*. Frankfurt am Main: Suhrkamp.

Löw, M. (2008) 'The constitution of space: the structuration of spaces through the simultaneity of effect and perception', *European Journal of Social Theory* 11(1): 25–49.

Lutz, H. and Wenning, N. (eds) (2001) 'Differenzen über Differenz – Einführung in die Debatten', *Unterschiedlich verschieden: Differenz in der Erziehungswissenschaft* (pp. 11–24). Opladen: Leske+Budrich.

Mathes, B. (2012) 'Teutonic shifts, Jewish voids. Remembering the Holocaust in post-Wall Germany', *Third Text* 26(2): 165–75.

Münkler, H. and Fischer, K. (2002) 'Einleitung', in *Gemeinwohl und Gemeinsinn im Recht: Konkretisierung und Realisierung öffentlicher Interessen* (pp. 9–23). Berlin: Akademie Verlag.

Nagel, A. K. (2012) 'Vielfältige Verunsicherung in der Mittelschicht – eine Herausforderung für Sozialen Zusammenhalt?', in L. Pries (ed.), *Zusammenhalt durch Vielfalt? Bindungskräfte der Vergesellschaftung im 21. Jahrhundert* (pp. 233–49). Wiesbaden: Springer VS.

Nassehi, A. (2012) 'Der Ausnahmezustand als Normalfall. Modernität als Krise', in A. Nassehi (ed.), *Kursbuch Nr. 170 – Krisen Lieben* (pp. 34–49). Hamburg: Murmann Verlag GmbH.

Ostrom, E. (1990) *Governing the Commons: The Evolution of Institutions for Collective Action.* Cambridge: Cambridge University Press.

Ostrom, E. (1999) 'Vorwort zur Deutschen Ausgabe', in *Die Verfassung der Allmende. Jenseits von Staat und Markt* (pp. xvii–xx). Tübingen: Mohr Siebeck.

Ostrom, E. (2011) *Was Mehr Wird, Wenn Wir Teilen. Vom Gesellschaftlichen Wert der Gemeingüter.* München: Oekom.

Otte, G. (2010) '"Klassenkultur" und "Individualisierung" als soziologische Mythen? Ein Zeitvergleich des Musikgeschmacks Jugendlicher in Deutschland, 1955–2004', in P. A. Berger and R. Hitzler (eds), *Individualisierungen: Ein Vierteljahrhundert, 'Jenseits von Stand und Klasse'?* (pp. 73–95). Wiesbaden: VS Verlag.

Pape, S., Rössel, J. and Solga, H. (2008) 'Die visuelle wahrnehmbarkeit sozialer ungleichheit – eine alternative methode zur untersuchung der entkopplungsthese', *Zeitschrift für Soziologie* 37(1): 25–41.

Pries, L. (2012) 'Erweiterter zusammenhalt in wachsender vielfalt', in L. Pries (ed.), *Zusammenhalt durch Vielfalt? Bindungskräfte der Vergesellschaftung im 21. Jahrhundert* (pp. 13–48). Wiesbaden: Springer VS.

Raman, B. (2011) *The Fuzzy Logic Of Urban Commons.* Online. Available HTTP: <http://infochangeindia.org/agenda/enclosure-of-the-commons/the-fuzzy-logic-of-urban-commons.html> (accessed 25 October 2014).

Rössel, J. and Bromberger, K. (2009) 'Strukturiert kulturelles kapital auch den konsum von populärkultur?', *Zeitschrift für Soziologie* 38(6): 494–512.

Scharpf, F.W. (1992) 'Die Handlungsfähigkeit des Staates am Ende des Zwanzigsten Jahrhunderts', in B. Kohler-Koch (ed.), *Staat und Demokratie in Europa. 18. Wissenschaftlicher Kongress der Deutschen Vereinigung für politische Wissenschaft* (pp. 93–115). Opladen: Leske+Budrich.

Schnell, R. and Köhler, U. (1998) 'Eine Empirische Untersuchung einer Individualisierungshypothese am Beispiel der Parteipräferenz von 1953–1992', in J. Friedrichs (ed.), *Die Individualisierungs-These* (pp. 221–47). Opladen: Leske+Budrich.

Schütz, A. and Luckmann, T. (1975) *Strukturen der Lebenswelt. Band 1.* Neuwied: Luchterhand.

Semi, G., Colombo, E., Camozzi, I., and Frisina, A. (2009) 'Practices of Difference: Analysing Multculturalism in Everyday Life', in A. Wise and S. Veayutham (eds), *Everyday Multiculturalism.* Houndsmill: Palgrave Macmillan.

Simmel, G. (1992) *Soziologie. Untersuchungen über die Formen der Vergesellschaftung, Bd. 11.* Frankfurt am Main: Suhrkamp Verlag.

Thaa, W. (2009) 'Das Ungelöste Inklusionsproblem in den Partizipatorischen Neubewertungen Politischer Repräsentation', in M. Linden and W. Thaa (eds), *Die Politische Repräsentation von Fremden und Armen, Baden* (pp. 61–78). Baden: Nomos.

Twickel, C. (2010) *Gentrifidingsbums oder Eine Stadt für Alle*. Hamburg: Edition Nautilus.

Vinken, G. (2013) 'Unstillbarer hunger nach echtem. Frankfurts neue altstadt', *Die Alte Stadt* 40(2): 119–36.

Vobruba, G. (1994) *Gemeinschaft ohne Moral. Theorie und Empirie moralfreier Gemeinschaftskonstruktionen*. Wien: Passagen Verlag.

Young, I.M. (1997) 'Deferring Group Representation', in I. Shapiro und W. Kymlicka (eds), *Ethnicity and Group Rights* (pp. 349–76). New York: New York University Press.

Chapter 6

Mediated exclusions from the urban commons

Journalism and Poverty

Greg M. Nielsen

A commonwealth is said to be instituted, when a Multitude of men do agree, and Covenant, every one, with every one [. . .] to live peacefully among themselves, and be protected against other men.

(Hobbes, 1651/1987: 90)

A democracy of the multitude is imaginable and possible only because we all share and participate in the common. [. . .] We consider the common also and more significantly those results of social production that are necessary for social interaction and further production, such as knowledges, languages, codes, information, affects, and so forth.

(Hardt and Negri, 2009: viii)

Commons is a general term that refers to a resource shared by a group of people. In a commons, the resource can be small and serve a tiny group (the family refrigerator), it can be community-level (sidewalks, playgrounds, libraries, and so on) or it can extend to international and global levels (deep seas, the atmosphere, the internet and scientific knowledge). The commons can be well bounded (a community park or library) transboundary (the Danube river, transmigratory wildlife, the Internet); or without clear boundaries (knowledge, the ozone layer).

(Hess and Ostrom, 2007: 4)

Introduction

Hobbes' seventeenth-century definition of the commonwealth as based in an 'us' and 'them' conflict continues to inform well-known conundrums for research on the commons like how the 'free rider', rival interests (subtractability), or monopoly rent (Harvey, 2012) inevitably lead to a denigration of shared resources. The so-called 'tragedy of the commons', the idea that unregulated comportments lead to the destruction of a given set of 'resource(s) shared by a group of people' and that only privatization or state regulation can stop the abuse or profiteering from occurring, flows out of classical contract theory even though contemporary versions avoid problematic assumptions about human nature. The normative argument points to a heuristic model that postulates the material culture of the commons can be used fairly, equitably, or efficiently.

This chapter takes a different trajectory in hopes of adding a critical dimension to research on the commons by arguing that it does not exist as a shared resource but is negotiated and argued over, and that antagonisms, infringements and metaphorical overgrazing against the 'covenant' or regulations have to be called by someone in order to be seen, to be made public – and this is the role that journalists and newspapers can play in public life. Hence, I propose to investigate how journalism produces an 'imagined urban commons' and names, depicts and writes about the urban poor and by implication their complex relations with the commons. The most important critique I offer is that the relationship is depicted without actually addressing the subjects themselves as audiences. However different and unique a city might be, the gap between rich and poor, between haves and have-nots, introduces a level of inequality for actors concerning access, usage, and nurturing of public places and goods.

In order to know more about the 'us' and the 'them' it is instructive to examine how institutions like mainstream newspapers define emotional, moral, and rational orientations of haves towards have-nots in the city and how external experts and internal experiences are cited to give authority and often affect to information and opinion about the commons. Based on a framing analysis of a selection of articles from 2010 on poverty in six North American cities I present a case study of how the voices of the North American poor and homeless find their way into public dialogue that almost always implies a problem for the urban commons. Below I first situate the argument in the literature on the commons so as to draw out a series of paradoxes between sustainability vs. access, usability vs. equality, justice vs. law, and an ethics of care vs. utilitarian calculations. Next I present the case study in a series of interpretive propositions that sketch out how some of the least well-off in the city are situated in relation to the commons via mainstream journalism and the medium of the big city newspaper. As I proceed I will introduce a study of different genres of narrative found in a year of reporting on poverty to illustrate my idea.

Theorizing the commons

Current policies around the world tend to favor privatization (for 'us') and enclosure (against 'them') and so require ever more hierarchical forms of governance and accompanying legal regimes to maintain order. Any theory of 'the well-ordered society' though needs to be challenged, even when it tries to take inequality and the fate of the multitude (Hardt and Negri, 2009), or that of the least well-off (Rawls, 1999, 2001), into consideration. At the same time, popular strategies for 'horizontal democracy' and self-government decision making are limited in terms of scale and numbers of participants, suggesting that some kind of 'nested hierarchy' emerges at some point in social movements so as to make rules at a variety of levels and contexts: local neighbourhoods, urban regions, the national, the continental and the global (Young, 2000; Harvey, 2012).

The knowledge commons (Hess and Ostrom, 2007), the cultural commons (Hardt and Negri, 2009) and the urban commons (Harvey, 2012) indicate an expanding conceptual arc in the literature that moves beyond the traditional theories of the commonwealth in significant ways. The expanded definition begins in a political economic challenge for public policy makers to go further than the binary solution of either privatization or increased regulation to every problem raised when a given population shares common assets. The research is not only trying to understand the paradox of a sustainable ecology where, for example, privately owned livestock can graze on public land, where private data can be bought and sold while maintaining universal internet access, or, as in my case, where commercial journalism can report on the place of have-nots in the urban commons and only address reports to the imaginary demos or 'normal people' that might buy newspapers. The sustainability of languages, the said and the sayable, diverse interpretive traditions, emotional-volitional tones of lifeworlds and narratives of everyday life all become objects of research on the commons. The shift toward a more emancipatory interest in recovering the urban commons for the 'multitude' or the least well-off so as to reduce the gaps between have and have-nots brings research on the commons into a messy history of the urban present.

My first point of departure then is that to theorize the material culture of a given urban commons it is necessary to raise symbolic questions about who are the uncommon against which the common resources are named and imagined. To talk about the urban commons, then, means there must be some who do not fit what seems to be normal. In other words, wherever a common place is defined in a city (a street, a park, a school, a clinic), there is a right that is put into place in the form of a law, a regulation, or a rule backed by either civil or penal sanctions. We can call this administrative citizenship, while wherever there can be an interpretive contradiction in which people stand up to argue that how they are being represented, or what is required of them, is unjust (Boltanski, 2011), we can call a citizens politics – or an act of citizenship (Isin and Nielsen, 2008; Isin, 2012). I take the gap between have-not subjects being reported on and the audience that is addressed as evidence of an interpretive contradiction where marginal subjects might object to the ways stories are told about them.

The multiple pathways leading in and out of the commons are structured as are the practices concerning its usage that in turn can be challenged so that new ways of accessing and appreciating a shared resource can be created. In this sense someone is always left outside or is marginal to the commons – be it the exploited worker, the criminal, the psychotic, the addict, the racialized, religiously orthodox, or sexually different subject. It seems also fair to state that to some extent the more than 3 million Americans and 300,000 Canadians that have become homeless since the 2008 recession are at best marginal to the use, access, and nurturing of the commons as are the more than 40 million living below the poverty line (Weisman, 2013). It may appear to many that everyone can walk in the street, sit in a park, or gain access to health care in North American cities. But many of these actors are harassed in parks, streets, and shuffled out of hospitals into prisons and other repressive facilities. They are either marginal to or removed from many common resources.

Simply empathizing more with the urban have-not population and their counter or heterotopic places in the North American context is not enough on its own to give new ideas for sharing a more just commons that may always be 'yet to come' – one that might bring the unjustly excluded or marginal into dialogue within a more just commons. New broader and more diverse acts of citizenship are needed to meet the coming challenges of inequality that the spectacularization of the city is preparing – *a la* Rio and Sao Paulo or any city hosting global events (Lenskyj and Wagg, 2012).

The field of journalism could contribute greatly to this new urban citizen politics but the craft would require much more dialogic work beginning by prioritizing a lively anticipated response from the subjects of reports as themselves the primary addressees. This would mean moving from a balance of external and internal sources toward a commitment to their stories and, with the same degree of accuracy via verification as required by the craft, toward activism. Such acts of journalism would distinguish themselves by breaking stories on social justice with the realization that once you take away the ultimate word from the subject on themselves and frame it for another audience, their representation becomes whatever they might appear to be for someone else (Bakhtin, 1984). Imagine if everyday working commercial journalists were to proceed through these principles. What kind of knowledge and information could the mass machine produce if it were to pursue this track? I approach this topic in more detail in a separate work. For this chapter I focus on how journalism helps define the actors in the contemporary North American urban commons.

The appearance of the have-not in the commons

Have-not subjects are not excluded from the commons by journalists in the sense that mediated public spheres in the main do not talk about them, quote their voices, show their faces, or explain their points of view. Most public talk and reportage on the urban poor or homeless addresses an ideal or normal 'common people' in a positive but conditional or charitable discourse. My point again is that the coverage does not address the subjects being talked about as an implied audience. This provides interesting keys to understanding the place of have-nots in the urban commons. Consider the addressee in the following quotes drawn from six North American newspapers in 2010:

The Montreal Gazette: 'Take me to the hospital, fill me up with morphine and tie me up for a month and maybe I'll stop', McHugh says. 'Till they let me out'.

(Linda Gyulai, 27 March 2010)

The New York Times: Daniel J. Langevin was 35, mentally ill and broke. A friend who visited him at the Rochester Psychiatric Center remembered that Mr. Langevin had pain in his jaw, eye and face that was not getting much attention from the staff. [. . .] Mr. Langevin sued New York State [. . .] But the state countered by demanding that Mr. Langevin reimburse it $1.7 million for 10 years of inpatient care he had received. A judge sided with the state.

(Alison Leigh Cowan, 25 December 2010)

The Miami Harold: The make-shift shantytown under the Julia Tuttle Causeway – once home to more than 100 sex offenders – is finally being dismantled. 'Even if I leave, how will I live? I have no job and no car to get there', said Wilson.

(Julie Brown, 26 February 2010)

The Toronto Star: Renee, whose pale, lined skin and mouth full of rotting teeth make her look worn down and older than her years, doesn't much care what happens with this new baby. 'I'd prefer her to come home with us', she says with a shrug. 'But I'm okay with whatever happens'.

(Megan Ogilvie, 13 March 2010)

The Los Angeles Times: 'on the ordinance forbidding overnight sleeping in vehicles', he said. 'The law is the law'. [. . .] But on the streets, the death of Hunter, is being seen as fallout from the recent crackdown. 'It really woke me up', said David Busch, 55, who said he has been homeless in and around Venice for the last dozen years.

(Martha Groves and Mike Anton, 12 December 2010)

The Vancouver Sun: a homeless woman died a brutal death one year ago when a candle ignited her shopping cart in Vancouver's West End. She is better known to the public by her street moniker, Tracy, 'She was outgoing', (her brother) recalled. 'She loved to paint. She was very artistic'.

(Lori Culbert, 9 January 2010)

Ask yourself who are the voices in the above quotes addressing? Is each not somehow outside or marginal to the commons both physically and symbolically? For example, the reported direct speech from the Montreal man gives a blunt emotional definition of the fate of the addict in the street but is his voice framed to anticipate a response from others in that world? The concept of rivalry developed in the field of public economics measures a well-functioning commons according to the level a given user subtracts assets away from any other user (Gosh, 2007). The clear message to the audience in selecting the quote from the addict is that he is going to continue to take from the commons by his presence in the street in ways that others would not. Because the article addresses someone else about his story, there is an appropriation of his last word on himself. He becomes a symbol for the extreme addicts in the street. In this sense his experience can be read as a shift in meaning from unsolvable problems of addiction toward the practical issue of the use of the streets as a commons asset.

In the next quote, can we say the journalist's reported speech about the suffering and the systemic injustice visited on Mr Langevin in the New York hospital is addressed to others in his position? Or is the report addressed to a more general audience and some sense of what is 'justice' vs. what is 'legal' in defence of the health commons? The problem of 'the free rider' seems to apply here. The free rider makes the commons vulnerable to deterioration by agents who do not contribute to its production and nurturing but who take from its assets. In this sense the counter-suite by the state would be the best way to balance the economic stability of the health care system as a whole. But in an act of citizenship the issue of justice is raised against the force of law. Who then are the free riders in this case? The patient or the State of New York? If it is the patient then the utilitarian calculation is that the correct solution is the one in favor of the state that is the best for all – or in Kantian terms, do it if you think everyone should do it this way. An ethics of care would start from the unique individual law and not the general law as Georg Simmel (2010) calls it. Here one has to weigh the life of the one within the community of the least well-off against the bodiless institution of the hospital.

Is the emotionally charged direct speech in the third quote from the displaced Miami man who has nowhere to go addressed back to the group living in the shanty town sharing resources under the causeway, or is it directed toward the same abstract 'generalized other' that already understands the difference between who are sane and who are not, as well as who are the most despicable, outcast, expendable or precarious in society? What can we make of that place under the causeway as counter-commons, a heterotopia outside the mainstream? Is the direct speech of the homeless pregnant woman in Toronto and of the man living out of a car in the Los Angeles area (as well as the indirect speech from the brother of the deceased homeless woman in Vancouver) in the final quotes above addressed back to the voices of those in these places or are they framed to maximize the attraction of the story for the newspaper's 'super-addressee' – a third larger ideal or implied commons and its 'normal' citizens?

Journalist narratives on poverty: a case study

To respond to these questions I want to examine more closely a pattern of journalistic narrative strategies that seek to represent poverty as something to be seen as outside the urban commons understood as both place and time that forms 'a shared, inherited knowledge of scientific research, historical knowledge, and folk wisdom, all of which contribute to the public domain' (Bolier, 2002). I draw the case study from a modest 2010 sample of mass circulated newspapers in Vancouver, Los Angeles, Toronto, Miami, Montreal and New York. The narrative types discussed below include: (1) the fall into poverty; (2) the social facts of poverty; (3) the dialectics of policy on the commons; (4) class and racialization; and (5) the (in)justice of law. Each narrative is theorized according to how voices of urban poverty enter into public dialogue and are used as a source to establish authority and especially to attract the emotional interest of the implied audience regarding the symbolic framing of the urban commons.

To demonstrate multiple levels that this idea suggests, I develop a sociological framing analysis of how the voices of urban suffering among the poor and homeless find their way into the public domain without being the implied audiences of the stories about them. Both mainstream journalism and mainstream sociology construct meaning at a second level for their audience by observing first level observers who act in the world (Luhmann, 2002). Neither of these disciplines or crafts is required to address the subjects they speak of as audiences. For journalism the voices of the urban poor find their way into public dialogue without being the implied audiences of the stories they tell. Some alternative or civic media look to move journalism in a more inclusive direction by directly anticipating and addressing rejoinders from the person, group, or community who are also the subject(s) of the report – but this is rare in mainstream coverage on topics of social exclusion.

For mainstream sociology, voices of urban suffering are constructed in the form of research objects that are transformed into policy recommendations for managing populations at risk. Critical sociology, like some alternative journalism, addresses itself to the subjects it speaks of by pinpointing enduring forms of domination that confine them (Boltanski, 2011; Jackson et al., 2011). My research seeks to undo the separation between subjects of representations or the actors that are reported on and the framing of perceptions for implied audiences. In addressing this as a relation of domination, critical sociology asks how is it that the voices of those excluded from the urban commons are so often quoted as sources at the first level of observation and yet are rarely if at all at the second level, a level where the audience is implied through tonal orientation, mode of address, and judgement. Keep in mind from the onset though that my object of analysis is the role of mainstream journalism in producing narratives about the commons and not the journalist's personal intention, the pattern of corporate ownership, editorial consistency, professional culture, and economic interest, or the decoding of the message by the empirical audience. The critique is aimed at opening the interpretive contradiction, the way in which subjects of reports might contest the way stories are told about them in acts of journalism, or how they might contest other injustices, rather than developing intersectional 'field' analysis that would examine this complex combination of political, organizational, and creative forces that 'struggle' with and against each other to structure the journalistic practice (Bourdieu, 2005; Benson, 2013).

Every year there are thousands of stories that include the voices of urban poor in daily newspapers around the world. The first level of our analysis draws a sample of news and commentary from six North American cities for a case study. 464 articles are selected as relevant for analysis from a total of close to 1,538 published in 2010. The articles are taken from the newspapers located in the cities cited above as well as the French language publication from Montreal: *La Presse*. The sample is generated using keyword searches (poor, poverty, homeless*, and pauvre*, 'sans abri') on the Factiva search engine. The keywords are paired with the name of the newspaper's city wherever they occurred in the same paragraph. We code the articles on both procedural and substantive levels: (1) how the article frames judgements on a positive or conditional opening toward, or outright rejection of, key issues that connect the urban commons with the subjects of poverty and the contemporary phenomenon of homelessness; (2) the external or internal sources that are cited to establish authority for the stories; and (3) the rational, moral or emotional tones used in the address. The following table presents the coding results:

Judgment frame:

- Positive opening 90%
- Conditional 7%
- Rejection 3%

Judgment tone:

- Rational 69%
- Moral 19%
- Emotional 11%

Sources or authority: types

- External 51%
- Internal 49%

Number of selected articles: 1,538 articles; coded articles: 464.

For the group of 464 articles, coders are asked to classify the judgments toward the issue of poverty, the poor and/or the homeless and whether they frame a positive opening or hospitality toward the issues raised, a conditional acceptance or hospitality toward the issues, or an outright rejection. Overall, a stunning 90 per cent of the articles we examined can be said to display a positive opening toward 'helping' the poor and homeless while 7 per cent were clearly conditional and a mere 3 per cent expressed an outright rejection. Although journalists, intellectuals, activists and 'concerned citizens' writing in newspapers frame positive openings toward issues of poverty and homelessness, our point is, they are writing about have-nots toward haves. To expose this contradiction further we also asked coders to determine whether the sources that support the story are framed with external sources or authorities (51 per cent) like quotes from scholarly experts or government officials or from internal sources such as direct quotes from the subjects themselves or from support groups such as community activists, religious groups, or shelters and other organizations that work with the poor or homeless (49 per cent). The balance between external and internal sources indicates a distance from the subjects being reported on as part of establishing credibility, especially given that only 19 per cent of the articles actually use first hand personal references or quotes. This distancing is also supported in the finding that judgments are seldom expressed with emotional tones (11 per cent), as based on personal feelings and experiences either of the subject or by the authorities being cited. Given the imperatives of the culture of professional journalism, that is, balance, the rigorous verification of facts, and a measure of editorial autonomy from purely economic interests (Curran, 2005), we are not surprised to see that the strong majority of the judgements are expressed in rational (69 per cent) tones, emphasizing logical or objective considerations or broader moral (20 per cent) tones offering arguments such as 'this is how things should be' or 'because this is the right thing to do'. These findings are taken as ways to measure the separations or distances between the implied audiences and the subjects of the reports and to point out the possibility of interpretive contradictions subjects of reports might bring against stories being told about them.

The framing analysis helps reveal the distance or the proximity between voices of urban exclusion or marginality from the commons and the implied audience but does not situate the voices according to types of direct or indirect speech that newspapers use to maintain the distance. In order to get a better idea of the way the voices are used we selected another 114 articles from the coded sample of 464 articles. This smaller group was selected on criteria that they best exemplified or gave the most in depth coverage of the themes. We were able to group several of them into the five genres. We categorized each of these according to how voices of urban suffering entered the discourse and were used as a source to establish authority and especially to attract the interest of the implied audience regarding the framing of the judgement.

1. The fall into poverty

> Body-place-commons has to do with practices of liveability – with the
> generative powers of life battening, hungering, sating, fearing, enjoying,
> sensing, resting, and playing within generative matrices co-constituted
> from earth, air, water, nutrients, energies and co-evolved creatures.
>
> (Reid and Taylor, 2010)

Who exactly are 'the people' who own the commons and who are the ones
that fall out? Stories about the fall into poverty connect the have audience to
urban have-nots on several levels. Stories of extreme marginalization or
exclusion from the commons (15) are often framed in newspapers as
psychological troubles within the contexts of dysfunctional systems such as
affordable housing programs or medical facilities rather than as critical social
issues (e.g. the political economy of class, or effects of cultural capital). Not
having a phone, an address, or being sane and sober can take away access to
the commons which is protected by law and backed by force. Such articles
draw the implied audience close to the subjects via the employment of
emotional and psychological rather than rational or moral tones in both direct
speech quoted from the subjects and indirect speech where journalists relate
the stories themselves. The themes tend to connect tragic forms of poverty
to corporal issues similar to the opening report on the physical condition of
the mental health patient who tried in vain to sue the state of New York for
heinous malpractice, or the drug addict from Toronto who is about to give
birth on the street to her fourth child. The more typical story of the fall into
poverty begins when the subject is still on the 'have' side of the urban
commons. A good example is seen in the story of a Toronto man named Creek:

> After working his way up in the hotel industry from dishwasher to head
> office manager, Creek lost it all in 1993 when he was diagnosed with
> cancer. He was just 37. When his Employment Insurance ran out, he
> washed up on welfare. Within a year, he had lost his downtown Toronto
> apartment, overstayed his welcome with friends and was sleeping in
> homeless shelters. He was frightened, depressed and alone. 'I was very
> sick. Basically, I was just waiting to die'.
>
> (Monsebraaten, 2010a)

First, this is a story that identifies a series of personal troubles in the shift
from the have to the have-not side of the divide. Second, the story situates
the shift from 'normal' recognizable institutions, systems or activities
(industry, work, unemployment insurance, housing) to the abnormal state of
'loneliness', illness, homelessness, and poverty without situating a social issue
that could identify solutions. Creek's cancer went into remission. After 12
more years of living in sub-standard public housing, he was able to work

again and find his way out of 'poverty'. The article provides a positive opening that hope for the most extreme personal cases is never lost, but the question arises: is this addressed to those who find themselves in similar circumstances or to a general implied audience who have no knowledge of this kind of tragedy and never will?

Framing stories about the fall into extreme poverty and dramatic narratives about the psychological effects of urban suffering like the one for Mr Creek, recalls the lesson of modern critical sociology. That lesson teaches that a personal trouble is at issue when it is about the fate of a single individual. A personal problem is when one pregnant drug addict is homeless, when one guy in a neighbourhood lives out of a car, or when a single displaced sex offender has nowhere to go. But when dozens of folks live out of their vehicles as they do in one Los Angeles area; when 100 displaced former sex offenders are forced out from underneath the same tent city in Miami; or when there are actually 300 homeless pregnant women living in the streets of Toronto every year, then the personal trouble needs to be understood as a social issue for the urban commons as a whole.

2. The social facts version of journalism

The dominant media by no means drown us in a torrent of images testifying to horrors that make up the present state of the planet. Quite the reverse, they reduce the numbers, taking good care to select and order them.

(Rancière, 2011: 96)

Several of the most informative articles (12) about life distinctly outside the commons are cast in more macro terms than the stories of personal/psychological tragedy or triumph. Almost all seem to assume the general as criteria for the norm without discussing the forced effects on individual cases. A significant number of articles focus on macro data (12) that define poverty according to shifts with income levels (Roberts, 29 September 2010, *New York Times*; Lee and Samuels, 17 September, 2010, *Los Angeles Times*) or 'facts' regarding the fate of a given city in national or more rarely in global terms (Leduc and Perreault, 21 April 2010, *La Presse*). A *New York Times* article gives a positive description of the way the city's most vulnerable poor (adjusted locally at $30,000 USD for a family of four per year) are absorbing the shock waves from the 2008 recession compared with other areas in the country. The *Los Angeles Times* reports a positive opening toward developing better policy for the least well-off. However, it expresses a negative rejection of Los Angeles's and California's position vis-a-vis the rest of the country:

California's poverty rate jumped 15.3% last year, the highest in 11 years. Analysis by the California Budget Project showed that 2 million children in the state lived in families with incomes below the poverty line last year. For the U.S. as a whole, the rise in the poverty level that began a decade ago and accelerated during the recession has wiped out all the gains made during the long run of economic growth and prosperity in the 1990s.

Like the *New York Times* article, a piece from *La Presse* situates Montreal's lower levels of poverty (at $28,000 CDN for a family of four) more positively in relation to other Canadian cities but also against the more macro definitions of poverty from the World Bank along with a figure sited in the millennium goals for 2015 (providing education for more than 72,000 children in developing countries). Still the message from the same article in *La Presse* is not all positive as one of the experts puts it: 'Le plus difficile, c'est de convaincre les gens que la pauvreté n'est pas un phénomène "normal", inéluctable, mais qu'on peut l'enrayer", a pour sa part déclaré M. Klein, de la Colombie-Britannique'.

For the most part articles from the second group of narratives present a positive opening toward solving social problems related to poverty so as to provide better access and appreciation of the particular urban commons they are marginalized from and they do so in mostly rational and moral tones. They rarely quote personal sources with emotional tones from the voices of urban suffering when establishing the authority for the article. Exceptions seem to occur in the more negative framing of the macro issue, as in the *Los Angeles Times* quote from the woman who lost her job at a law firm and has run out of unemployment benefits. She is quoted in a haunting emotional pragmatism: '"If it has to be that I live in my car, I accept it", Evans said Thursday, breaking down in tears. "It's reality"' (Lee and Samuels, 17 September, 2010, *Los Angeles Times*). Both the rational description of the general perception of poverty in *La Presse* article and the emotional tone of the woman from Los Angeles ironically present the general reality as a norm almost as if the person as well as the society were to see it as a personal trouble rather than a commons issue.

Understanding poverty as outside or marginal to the commons means taking into consideration both the local, urban or national perspective that newspapers report on and a wider global and longer historical perspective that they rarely contextualize. Both local perspectives and contextual levels are built on social divisions that are generally inhospitable toward have-nots or the least well-off in a given urban commonwealth. Haves and have-nots are kept in place through a number of conditions like being born or identified within a racialized group; a marginal (or even non-) citizenship category; an oppressed social class; a rigidly pre-assigned gender; or other conditions that vary from region to region like having a fixed address; having a telephone number; speaking a language well enough; or being qualified, sober, and sane.

Social issues need to be situated locally and nationally across such categories, as well as on a global and historical level. For example the above-mentioned 300,000 homeless in Canada and more than 3 million homeless Americans are not a new phenomenon for cities. Yet, the very concept of homelessness only came into common parlance in the 1970s. Before that the term homeless referred to someone without a home. The voices of those outside the commons becomes even more of a social issue when we consider the gap between the very rich and what the Occupy movement calls the remaining 99 per cent (a large mass of working poor and the remaining middle or even upper middle classes in North America) who could find themselves steps away from losing their livelihood and their lodging. But the most important step in developing a critical explanation of how to situate homelessness into commons issues that shape the meaning of the city is to consider the even larger division between the official measures of poverty in Canada ($29,000 CDN) and the US ($21,000 USD) for families of four with the World Bank definitions of extreme ($1.00 USD a day) and relative poverty ($2.00 USD a day) at the global level. When put in a global and historical perspective, the question arises as to whether or not it is appropriate to calculate facts or norms for the voices that fall outside the urban commons in the North American context. Nonetheless, voices of exclusion from the commons among the poor and homeless in the North American city are cited, reported, named and framed in terms of social facts and general norms. Placing the voices of urban suffering into these different contexts helps shift analysis back and forth between the virtual world of the news report and a critical realism that might be developed with the subjects under discussion.

3. Poor policy dialectics

The commons [is] an unstable and malleable social relation between a particular self-defined social group and those aspects of its actually existing or yet-to-be created social/and or physical environment deemed crucial to it.

(Harvey, 2012: 73)

The majority of the most informative articles in 2010 (17) addressed reviews of policy issues that often posed critiques through rational as well as more emotional tones (from severity to anger). If we can say that the review of policies orientated toward the solution of social problems for the commons are going to be value orientated then we can also say they address themselves to cultural phenomena or pre-established world views. A great example of the opposite ways of framing policy stories and world views in the news is seen in articles from the *Montreal Gazette* (Fidelman, 2010) and the *New York Times* (Buckley, 2010). The two articles give opposite presentations of the same class of programs to help some of the severe have-nots in the two cities.

One presents a positive policy model in rational and moral tones while the other provides a sharp condemnation in equally moral and emotionally polemic tones against the same policy type.

The Montreal Gazette article gives a positive review of a federally financed housing experiment to provide lodging for both moderate and severely affected groups of mentally ill homeless regardless of competency or state of sobriety. 400 are to be housed in Montreal apartments. The policy is presented as an experiment to demonstrate that housing the most chronically homeless will cost the commons less than what it costs for policing public places and providing hospital and emergency services (estimated at $55,000 CDN per person, per year) if left outside to languish in the streets. To demonstrate the hypothesis, the project's research team provides care and regular follow-ups with 400 users. It also keeps records on a control group who are not provided with housing or care outside the existing system in order to estimate the cost they represent for those services.

The article in question introduces us to Sam Tsemberis, a Montrealer outreach worker who helped create the research design that became the model policy for dozens of other cities. While working in the streets of New York in 1992, Tsemberis observed that the growing population of homeless suffering from mental illness and addiction were excluded from emergency shelters (as they require sobriety and a level of competency) while others were shuffled through emergency care or the prison system only to end up back on the street. In describing the origins of the Paths to Housing Program in New York (called Chez Soi/At Home in Montreal, and At Home in Toronto, Vancouver and Moncton), he recalls the conversation he had with someone in the street when asked what he thought was the solution:

> 'I need a place to live – isn't it obvious? Like, open your eyes and see', the transient says. 'Well, what about your schizophrenia and your addiction?' the worker asks. 'I just need a place to live – I don't need treatment', replies the transient, an addict since his teens, schizophrenic since his 20s, but homeless only for the seven years since his mother died.

Here the voice of those excluded from or marginal to the urban commons enters the newspaper through two speakers in the sense that the journalist quotes a care giver who recalls the speech of someone from the street in order to get at the most unique meaning of the phenomenon. The Montreal 'experiment' is presented as a 'normal' continuation of the de-institutionalization of psychiatric patients that began in the 1970s and the resulting absorption of the mentally ill into community public places in the city. The Chez Soi project does not cover the entire cost of housing, as users must pay 30 per cent of the rent, but the project's teams provide the necessary medical care and follow-up social work for the users. As Tsemberis says:

Society is simply transferring health and social services from hospitals to a community setting where individuals can live 'like the rest of us', going to movies, taking the metro, hanging out with family and friends. It's not like 'housing first' will end schizophrenia – it will end homelessness.

Consider though further historical and contextual points left out of the *Gazette* article. First, 1992 was a time of extremes in New York – the city was on the verge of bankruptcy and in the midst of the infamous crack cocaine war while the country was facing a massive decrease in public housing budgets that had already begun under Bush 1 along with a sharp rise in the numbers of homeless (Weisman, 2013). The paths to housing program is generally acknowledged as contributing positively to the recovery of New York from one of its darkest periods but the *New York Times* article in 2010 presents quite a different version of the same ideal typical program today. It begins by contesting an obvious moral dilemma in the project's founding logic. The dilemma lies in which subjects are chosen to benefit from the program and which are to be left out. 'It has long been the standard practice in medical testing: give drug treatment to one group while another, the control group, goes without. Now, New York City is applying the same methodology to assess one of its programs to prevent homelessness. "I don't think homeless people in our time, or in any time, should be treated like lab rats", Ms. Palma said' (Buckley, 2010). The critique and moral tone is aimed against the federal Homebase program that would track people on the verge of eviction and provide funds for a certain number to allow rent payment but refuse funds to a control group much along the same lines as the Chez Soi program in Montreal. The article draws attention to how the methodology for similar programs is being applied internationally (with specific reference to India) ostensibly to provide data that will maximize efficiency in the dispensing of the decreasing availability of public funds. In contrast the article also cites the emotional tones used by one individual to describe the anxiety she is forced to endure resulting from her arbitrary rejection from the user group: '"I wanted to cry, honestly speaking", Ms. Almodovar said. "Homebase at the time was my only hope"' (op cit.).

These voices are excluded not just from access and their capacity to appreciate the urban commons (because they are forced out from one public space to another) but also from their ability to nurture it and contribute to its governance and political life. The two newspapers bring these subjects into articles for different purposes and with different results. The *Gazette* article provides a strongly framed positive opening toward the ideal typical Path to Housing policy in both rational and moral terms through quoting Mr. Tsemberis' recollection of an imaginary conversation with the itinerant encountered in his work. The reported speech is telling the implied audience what is clearly and practically needed is housing beyond all other necessities.

Ms. Palma's criticism of the Homebase program appears to speak for the homeless but not to them either directly or implicitly. Her sharp polemic offers moral opposition to what has become a typical municipal housing strategy for the least well-off that justifies expenditures based on the measure of the lesser cost for treating a control group vs. a greater cost for the group, offers no remedial measure. The final emotional tones from Ms. Almodovar don't address others who are left without subsidies but add an individual emotional polemic addressed to the implied audience against an official policy meant to provide support.

4. Racialization

How does it feel to be a problem [. . .] It is a peculiar sensation, this sense of always looking at oneself through the eyes of others.

(Dubois, 1903: 5)

Race differences and class differentials have been ground together in this country in a crucible of misery and squalor.

(Henry Louis Gates Jr. and Cornell West,
cited in Hardt and Negri, 2009: 49)

The legacy of poverty for Aboriginal people in urban centres continues today. [. . .] Aboriginal peoples in urban areas were more than twice as likely to live in poverty as non-Aboriginal people.

(Center for Social Justice, 2014)

Several articles reported on the links between racialization (11) and how it can structure vulnerability to issues of poverty, education, income levels and employment. None, however, seem to arrive at the critical insights that Dubois or Gates and West express more than a hundred years apart. While all six cities grapple with hierarchies of race and ethnicity, the Canadian newspapers highlight urban aboriginals as a key voice of Otherness among the urban poor and homeless. Aboriginals are the only racialized community named in a *Toronto Star* article that discusses a federal government report on poverty in Canadian cities. Statistically this group is most likely to be among the most affected by poverty in Canada. The articles present a definition of who the poor are in Canada:

3.1 million, or 9.4 per cent, of Canadians; 27.2 per cent of single, working-age adults; 6.3 per cent of couples and families; 1.6 million, or 9.9 per cent, of women; 610,000, or 9 per cent, of children; 18 per cent of single-parent families; 700,000 working poor in 2007; 250,000, or 5.8 per cent, of seniors; 42 per cent of single aboriginals; 58.3 per cent of single immigrants and 32.6 per cent of immigrant couples and families.

(Monsebraaten, 2010b)

Bruce Miller, an anthropologist from The University of British Columbia who specializes in problems faced by British Columbia's urban aboriginals provides an analysis of how a vigilante group in downtown Vancouver harassed 518 individuals said to be 'loitering' in common public spaces, one-third of whom were aboriginal (Pemberton, 2010). Homeless aboriginals are cited again in the *Montreal Gazette* as the population most at risk. Inuit make up one-10,000th of the population of the city but are 50 per cent of the homeless living in one of the inner city's poorest neighbourhoods called Shaughnessy Village. Many of the articles in this group are close to the social facts narrative (see above) but some use a direct form of speech from those suffering in the street, as in the following:

> This summer will mark 11 years that Connie has been in Montreal [. . .] She followed her younger brother out of Nunavik. 'I was supposed to just visit and I wound up living here', she says, tossing back her long black hair. He's dead, she says matter-of-factly. 'Alcohol poisoning', she says. He was 25.
>
> (Gyulai, 2010)

American focus in this narrative is on comparable racial categories. In Los Angeles, for example, a report by Alana Samuels states that even though Asian Americans have lower unemployment rates in the region ('9.5% compared with 17.1% for blacks, 14.9% for Latinos and 12.0% for whites'), they take much longer to find work and so are at risk of entering a fall into poverty (see category 1 above). This is because most Asians work with other Asians and about half the Asians who are laid off cannot speak English and have 'cultural differences' that hinder their job applications. Shirley Tam, a 50-year-old widow is trying to return to work after a long absence taking care of her husband: '"I don't have any more money", said Tam, pulling out a bank statement that showed she had $54 left in her savings account. "I need a job. I just need a chance"' (Samuels, 7 September, 2010, *Los Angeles Times*). 'The Miami demographic is elaborated in a similar racialized division – Hispanic/brown, black and white. Recent census data for the Miami area suggests that while the income disparity between the three groups has not changed, the levels of college graduates improved by more than 10 percent for black and Hispanics in a city where 49 percent of the population is foreign born' (Viglucci, 2010).

Few newspapers are as adept at documenting racialization and ethnic divisions of alterity among the urban poor as the *New York Times* (Nielsen, 2009). In 2010 it reports that Puerto Ricans are among the most vulnerable communities in New York to suffer from poverty:

> Roughly 17 percent of young Puerto Rican men were not in school, employed or looking for work, compared with 9 percent of Dominicans and 8 percent of Mexicans. [. . .] Regardless of birthplace, about 33

percent of Puerto Rican families lived below the poverty line, compared with 29 percent of Dominicans and 27 percent of Mexicans.

(Dolnick, 29 October 2010)

Despite enjoying the status of being one of the oldest immigrant groups to arrive in the City, Puerto Rican youth also fall behind African Americans in these categories. Another article on poverty and racialization entitled 'Amid Joblessness: Mexican Workers are a Steady Force' provides an odd take on immigration and describes how despite their difference, Mexican workers have an extraordinary work ethic. This ethic has led them to take jobs no one else will do. As a result, the article concludes, they are employed at twice the rate of the other groups:

> 'That success, though, has a flip side', the journalist says. 'One reason Mexicans have found work in such numbers, experts say, is that many are illegal immigrants, and less likely to report workplace abuses to the authorities for fear of deportation'. Alex, 35, says: 'It's not necessarily what we want to do', he said, 'but it's what we can get to survive'.
>
> (Semple, 2010)

Once again a voice of urban suffering enters the news narrative in a supporting role and lends an emotional tone to the story's appeal.

Perhaps the most compelling story from New York in the sample though was not about the precarious future for Puerto Rican youth or the exploitation of the Mexican working poor but a parallel biographical account of two African Americans named Wes Moore who have the same name and background but have never met:

> The successful writer Wes grew up in a poor, drug-ravaged neighborhood of the Bronx. [. . .] Despairing, Wes's mother dispatched him to a military school. There he finally began to soar [. . .] The other Wes Moore will spend every day until his death behind bars. [. . .] Both came from poverty but one becomes a successful college graduate, a Rhode Scholar, and an author. The other is on death row for killing a police officer. 'American antipoverty efforts have been disgracefully inadequate' (Wes the writer concludes). It should be a scandal that California spends $216,000 on each child in the juvenile justice system, and only $8,000 on each child in the Oakland public schools.
>
> (Kristof, 2010)

Again we need to ask the question about who this direct speech is addressing. Is it the have, who used to be a have-not, speaking with or about the have-not?

Quoting direct speech from urban actors excluded from or marginal to the commons occurs more often in these articles, whether from the US or Canada, and plays a supporting role to the data that is reviewed. They tend to dramatize the worse cases and the theme of the fall – the citing of the death sentence for Wes Moore discussed by Wes Moore the writer, the quote from the Mexican worker, the first nations homeless being chased from public spaces in Vancouver, or Connie's telling of her brother's death in the streets of Montreal are examples. Voices that come through racialization discourse tend to anticipate larger social issues of poverty and the new racism that cites cultural essentialism as a cause. This differs from the more psychological and individualized scenarios that introduce the extreme examples of falling into poverty from the first narrative we discussed. Here injustice is at the edge of the emotional tones used in the direct quotes. The charge of injustice extends into interesting critiques of laws and how unjust or imperfect laws fill the urban commons as we can see in the fifth and final narrative that can be drawn from the sample.

5. The (in)justice of law

Justice: 'infinite, incalculable, rebellious to rule, and foreign to symmetry, heterogeneous and heterotopic'.

Law: 'legitimacy or legality, stabilizeable and statutory, calculable, a system of regulated and coded prescriptions'.

(Derrida, 1992: 22)

For Derrida, justice and law are not equivalent terms. He argues that law is not justice and that acting within the law does not make an act just. A number of articles (12) demonstrate this same thesis either through a protest against the justice of existing law or against its strict use as an authority in aggressive gentrification arguments that assume or pose outright rejection toward complex problems faced by the homeless and their relation to the streets (a 3 per cent rejection toward helping the poor or homelessness according to our coding). Examples that argue for positive openings for the poor are seen in several *New York Times* articles that have judges arguing for better legal aid to make law more just for have-nots (Glaberson, 2010a), or that condemn the 'system of regulated and coded prescriptions' of crimes against the commons. One article in this example cites the 19,137 non-felony public nuisance cases from 2008 in New York. For these cases bail was set at $1,000 USD or less. '87 percent of the defendants in those cases did not post bail and went to jail to await trial. They remained for an average of 15.7 days' (Secret, 2010). In Toronto, one in five men who go off to prison are homeless and one in three are homeless when they leave prison. 43 per cent have health issues:

'[Prison is] the modern version of the poorhouse', says Sylvia Novac, a researcher with the University of Toronto's Cities Centre. 'These are people who had nothing to begin with. They're worn down, in this middle-aged group, and they have health issues. These people need a lot of help'.

(Rankin, 2010)

There is an important distinction here between public places and public goods, on the one hand, and the commons on the other, as David Harvey puts it. Public places like streets and goods or services are subject to administrative citizenship. And while the spaces and the goods are needed for the commons they are not on their own what constitutes the commons. The commons is kept in order by what I called an administrative politics but remains dynamic because of its citizen politics where acts of citizenship evoke an interpretive contradiction and make a claim for justice that ruptures either traditional ways of doing things or oppressive laws. As Harvey puts it 'there is always a struggle over how the production of and access to public space and public goods is to be regulated, by whom, and in whose interest' (2012: 73).

Among the most striking examples of using law as a force to maintain social division around public place and public goods are seen in the 'not in my back yard' type rejection examples from Miami and Vancouver articles. 'Homeless and panhandlers referred to as "scum of the earth", a hearing in Vancouver is told' (Pemberton, 2010). The headline is a quote from an undercover artist who posed as a volunteer for the Ambassadors for the Downtown Vancouver Business Association. For the last ten years the Ambassadors have been patrolling the downtown core and asking the homeless to move on from their spot, or staying with them until they are intimidated enough to leave. If they don't leave they call the police to lodge a complaint. The artist gave testimony about his experience to a public hearing looking into the activities of the Ambassadors. Several internal support groups advocating for the homeless sponsored the hearings including the Pivot Legal Society, the United Native Nations and the Vancouver Area Network of Drug Users (Pemberton, 2010).

While the Vancouver stories in this typology are about how the law allows a version of citizens policing to displace the homeless, the *Miami Herald* articles are slightly different. They are about first creating municipal laws to ban activities that support the homeless and then about the internal support groups defying the law and acting in the name of justice. Headlines from several articles in the *Miami Herald* show how local ordinances are used to try and remove homelessness and the poor from plain sight while the articles also discuss how groups organize to oppose support groups working to give relief to the voices of those being excluded from or kept marginal to the urban commons:

North Miami Beach bans panhandling on city's largest roads, intersections: North Miami Beach has now joined the list of cities that criminalizes street vending and panhandling, a law it may soon have to defend in court.

(Pagliery, 2010)

Ordinance aims to ban unrestricted feeding of downtown homeless: Churches flock to downtown Miami to feed the homeless, but under a proposed ordinance that's gaining support, these unrestricted street feedings would be banned.

(Kaleem, 2010)

No-panhandling zone widens near arena, theater.

(Mazzei, 2010)

Although Key West is named by one homeless advocate from the Miami articles as the meanest city in America after a legal crackdown that saw more than 70 homeless put in jail over two months (Clark, 2010), the above headlines suggest that Miami may be taking the lead in the same category. The 5 February ban took seven years of debate before coming into law. It pitted support groups working with the homeless against business interests looking to create a more attractive environment for tourists. The justice of the law continues to be questioned by its adversaries. For example, the *Homeless Voice*, an alternative newspaper that employs the homeless to sell copies of the paper in the streets, is cited for its protest against the move. '"You cite safety, but it's all written about prejudice", *Homeless Voice* founder Sean Connie told the council Tuesday' (Clark, 2010).

The ban on feeding the homeless in a Miami area undergoing gentrification has a similar controversial history. Dozens of volunteers had been descending on the area over the years every Sunday after church to set up makeshift soup kitchens. Local businesses argued it was hurting their trade. As one local condominium owner put it: 'As soon as these cars and trucks pull up to feed, all hell breaks loose in the neighborhood', 'It's violent when 200 people are trying to push and shove to get food' (Kaleem, 2010). While the ordinance requires seemingly sensible regulations such as serving food within four hours of its preparation or providing proper sanitary conditions at the site, the measures would have the effect of stopping the present practices. Opposition groups claim there are other solutions such as the city providing garbage cans and other public facilities and vowed they would continue the practice without compliance. It appears the conflict between advocates for the homeless and those defending private property or business interest date back to 1998 when police were no longer allowed to arrest the homeless for sleeping in public places. '"They can't arrest the homeless for eating", said Burton of the Miami

Coalition for the Homeless. "This is why they go after the people that are serving the food"' (Kaleem, 2010).

Unlike administrative citizenship, citizenship politics are not divorced from subjective culture and a sense of justice that is not so calculable. Administrative acts define who is a citizen with rights to the commons or an outcast in the same neutral disengaged language of right or law. Civil disobedience can be a flash point that breaks-open the barriers of the commons and the very definition of citizenship. When these boundaries are transgressed, the meaning of walking or standing in the street is in turn transformed into a subjective state of confrontation. This condition is parallel to the manifest division between emotionally engaged moments when rights are publicly claimed in the name of justice, on the one hand, and where administrative fiats define citizenship in the neutral disengaged language of law, on the other.

In summary we have examined several levels on which the voices of those excluded from the urban commons are named in news and commentary without themselves being interlocutors in the dialogue with the implied audience. We established how this occurs in framing positive, conditional, or negative judgements about them backed with external or internal sources and expressed through rational, moral or emotional tones. Unraveling how acts of journalism appropriate the voices of those who are excluded from the urban commons and plea for a positive opening that would support those voices, on the one hand, while addressing the subjects they speak of at best in a secondary sense, on the other; points to an interpretive contradiction. We opened this contradiction further by examining a series of narratives ranging from the most abstract forms of social fact reporting and policy evaluation to the most concrete reports on personal troubles such as the fall into poverty, racialization or claims for justice against laws. Where both the social facts reporting and the dialectics of policy on poverty do quote the indirect voices of those excluded or who are marginal to the commons, it is in a minor way of providing support or contrast to a story. The stories of extreme cases emphasize the psychological or physical effects in the narrative of the fall and use quotes from the direct speech of the subject to provide an emotional hook but still do not put the address back to the subjects being discussed.

Conclusion

Research on the commons comes out of classical assumptions about conflicts between 'us' and 'them' as the inevitable outcome of human nature, limited economic goods and material cultures, or other imperfections regarding the use and caring for what should or could be shared resources. While this chapter does not negate the importance of normative approaches toward the commons it has taken a more deconstructive approach to the problem, arguing instead that an equal distribution and enjoyment of the urban commons is unlikely.

It is unlikely in that even if every urban actor were allowed to use the commons, there is always the question of whether or not all can access it and appreciate it equally given the social divisions that divide every city.

The question remains concerning the kinds of shifts that would be needed if journalism in the mainstream were to contribute to a more inclusive politics for the urban commons. The results of our analysis suggest we need to create new ways to do journalism and mediate dialogue that would give recognition to those who from generation to generation are not part of the implied audience. First, this requires undoing the journalistic address that names an imaginary commons to an implied audience. It would mean changing the identification toward some representations and aversion toward others. In the sense those most in need of having their stories told about their exclusion or unequal appreciation of the commons would be better told. This would require a shift from constative to more performative acts of journalism, from balance to more commitment to the story, from external to more internal sources, from rational to more adversarial tones; from the verification of facts to more co-authored facts, and from editorial autonomy to increased community input.

Writing narratives that address themselves back to the subjects of the reports, writing more from the subject position rather than relying on the external view, shifting from rational to moral and more emotional tones, taking an advocate role for justice while staying accurate, taken all together could transform journalism into dynamic acts of citizenship that could challenge the habitus of the commons so that its sense of justice would always be to come. One might say all this is already being done and yet it needs to be acknowledged that social media along with alternative, citizens, and public journalism so far have had little impact on the mainstream forms of address. And yet the mainstream newspaper continues to be the most important source for original news reporting on public issues compared to all other media. The naming of 'us' and 'them', of inclusion and exclusion in the commons is not only in the law, or in the administrative apparatus, it is in the public imaginary. Any change that might be effected for the urban commons would do better if it were to challenge the framing of the news address that dominate fully mediated societies.

References

Bakhtin, M. (1984) *Problems of Dostoevsky's Poetics*. Minneapolis: University of Minnesota Press.

Benson, R. (2013) *Shaping Immigration News: A French-American Comparison*. New York: Cambridge University Press.

Bollier, D. (2002) 'Reclaiming the commons. Why we need to protect our public resources from private encroachment'. Online. Available HTTP: <http://yin.arts.uci.edu/~studio/resources/236/Bollier_commons.pdf> (accessed 1 September 2014).

Boltanski, L. (2011) *On Critique: A Sociology of Emancipation*. London: Polity.

Bourdieu, P. (2005) 'The Political Field, the Social Science Field, and the Journalistic Field', in R. Benson and E. Neveu (eds), *Bourdieu and the Journalistic Field*. Cambridge: Polity Press.

Center for Social Justice (2014) 'Aboriginal issues'. Online. Available HTTP: <http://www.socialjustice.org/index.php?page=aboriginal-issues (accessed 1 September 2014).

Curran, J. (2005) 'What Democracy Requires of the Media', in G. Overholser and K.H. Jamieson (eds), *The Press*. New York: Oxford University Press.

Derrida, J. (1992) 'Force of Law: The "Mystical Foundation of Authority" ', in D. Cornell et al. (eds), *Deconstruction and the Possibility of Justice* (pp. 3–29). London: Routledge.

Dubois, W.E. ([1903] 2008) *The Soul of Black Folks*. Rockville Maryland: Arc Manor Press.

Gosh, S. (2007) 'How to Build a Commons: Is Intellectual Property Constrictive, Facilitating or Irrelevant', in C. Hess and E. Ostrom (eds), *Understanding Knowledge as a Commons: From Theory to Practice* (pp. 209–46). Cambridge: MIT Press.

Hardt, M. and Negri, A. (2009) *Commonwealth*. Cambridge, Massachusetts: The Belknap Press of Harvard University Press.

Harvey, D. (2012) *Rebel Cities: From the Right to the City to the Urban Revolution*. London: Verso.

Hess, C. and Ostrom, E. (eds) (2007) *Understanding Knowledge as a Commons: From Theory to Practice*. Cambridge: MIT Press.

Hobbes, T. (1987/1651) *The Leviathan*. London: Everyman's Library.

Isin, E. (2012) *Citizens Without Frontiers*. London: Bloomsbury.

Isin, E. and Nielsen, G.M. (2008) *Acts of Citizenship*. London: Zed Books.

Jackson, J., Nielsen, G. and Hsu, Y. (2011) *Mediated Society: A Critical Sociology of Media*. Don Mills: Oxford University Press.

Lenskyj, H. and Wagg, S. (2012) (eds) *The Palgrave Handbook of Olympic Studies*. Houndmills: Palgrave Macmillan.

Luhmann, N. (2002) *The Reality of Mass Media*. Stanford: Stanford University Press.

Nielsen, G.M. (2009) 'Framing immigration in the *New York Times*', *Aether: the Journal of Media Geography* IV: 37–57.

Rancière, J. (2011) *The Emancipated Spectator*. London: Verso.

Rawls, J. (2001) *Justice as Fairness: A Restatement*. Cambridge, Massachusetts: Harvard University Press.

Rawls, J. (1999) *The Law of Peoples*. Cambridge, Massachusetts: Harvard University Press.

Reid, H. and Taylor, B. (2010) *Recovering the Commons: Democracy, Place, and Global Justice*. Chicago: University of Illinois Press.

Simmel, G. ([1918] 2010) *The View of Life: Four Metaphysical Essays with Journal Aphorisms*. Chicago: The University of Chicago Press.

Weisman, E. (2013) *Spaces, Places and States of Mind: A Pragmatic Ethnography of Liminal Critique*. PhD. Dissertation. Montreal: Concordia University.

Young, I.M. (2000) *Inclusion and Democracy*. Oxford: Oxford University Press.

Newspaper references

Brown, J. (2010) 'Julia Tuttle causeway sex offender enclave being dismantled', *The Miami Herald* 26 February.

Buckley, C. (2010) 'To test housing program, some are denied', *New York Times* 9 December.

Clark, C. (2010) 'Vagrants tax Key West as tourist capital', *The Miami Herald* 28 March.

Cowan, A.L. (2010) 'When mental patients pursue damages, hospitals send bill', *The New York Times* 25 December.

Culbert, L. (2010) 'Tracy's legacy: More shelter for the homeless; She died horribly on the street. The coroner called for increased help for those like her. That is happening', *Vancouver Sun* 9 January.

Dolnick, S. (2010) 'Report shows plight of Puerto Rican youth', *The New York Times* 29 October.

Fidelman, C. (2010) 'Program to give 300 homeless a home; No strings; Radical concept a success in U.S.', *Montreal Gazette* 21 January.

Glaberson, W. (2010a) 'Top New York judge urges greater legal rights for the poor', *The New York Times* 4 May.

Glaberson, W. (2010b) 'Judge's budget will seek big expansion of legal aid to the poor in civil cases', *The New York Times* 29 November.

Groves, M. and Anton M. (2010) 'Homeless advocates hit the street; Activists in Venice allege police unfairly target people who live outdoors and in RVs.', *Los Angeles Times* 12 December.

Gyulai, L. (2010) 'Life among the ruins', *The Montreal Gazette* 27 March.

Kaleem, J. (2010) 'Ordinance aims to ban unrestricted feeding of downtown homeless', *The Miami Herald* 28 March.

Kristof, N.D. (2010) 'Two men and two paths', *The New York Times* 13 June.

Leduc, L. and Perreault, L.J. (2010) 'Québec félicité pour sa lutte antipauvreté', *La Presse* 21 April.

Lee, D. and Samuels, A. (2010) '1 in 7 in U.S. lives below poverty line; Last year, nearly 4 million Americans joined the ranks of the poor. California's rate is highest in 11 years', *LA Times*, 17 September.

Mazzei, P. (2010) 'No-panhandling zone widens near arena, theater', *The Miami Herald* 19 November.

Monsebraaten, L. (2010a) 'Hope found in escaping poverty trap; It was being destitute, not having depression or cancer, that almost broke activist's spirit', *Toronto Star* 19 July.

Monsebraaten, L. (2010b) 'Wrong answer to problem', *Toronto Star* 18 November.

Ogilvie, M. (2010) 'Is it ever okay for a pregnant woman to smoke crack? A. If it means not getting her fix from booze, then yes. The hardest cases: More than 300 homeless women give birth in Toronto each year amid huge risks', *Toronto Star* 13 March.

Pagliery, J. (2010) 'North Miami Beach bans panhandling on city's largest roads, intersections', *The Miami Herald* 5 February.

Pemberton, K. (2010) 'Homeless and panhandlers referred to as "scum of the earth", hearing told', *Vancouver Sun* 1 June.

Rankin, J. (2010) 'The struggle to stay straight. By the numbers; Each year, more people are released from jail only to face homelessness, a new report shows', *Toronto Star* 10 August.

Roberts, S. (2010) 'Census data shows, in new ways, how the recession hit New Yorkers', *The New York Times* 29 September.

Secret, M. (2010) 'Low bail, but weeks in jail before misdemeanor trials', *The New York Times* 3 December.

Samuels, A. (2010) 'Asian Americans; Ethnic barriers in job hunts?; Unemployment is lower among people of Asian heritage, but it drags on longer', *Los Angeles Times* 7 September.

Semple, K. (2010) 'Now arriving; amid joblessness, Mexican workers are a steady force', *New York Times*, 23 September.

Viglucci, A. (2010) 'Miami-Dade is rich, poor, polarized and getting better educated', *The Miami Harold* 19 December.

Chapter 7

Communities and the commons

Open access and community ownership of the urban commons

Maja Hojer Bruun

Introduction

> The sale of my cooperative flat was perceived differently than it would if it had been a condominium. It is as if one is selling something that is not one's own.
>
> (Former member of a housing cooperative, Copenhagen, 2008)

During the housing boom in Copenhagen, from the beginning of the 2000s until the credit crisis in 2008, the members of many housing cooperatives, a common form of collectively-owned housing in Danish cities, decided to raise the prices of their cooperative shares, so that individual members could sell their cooperative flats at small, and sometimes even large, profits. The Danish media and general public frowned at these decisions and were morally offended. Members of housing cooperatives were criticized for displaying a lack of solidarity; they were accused of greed and of having enriched themselves at the expense of others who could have benefited from good and cheap dwellings, the consequence of their decision being that now only the well-to-do could afford cooperative living.

This moral outcry in Danish society made me think more about ownership and property rights in Danish housing cooperatives, where I subsequently carried out 15 months of anthropological fieldwork in 2008–2009.[1] Though housing cooperatives are formally owned by their members, who have shares in the whole building and user rights on their flats, I argue in this chapter that the moral struggles around housing cooperatives show that members should perhaps not be seen as the only legitimate owners of cooperatives.

---

1 Fieldwork was carried out in eight housing cooperatives in the metropolitan area of Copenhagen where I participated in general assemblies, committee meeting, work parties and other social gatherings (Bruun, 2012). As part of the eight case studies, I collected archival documents and legal documents and followed newspaper and other media debates, including social media. The study also included interviews with 48 members, former members of cooperatives and other residents in cooperatives, many of whom were interviewed several times during the fieldwork.

Rather, housing cooperatives can be seen as an urban commons shared by the whole of Danish society, and cooperative members as caretakers or stewards of the commons, which they depend on as their homes but hold only temporarily. In this light, the moral outcry can be interpreted as a reaction to a felt loss of something that was regarded as a kind of common good, without explicitly being articulated as such. This opens up a perspective for a new understanding of urban commons that encompasses a variety of claims to commons and rights in commons.

The concept of commons is used by a growing number of people within and outside the academy, and commons are today as much an expression of political movements as they are expressions of different strands of theory, covering traditional commons property regime theory (Ostrom, 1990; McCay and Acheson, 1987; Bromley, 1992; Feeny et al., 1990) and a more recent debate about 'new commons' such as 'knowledge commons' (Hess and Ostrom, 2007), 'global commons' (Soroos, 1997), 'social commons', 'intellectual and cultural commons', 'musical commons', 'species commons' and many more (Bollier, 2003; Nonini, 2007), including also 'urban commons' (Harvey, 2012; Blomley, 2008; Susser and Tonnelat, 2013). 'New commons' are not necessarily new per se, but framing collective resources such as knowledge or music as commons is a way of pointing out that these resources used to be or should be owned and managed collectively as a common good.

With so many different uses of 'commons' it is probably impossible to formulate one generic definition of commons or to define one set of features that covers all the different kinds of existing and emergent commons. In this chapter, I focus on one important aspect that is missing in current theoretical debates on urban commons: the people and communities who live in commons. I define commons in relation to the people who 'hold' the commons and the activities that constitute and reproduce the commons, because this perspective lends new insight into the workings of actual practiced commons. These communities do not necessarily frame their moral struggles over resources as a fight for a commons, but I will argue that commons are characterized by overlapping claims to and rights in the commons and that focusing on the people and communities who make such claims helps us recognize this important feature of commons.

Anthropologist Stephen Gudeman (2001) points out that most economists and political scientists who have described commons and developed commons theory, for example Ostrom (1990), who has a background in political science and won the Nobel Prize in economics in 2009, treats commons as real property and, within their discourse, separate objects from subjects and the material resources of commons from human communities and activities, thereby tending to naturalize and reify the concept of commons and de-emphasize the commons' dependence on cultural behavior (Wagner, 2012). In an anthropological use of the term, however, commons are closely tied to the communities that 'keep them', and commons and communities are co-constitutive of each other. Commons refer not only to material resources and physical space but also to social and cultural values and anything that contributes to the material, social and cultural sustenance of communities (Gudeman, 2001: 27). Many anthropologists and other social scientists have pointed to the 'trouble' with the concept of community due to its many variable, normative and vague uses (Amit and Rapport, 2002; Creed, 2006). In this chapter I will employ the nexus of commons and community without being blinded by the persuasiveness of the term 'community':

> A commons is regulated through moral obligations that have the backing of powerful sanction. But communities are hardly homes of equality and altruism, and they provide ample space for the assertion of power and exploitation from patriarchy to feudal servitude.
>
> (Gudeman, 2001: 28)

In other words, to focus on communities also involves investigating the relationships of power that maintain commons and social and cultural norms that may not be written laws but moral obligations that are sanctioned through social relations. A focus on communities foregrounds the concrete practices of 'commoning' (Harvey, 2012; Linebaugh, 2009) that social agents engage in to produce and reproduce the commons.

I begin the chapter with an examination of the existing literature on commons in relation to the relationship between commons and communities. I point out that traditional commons theory, the common property regime literature of Ostrom (1990), McCay and Acheson (1987), Bromley (1992) and Feeny et al. (1990), is based on institutional economics and mainly occupied with refuting Hardin's theory of 'The Tragedy of the Commons' (1968) and with showing the different ways in which commons are governed by communities through community rules and norms. New commons theory largely ignores communities and questions of governance, but renews the debate on commons significantly by considering social justice, the common good and the link between commons, the social order and political economy in wider society. Combining insights from both approaches to the commons and bearing in mind that 'ownership' of the commons involves several commoners and commoning economies, as in the Old English open field commons, I reach for an image of the commons as a layered pattern of nested and overlapping claims and rights of access and use.

In the second part of the chapter, an empirical exploration of the everyday management, political decision making and moral debates in an actually practiced commons, Danish housing cooperatives in the city of Copenhagen, enables me to make three important points that add to the theoretical understanding of practiced urban commons: I argue that the housing cooperatives are an instance of an urban commons characterized by overlapping claims to and rights in the commons and that they are 'owned' both by local communities of cooperative members and the larger Danish society. Commons challenge liberal-economistic notions of property, because ownership of commons depends not on a single titleholder but on layers of social relations and mutual obligations and there can be varying scales of claims to the commons. Bodies of commoners on different scales of the social, such as the community of local residents, the city or the nation, can make claims on the same commons, which can result in tensions among these groups. In addition, 'open access' to the urban commons must not be seen, as it is in the common property regime literature, as a form of 'non-property' or no one's property, and therefore intrinsically destructive, but can be seen as a central social value arising from democratic open societies that implies an aspiration for the commons as everyone's property. As a third point, the history of the Danish housing cooperative tells us that public claims to the urban commons are challenged in several ways. Apart from enclosure through (quasi-)privatization and commodification, nepotism and other manifestations of favoritism are exclusionary practices that threaten to break up the commons as a social institution with many possible users.

Commons theory and urban commons

When Elinor Ostrom and other scholars in the 1980s began working on common property regime theory (Ostrom, 1990; McCay and Acheson, 1987; Bromley, 1992; Feeny et al., 1990), it was in response to Garret Hardin's famous 'Tragedy of the Commons' (1968). Hardin's classic essay maintains that natural resources should be held as private property or regulated by governments so as to not be overexploited by free riders and ultimately deplete. Based on a long range of case studies from all over the world, however, Ostrom and her colleagues refuted Hardin's simplified model and demonstrated that there are alternatives to private and public property regimes and that forests, irrigation systems, fisheries and stocks of wildlife can be efficiently managed by local communities as common property, also called commons.

In the 1990s, a new literature on the commons developed that was not based on studies of natural resource management but in new types of commons that were in danger of being privatized or enclosed: 'knowledge commons' (Hess and Ostrom, 2007), 'social commons', 'intellectual and cultural commons', 'musical commons', 'species commons', and many other types of commons (Bollier, 2003; Nonini, 2007), including also 'urban commons' (Harvey, 2012; Blomley, 2008; Susser and Tonnelat, 2013). In this new literature, the commons are usually seen in relationship to larger changes in the world's political economy of neoliberalization, privatization and marketization, where more and more public goods are marketized and put under market-like regimes (Bollier, 2002; Hardt and Negri, 2009). Urban commons and other 'new commons' are sometimes discussed in relation with the common property regime literature, but in fact debates about them are much more informed by the history of enclosures, and commons become a question of open and inclusive societies, that is, democracy and freedom, in modern societies (Hess and Ostrom, 2007: 12).

This is also the case in debates about urban commons. In the name of enforcing public safety and homeland security there has been an encroachment of public space, especially in American cities (Mitchell, 2003; Smith and Low, 2006). Similar developments have been studied elsewhere (e.g. Caldeira, 2000; Sassen, 1991). Though commons are different from public space, there is common ground in the claim for open access and social justice that is challenged by privatization. Recently, David Harvey (2012) has revived the concept of urban commons building on Lefebvre's idea of *The Right to the City*. Harvey (2012) and Susser and Tonnelat (2013) mainly use 'urban commons' to describe whole cities as resources for people living in them, and to assert that all urbanites have 'a right to an equitable usufruct of cities within the principles of sustainability, democracy, equity and social justice' (Lefebvre in Susser and Tonnelat, 2013: 110). If the world's large cities, which are today spaces of political, economic and social inequality, are realized as urban commons, they claim, this would be the greatest transformative potential for social movements.

The strength of employing the concept of commons instead of public space to discuss social justice in urban contexts is a more comprehensive approach to the political and economic resources fundamental to social life. Urban commons and the right to the city are about much more than securing public *access* to physical spaces such as the street, parks and other cityscapes and to social spaces, knowledge, media and information infrastructures such as the internet; urban commons and the right to the city are about securing people a *life* in the city. Susser and Tonnelat (2013) identify three aspects of urban commons that, if they came together, would ensure people an equitable life. First, labor, social services, reproduction of neighborhoods, housing, transportation and other consumption are seen as commons that urbanites have a right to use and control collectively. These resources and services are the closest we get to the traditional rural natural resource commons, such as grazing lands and lakes, albeit on a much larger scale (2013: 110). Second, public space and the public sphere are seen as commons; they include all 'public space, the public infrastructure, such as streets and squares, train stations, cafés, public gardens, and all forms of space where urbanites can rub shoulders and gather' (2013: 111). And third, Susser and Tonnelat refer to collective urban visions, art and creative endeavors like the community garden movement as commons, because they can transgress boundaries and transform people's perception of their city. This mapping out of different aspects of the commons, which are of course impossible to separate in social life, makes it clear how comprehensive commons are and that commons cover both material and immaterial resources.

While Susser and Tonnelat do, however, mainly focus, optimistically, on the public goods, public services and public spaces that *could become* the commons of tomorrow, in this chapter I want to offer insights into the practices and pragmatics of commons that are already enacted. I agree with Harvey (2012) when he states that spaces become urban commons through social action; he describes the commons as 'an unstable and malleable social relation between a particular self-defined social group and those aspects of its actually existing or yet-to-be-created social and/or physical environment deemed crucial to its life and livelihood' and, in other words, as 'a social practice of commoning' (2012: 73).[2] However, in Harvey's work, we do not get very close to people and their concrete actions, and we do not follow them over time or learn about their culture and history.

Before I flesh out in the second part of this chapter what concrete activities of commoning may look like in a practiced urban commons – activities such as working together to taking care of the common property as well as political decision making – I want to draw attention to the economic aspect of commoning activities, and the relationship between commons and markets, commodities and money. Harvey (2012: 73) writes that:

> at the heart of the practice of commoning lies the principle that the relation between the social group and that aspect of the environment being treated as a common shall be both collective and non-commodified-off-limits to the logic of market exchange and market valuations.

Applied as ideological terms, it may be easy to keep a sharp distinction between commons and commodities, where commodification destroys the commons, typically through privatization and enclosure. Anthropologists and other social scientists who have studied communal and community economies have pointed out, however, that it is difficult to keep commodities and market exchange separate from other forms of exchange in actual life and that it is not the introduction of commodities and commodity relations per se that undermines 'traditional' or 'communal' economies (e.g. Parry and Bloch, 1989).

One of the problematic effects of demarcating commons completely from commodities is that commons are often depicted as practices that 'have survived in many little-known places' (Susser and Tonnelat, 2013: 108), but are long gone in the modern world that is so characterized by market exchanges. In modern large-scale societies, urban commons are either defined as not-yet-realized social practices (e.g. Susser and Tonnelat, 2013) or they are restricted to physical public spaces such as parks and community gardens that do not encompass people's sustenance, except for marginalized groups

---

2 The term 'commoning' was coined by historian Peter Linebaugh in his book *The Magna Carta Manifesto: Liberties and Commons for All* (2009), because an active verb for the commons emphasizes that commons are matters of social activity and not just material resources.

such as the homeless and squatters. In a third approach, commons are defined as 'neighborhood commons' that resemble homeowner associations or gated communities and are more or less co-opted by market interests in that they benefit only the owners and residents themselves (Blackmar, 2006; Foster, 2011). The possibility that modern urban commons exist with a claim for open access and social justice, although they are continuously contested, while being connected to market economies, is left out of the purview of this particular formulation.

Speaking of such modern urban commons, such as certain forms of collectively owned housing, it is impossible to separate them completely from the surrounding urban real estate markets, just as they also relate to public housing policies. That housing commons include values that correspond with and can be realized in the housing market does not, on the other hand, prevent people from sharing communal economies and collective property. When we only find *either* markets *or* commons we risk reproducing the contradiction between 'economy' and 'the social' that reflects the modern compartmentalization of social life institutionalized through modern economics (Polanyi, 2001).

In this chapter I want to discuss an example of a modern urban commons that includes both material resources and physical space as well as social and cultural values, but that is continuously contested by different people's and communities' interests. Housing cooperatives in the city of Copenhagen are managed by local communities as common property and are at the same time embedded in the larger political and moral economy of the modern Danish welfare state and housing market. The simple narrative of gradual enclosure and commodification of the original commons is easily dismissed in relation to the housing cooperatives that originated in the beginning of the twentieth century as an alternative to private property, but were acquired by groups of people through market exchanges.

One of the obvious reasons why most theories on urban commons define markets and commodities in opposition to commons is because commodification and privatization usually imply a restriction of access, particularly access for the urban poor and underprivileged. In my discussion of the housing cooperatives we will see that neoliberal housing policies have led to an exclusion from the commons, but that exclusionary practices also spring from other causes than the market, for example nepotism and other ways of denying people their rights in the commons. This leads me to a discussion of open access, which is a central social value in modern urban commons, and community ownership.

Open access, public goods and rights in commons

One of the main points of criticism that post-Hardin commons theory raised was Hardin's (1968) failure to distinguish between 'open-access' and 'common property regimes' (Ostrom, 1990; McCay and Acheson, 1987; Bromley, 1992;

Feeny et al., 1990). What Hardin had described were not commons but 'open-access resources', which refers to resources that are unregulated and available to all, and thus vulnerable to overuse and free riding, because they are 'resources over which no property rights have been recognized' (Bromley, 1992: 4). Commons differ significantly, Ostrom and her colleagues argued, as they described a wide variety of sustainable and community-based institutional arrangements that delimit access and impose restrictions on the use of grazing lands, forests, water and other such resources. While public property is owned and managed by state agencies and private property by individuals or corporations, common property is 'held by an identifiable community of interdependent users. These users exclude outsiders while regulating use by members of the local community' (Feeny et al., 1990: 4). There are no general rules for the successful management of commons, but Ostrom (1990) identified eight 'design principles' to be found in all successful local commons, including clearly defined boundaries, rules regarding the appropriation and provision of resources, collective decision-making procedures, effective monitoring, sanctions against violating community rules, conflict-resolution mechanisms, recognition of the commons' self-determination by a higher-level authority and small local common property regimes at the base level of multiple layers of nested enterprises. In short, in the common property regime literature commons are well-defined resources that are managed by local communities that are recognized holders of the commons and exclude outsiders.

The economic distinction between common property and open access in the common property regime literature was important to demonstrate that common property regimes do exist and offer sustainable and efficient alternatives to privately held or state owned property. It is, however, an insufficient framework for understanding urban commons, and more generally new commons, where open access to common goods is a central value and has a different meaning. Many new commons cannot get depleted in the same way as do natural resources even though they do, of course, have to be maintained too and resources such as labor are limited. Much more importantly, however, what is of value in the commons has to be redefined to include not only economic resources but also social and political values. 'Open access', or 'public access', to the commons is a matter of freedom and democracy and citizens' moral right *not to be excluded* from the uses or benefits of the commons (Blackmar, 2006: 51; Blomley, 2008: 320). This does not, however, mean that commons are the same as 'public goods', at least not if public goods (or public property) is defined as resources owned and managed by a government body. I will discuss this issue in relation to the concrete case of housing cooperatives in the second part of the chapter. For now, I note that there seems to be confusion in the new commons literature between 'commons' and 'public goods' and between 'open access' and 'communal access' (see also Narotzky, 2013). One way to move towards conceptual clarity is to acknowledge that commons challenge the liberal-economistic notion of property that Singer (2000) calls the 'ownership model of property' and to recognize that the commons can be 'owned' in different ways and by more than one singular owner, such as the public, in the sense of 'the people', 'the nation' or other 'unorganized public' (Rose, 1994), and local communities of commoners at the same time.

In a liberal-economistic definition, property is a relationship of ownership between a resource and a titleholder, who can either be an individual or a corporation such as a state, or a community, and who possesses the full bundle of rights and privileges in the resource, including the power to exclude others from it and alienate it. Commons, however, do not depend on a singular titleholder with absolute ownership, but on social relations, mutual obligations and a variety of rights in the commons. In the Old English open field commons:

> the state, as represented by the king of the country, might thus have the right to the large trees most suitable for use in naval construction and a nobleman owning estates covering a large region might have the right to certain game animals, while a certain farmer from the village had the right to pannage for his swine, and a village cottar the right to gather firewood from the ground. The commons thus transcended a large number of spatial and social scales that overlapped within a commons that need not be clearly defined spatially.
>
> (Olwig, 2005: 307)[3]

The people sharing a commons did not form one narrowly-bounded community, and must not be seen as a kind of corporation with absolute ownership of a clearly bounded resource. Rather, the image is one of nested social entities and diverse bodies of commoners with different rights and different kinds of belonging in the commons. The Old English open fields commons has been called the 'patrimony of the poor' or 'the property of the poor' (Polanyi, 2001), but historians have shown that there were several different social groups of landed and landless commoners with rights in the commons and that commons included different, interlocking commoning economies (Neeson, 1993).

This image leaves communities holding commons with a different status. Communities using or benefiting from the commons are not singular owners: there are different bodies of commoners. In a modern urban context, local communities of residents can be seen as stewards or caretakers of the housing commons that they have the right to use and dwell in, but they may not have the moral right to sell their flats, because the housing commons is at the same

3 It is important to note that the Old English open field commons existed on the basis of custom and not rights; custom did, however, have the force of law. It was the introduction of modern capitalism with legal rights and modern markets that guided the enclosure movement and the attack on the commons (Neeson, 1993; Thompson, 1991).

time a common good that belongs to members of larger society who have a moral right of access to affordable housing and the right not to be excluded from the commons.

When we begin to think about nested or layered rights in the commons and recognize that different people and communities of commoners co-reside in the commons and make legitimate claims to the commons, we open the way for seeing conflict and moral argumentation within and among these communities. Battles for the right to the city and urban commons are not necessarily two-sided battles between, for instance, a developer who has bought a building and sees it as his private property and a community of activists and homeless people who claim it as a commons (Blomley, 2008). When we zoom in on 'the community' there can in fact be several social groups and bodies of commoners asserting power and claiming different rights in the commons.

In the next part of this chapter I discuss the case of cooperative housing, which is a commons both in the sense of constituting a resource held and managed by a local community that sets rules for inclusion and exclusion through relations of governance, power and hierarchy and in the sense of forming a common good that all should have access to. Also, the housing cooperatives are a symbolic commons for the modern welfare society that carries important social and cultural values.

Housing cooperatives as an urban commons

Housing cooperatives are a common, well-known and taken-for-granted form of collective ownership of housing in Denmark, with 7 per cent of all housing being in cooperatives (Kristensen, 2007). A large number of Danes either live or have lived in a housing cooperative themselves or know somebody who does. In Copenhagen, one-third of all housing is organized as self-governing cooperatives with ten to a few hundred cooperative flats in each cooperative. A housing cooperative is a voluntary member-based association, created with the goal of running a collectively-owned residential property. Cooperative members do not have private property rights to their individual flats, but own a share of their cooperative that holds the building as a legal entity and have the right to live in the particular flat that their share corresponds to. Members are obliged to live in the cooperative they have a share in. This prevents speculation and ensures that members participate in the upkeep and management of their building.

There are two events in particular that gather all members of a housing cooperative together: work parties where members work together to maintain their common property and the annual general assemblies where decisions are made about the maintenance of the building, the cooperative's finances and member recruitment.

It is a common tradition in many housing cooperatives that members are summoned for a work party once or twice a year, usually on a Saturday or Sunday when people are off work. Typically, people gather in the morning in the courtyard to divide the tasks and work on the cooperative's common spaces, painting staircases and cleaning up the courtyards, basements or attics for some hours or the whole day. The day often ends with a barbecue or other communal meal. On such occasions people's activities constitute the commons in a material, economic, physical, social and cultural sense (Gudeman, 2001). By working together people strengthen interpersonal relations and create a sense of community and egalitarian togetherness where hierarchies and social and economic differences and power relations are left aside. This egalitarian sociality extends the local community and manifests a cultural ideal in and of modern Danish society (Bruun, 2011). Participating in a work party is an activity that not only involves helping out one's neighbors, but symbolizes good public spirit and willingness to participate in society at large. In Norway, there is a special term – *dugnad* – that refers to voluntary and collective work that is conducted in a community. In pre-industrial Norway, peasants called upon their neighbors for assistance in particularly large tasks, such as renewing turf roofs, and this effort today extends into modern Norway for the accomplishment of common national goals (Klepp, 2001). Sociality on a small scale in housing cooperatives during work parties serves as a model for sociality on a larger scale, including the whole of society (Bruun, 2011).

The annual general assembly where each member has a vote is the highest authority of each cooperative. In the general assemblies members elect an executive committee that is responsible for the day-to-day work connected to maintaining the building and decide on the principles for recruiting new members into the cooperative. Most housing cooperatives have, or used to have, waiting lists that grant the larger public access to cooperative housing. Member recruitment through waiting lists in Danish housing cooperatives generally meant picking new members from the top of the waiting list, without any further interviewing, credit rating or other criteria for eligibility. Waiting lists build on a notion of social justice similar to public welfare institutions such as social housing and public day care, and they used to work as an instrument of social justice and accessibility for outsiders before the high prices of cooperative shares made waiting lists superfluous. There were, however, considerable differences in the way that waiting lists were managed in the cooperatives: in some cooperatives anyone could sign up, while others only accepted people with some prior connection to existing members of the cooperative. The latter, more closed, waiting lists were criticized for excluding others through nepotism, which I will come back to.

The general assembly also presents and passes the accounts and settles on a budget for the following year, including what the price of cooperative shares should be. In the 1980s and 1990s, share prices were generally low, often token, in line with the original non-profit ideology of cooperative housing and also because there were no incentives to raise the share prices. In this way, the cooperatives were 'non-commodified-off-limits to the logic of market exchange and market valuations' (Harvey, 2012: 73), even though, in theory, individual housing cooperatives had the opportunity to raise share prices according to market valuations of their building.

This changed in 2001 when a Liberal-Conservative government came to power and propagated neoliberal reforms and the free market model in Danish cooperative housing through what has been described as 'change without reform' (Nielsen, 2010). The Ministry of Housing was dismantled, and cooperative housing came under the jurisdiction of the Ministry of Economic and Business Affairs. The overall vision of the new housing policy, titled 'More Housing: Growth and Renewal on the Housing Market' (Government, 2002), was to 'set the stage for a gradually more market-oriented policy with increasing support for economic growth where the role of the state is reduced and aimed at the weakest groups in the housing market'. One of the objectives was the 'market-orientation of cooperative housing', which included the scaling down of subsidies and the introduction of mortgage-like loans secured on members' shares in housing cooperatives that became effective in 2005.

This presumably small and rather technical amendment did not cause much debate in the Danish Parliament, but it resonated with other important developments in Danish society – the introduction of new interest-only loans, a new demographic pressure on the cooperatives and, not least, the price boom in the housing market leading up to the financial crisis in 2008 – and had a significant impact on housing cooperatives. The opportunity that members now had to take individual loans against their cooperative shares formed an incentive to raise the prices of cooperative shares, and over the following years, cooperatives and their members were drawn into credit flows and the share prices in housing cooperatives increased dramatically, following the general upward trend in the market valuation of real estate.

While this development in the last decade is a history of commodification, quasi-privatization and enclosure of the commons, we have not seen the end of the story yet and there are other lessons to be learned from the case of Danish housing cooperatives about how we can conceptualize urban commons. Paradoxically, enclosures or attacks on the commons also invoke the commons and make us aware of their existence (Blomley, 2008). Paradoxically, as I will show in the next section, it was the moral disputes about the cooperatives' economic decisions on whether to raise prices and take loans, framed as a question of respecting the cooperative ideology (*andelstanken*), that made explicit the role of housing cooperatives as a commons that all members of Danish society have rights in, or at least have the right not to be excluded from. Open access to the housing commons has, however, continuously been challenged by exclusionary practices, such as of the local residents who favor their own friends and relatives or want to make individual profits.

The cooperative ideology and public rights in the commons

The cooperative ideology, *andelstanken*, literally the cooperative *idea*, outlines a set of organizational principles of open membership, participatory democracy and cooperation that originated in the cooperative movement. It does, however, also stand for values and virtues of equality in general, and notions of solidarity and sharing that circulate and are practiced in cooperatives – or *not* practiced, which some people then criticize or defend in particular ways.

Cooperative housing is one among many forms of cooperative association that have developed in Denmark since the formation of the cooperative movement (*andelsbevægelsen*) in the second half of the nineteenth century, inspired by the English Rochdale principles. The first Danish consumer society was set up in 1866 and, especially from the 1880s onwards, cooperative dairies, slaughterhouses and agricultural machinery stations were established all over the country. Together with the great popular movements of folk high schools and free farmers, the cooperative movement was essential in laying the groundwork for modern Danish society, and the formation of the modern Danish welfare state, especially after the Social Democratic part of the workers' movement, accepted the cooperative housing movement in 1913. Though it usually goes largely unnoticed, the cooperative ideology is still reflected in a range of cooperative and mutual organizations in Danish society.[4]

In contemporary housing cooperatives, many members who I interviewed during my fieldwork connect the cooperative ideology with general ideals of social justice, solidarity and the right to a home in Danish welfare society, though historically cooperative housing and other mutual housing associations predate the welfare state's provision of social housing. Housing cooperatives never became public property as such but continued to exist as an alternative to and in symbiosis with the social housing schemes initiated by the welfare state in the 1930s.

Carol Rose (1994) distinguishes between two types of 'public property' in the common law of Britain and America: one predictable from economic theory, namely public property owned and managed by a government body, and the other public property collectively 'owned' by society at large with claims that are independent of and superior to the government (1994: 110). I suggest that in a similar way, but without the legal backing of common law, which does not exist in Denmark, the 'unorganized public' has moral rights, with practical effects, in housing cooperatives, based in the cooperatives

---

4 In 2001, 1.6 million of the total Danish population of 5.5 million were members of the Fællesforeningen for Danmarks Brugsforeninger (United Danish Consumer Societies), just as some large energy suppliers, insurance companies, dairies and slaughterhouses are still organized as cooperatives or mutual societies.

being perceived both as a product and a symbol of collective life and collective history. Larger society's rights in the commons are claimed by referring or alluding to the cooperative ideology.

In public discourse, the cooperative ideology is often expressed as 'everyone ought to have the opportunity to get in and get a place to live', implicitly referring to a cooperative flat, or as 'cooperatives should offer affordable dwellings for all'. Importantly, these claims are not only made by outsiders. Also many cooperative members agree on this, even though it is not written anywhere in the cooperatives' statutes that cooperatives have the moral obligation to include others and make inexpensive and attractive cooperative flats available to all members of society. This moral axiom is not just talk, but also plays a role at committee meetings and general assemblies, for instance when a decision is made about waiting list rules or about whether two small cooperative apartments should be allowed to be merged into one large apartment. Keeping small apartments is framed as a sign of solidarity in relation to anonymous members of society in need of small, affordable places, who have a legitimate need for cheap housing and cannot afford to buy large apartments.

I also take it as a sign of the cooperatives being viewed as a commons that all members of society have a moral right not to be excluded from that some people were morally offended, more by the profits that members of cooperatives made from selling their cooperative apartments than by the profits that private home owners made from selling their condominiums during the same years. This is reflected in the quote at the beginning of this chapter where a former member of a cooperative says that he felt he was being accused of 'selling something that was not his own'. When housing cooperatives decided to 'follow the market', as a common formulation went, in the years of the housing boom, this was accompanied with nostalgia and moral concerns among cooperative members and other Danes. Many people were concerned that the original cooperative ideology and solidarity had vanished and that cooperatives no longer cared for people in need of affordable dwellings.

I once I interviewed a young couple who had just moved into a housing cooperative. They were lamenting the fact that cooperative flats had become too expensive, and the young man said:

> The flat prices are now so high that people from other social layers [i.e., those who are better off] get in because the poor cannot afford it – not anymore. The cooperative ideology is a little bit gone. I really think that is a shame. I think it is a great idea. But it is difficult to realize, because then you have waiting lists and so on and it is difficult to make it really democratic. Money under the table and so on.

The young man was concerned that it was no longer possible for everybody to 'get into' a housing cooperative. He did, however, also have a feeling that the cooperative ideology of openness and open membership allowing everybody to 'get in' had always been 'difficult to realize', and that actual cooperatives had never really lived up to this ideal anyway. For him, the cooperative ideology was under attack not only from people's greed and from market forces, but also from nepotism and other forms of favoritism. Before the housing cooperatives were drawn into the market, cooperative members had, for instance, received money 'under the table' when selling their officially cheap cooperative shares. He also explained to me that many cooperatives had allotted the cheap flats in attractive neighborhoods to their own relatives and friends. One common view was that the new wealth had corrupted the true cooperative ideology; another was that the recent flows of money simply exposed transactions, interests and calculations that were previously hidden behind an ideological smokescreen.

By no means all cooperative communities make affordable cooperative flats and cooperative living accessible to outsiders and lend themselves to open access to the commons. Given the pervasiveness of this trend, it is striking that even though the cooperative ideology has been challenged over the last decades, first by nepotism and the black market, and then by commercialization and quasi-privatization, people's moral concerns and reasoning reflect that a particular ethic of open access to a shared social good still plays a role in the housing cooperatives.

Conclusion

One important aspect that is missing in current theories on the urban commons is a view of the communities and the people who live in and maintain them. The essence of urban commons is not just ensuring access to parks or other public spaces, but of offering people an equitable life in the city, and commons are not the same as economic resources or real property. Most social theory on the urban commons (e.g. Harvey, 2012) conveys very general or global claims to the right to the city, but few people treat the whole metropolis as a commons in their everyday life. In order to grasp urban commons from an experiential view I have zoomed in on local cooperative communities and the way they maintain and make decisions about their common property. I have shown that the housing cooperatives have several 'owners' and groups of users and beneficiaries who make claims on the commons: those cooperative members who have lived in the cooperatives for many years and taken care of the buildings; all members of Danish society, who should have the option of obtaining a cheap cooperative flat; and cooperative members who owned a share in a cooperative during the years of economic boom and capitalized on the commons by selling expensive shares. Space does not allow me to go deeper into the different ways that these ownership claims are negotiated in the cooperatives, but I have shown how the cooperative ideology, as a powerful norm for cultural and moral behavior in the commons, plays an important role in making decisions, or at least makes initiatives to privatize the commons morally suspect. Obviously, housing and people's homes cannot be everyone's property at the same time, and there are local stewards or caretakers of the commons who enjoy the benefits of living in the commons and have the duty of managing it – and the temptation of appropriating it for themselves. Once the public has become aware of the existence of a commons, and paradoxically this often happens when the commons is threatened by enclosure, new ways to protect the commons may have to be found.

It has been claimed that 'new commons have no history and often have no rules or governance systems in place' (International Association for the Study of the Commons [IASC], cited in Wagner, 2012). The urban commons that this chapter has looked at does, however, have such a history, and within it we can trace layers of governance systems, unwritten laws and the cooperative ideology, as important factors structuring what goes on here. The story of a practiced urban commons challenges the simple narrative of enclosure and commodification that commons always originate in pre-capitalist societies and will eventually be enclosed, and that commodification and the market are the only threats to urban commons. This chapter has shown how nepotism and other self seeking exclusionary practices which do not necessarily have anything to do with processes of commodification have influenced the dilution of the cooperative ideology. The commons can indeed be threatened 'from within', but not necessarily in the tragic ways envisioned by Harding (1968). We need to go beyond the question of whether a resource is or should be held in common, and to ask how these commons are, concretely and every day, lived and organized. This means that we need to ask which communities act as stewards or caretakers of the commons, and how these communities can be supported in ways that keep the commons open and inclusive. In short, we need to think the commons within the broader framework of political economy, and to neither idealize them as problem-free, nor stigmatize them as inevitable tragedies.

Acknowledgements

I would like to thank Patrick Cockburn for his encouragement and valuable comments on various drafts of this chapter.

References

Amit, V. and Rapport, N. (eds) (2002) *The Trouble with Community. Anthropological Reflections on Movement, Identity and Collectivity*. London: Pluto Press.

Blackmar, E. (2006) 'Appropriating "the Commons": The Tragedy of Property Rights Discourse', in S.M. Low and N. Smith (eds), *The Politics of Public Space* (pp. 49–80). New York and London: Routledge.

Blomley, N. (2008) 'Enclosure, Common Right and the Property of the Poor', *Social & Legal Studies* 17(3): 311–31.

Bollier, D. (2003) *The Silent Theft: The Private Plunder of Our Common Wealth*. New York: Routledge.

Bromley, D.W. (ed.) (1992) *Making the Commons Work: Theory, Practice, and Policy*. San Francisco: ICS Press.

Bruun, M.H. (2011) 'Egalitarianism and Community in Danish Housing Cooperatives. Proper Forms of Sharing and Being Together', *Social Analysis* 55(2): 62–83.

Bruun, M.H. (2012) *Social Life and Moral Economies in Danish Cooperative Housing. Community, Property and Value*. PhD thesis, Department of Anthropology, Faculty of Social Sciences. Copenhagen: University of Copenhagen.

Caldeira, T.P.R. (2000) *City of Walls. Crime, Segregation, and Citizenship in São Paolo*. Berkeley, Cal.: University of California Press.

Creed, G.W. (2006) 'The Seductions of Community. Reconsidering Community', in *The Seductions of Community: Emancipations, Oppressions, Quandaries* (pp. 1–25). Santa Fe: School of American Research Press.

Feeny, D., Berkes, F., McCay, B.J. and Acheson, J.M. (1990) 'The Tragedy of the Commons: Twenty-Two Years Later', *Human Ecology* 18(1): 1–19.

Foster, S.R. (2011) 'Collective Action and the Urban Commons', *Notre Dame Law Review* 87(1/2): 57–134.

Government (2002) *Flere Boliger. Vækst og Fornyelse på Boligmarkedet*. Copenhagen: Økonomi og Erhvervsministeret.

Gudeman, S. (2001) *The Anthropology of Economy: Community, Market, and Culture*. Oxford: Blackwell Publishing.

Hardin, G. (1968) 'The Tragedy of the Commons', *Science* 162: 1243–8.

Hardt, M. and Negri, A. (2009) *Commonwealth*. Cambridge, MA: Harvard University Press.

Harvey, D. (2012) *Rebel Cities: From the Right to the City to the Urban Revolution*. London and New York: Verso.

Hess, C. (2008) 'Mapping the New Commons', *12th Biennial Conference of the International Association for the Study of the Commons*. Cheltenham, UK.

Hess, C. and Ostrom, E. (eds) (2007) *Understanding Knowledge as a Commons: From Theory to Practice*. Cambridge, Mass.: MIT Press.

Klepp, A. (2001) 'From Neighbourly Duty to National Rhetoric: An Analysis of the Shifting Meanings of Norwegian "Dugnad"', *Ethnologia Scandinavica* 30: 82–98.

Kristensen, H. (2007) *Housing in Denmark*. Copenhagen: Centre for Housing and Welfare. Online. Available HTTP: <http://boligforskning.dk/sites/default/files/Housing_130907.pdf> (accessed 1 September 2014).

Linebaugh, P. (2009) *The Magna Carta Manifesto: Liberties and Commons for All*. Berkeley and Los Angeles: University of California Press.

Mitchell, D. (2003) *The Right to the City*. New York: Guilford.

McCay, B.J. and Acheson, J.M. (eds) (1987) *The Question of the Commons: The Culture and Ecology of Communal Resources*. Tucson: The University of Arizona Press.

Narotzky, S. (2013) 'What Kind of Commons are the Urban Commons?', *Focaal: The European Journal of Anthropology* (66): 122–14.

Neeson, J.M. (1993) *Commoners: Common Right, Enclosure and Social Change in England, 1700–1820*. Cambridge: Cambridge University Press.

Nielsen, B.G. (2010) *The Hidden Politics of a Haunted Sector – Retrenchment in Danish Housing Policy 2001–2009*. PhD thesis, Department of Political Sciences, Faculty of Social Sciences. Copenhagen: University of Copenhagen.

Nonini, D.M. (2007) 'Introduction: The Global Idea of "the Commons"', in D.M. Nonini (ed.), *The Global Idea and the Commons* (pp. 1–26). Oxford: Berghahn Books.

Olwig, K.R. (2005). 'The Landscape of 'Customary' Law Versus that of "Natural" Law', *Landscape Research* 30: 299–320.

Ostrom, E. (1990) *Governing the Commons: The Evolution of Institutions for Collective Action*. Cambridge: Cambridge University Press.

Parry, J. and Bloch, M. (1989) 'Introduction: Money and the Morality of Exchange', in *Money and the Morality of Exchange* (pp. 1–33). Cambridge: Cambridge University Press.

Polanyi, K. (2001/1944) *The Great Transformation*. Boston: Beacon Press.

Rose, C. (1994) *Property and Persuasion: Essays on the History, Theory, and Rhetoric of Ownership*. Boulder: Westview.

Sassen, S. (1991) *The Global City*. New York, London, Tokyo, Princeton: Princeton University Press.

Singer, J.W. (2000) *Entitlement: The Paradoxes of Property*. New Haven: Yale University Press.

Smith, N. and Low, S.M. (2006) 'Introduction: The Imperative of Public Space', in S.M. Low and N. Smith (eds), *The Politics of Public Space* (pp. 1–17). New York and London: Routledge.

Soroos, M.S. (1997) *The Endangered Atmosphere: Preserving a Global Commons*. Columbia, SC: University of South Carolina Press.

Susser, I. and Tonnelat, S. (2013) 'Transformative Cities: The Three Urban Commons', *Focaal: The European Journal of Anthropology* 66: 105–32.

Thompson, E.P. (1991) *Customs in Common*. New York: The New Press.

Wagner, J.R. (2012) 'Water and the Commons Imaginary', *Current Anthropology* 53(5): 617–41.

Index

act of citizenship 129–30, 132, 146, 148–9
activism: flawed historical methodology of 62–3
affective energies 84
Agrawal, Arun 64
Althusser, Louis 61
Anderson, Ben 71
animals 23–5, 29, 33, 35–7, 39–43, 58
Anthropocene, the 23, 37, 40, 42
anti-capitalism 48, 55
anti-globalisation 48
Arendt, Hannah 87, 116
Arias, Víctor 92
Athens 111
Atkins, Peter 35
atmosphere 2, 47, 68–72 , 107, 121, 127; and urban commons 8–11, 74, 76, 85–7, 89

Bachelard, Gaston 86
Banham, Reyner 12
Barad, Karen 22–3
Barcelona 111
Benjamin, Walter 18–9
Berlin 17, 36, 49, 50, 53, 61, 113, 116
biopolitics 3, 10, 29, 39, 43
Birmingham 36
Borch, Christian 71
Braudel, Fernand 26
Brennan, Teresa 68, 70–1, 76–7
Bruun, Maja Hojer 6, 18
Buckingham, Richard Derby of 58
Bylund, Jonas and Saunders, Fred 33
Böhme, Gernot 2, 8, 10–11, 70–1, 77

Cairo 105, 111
Campos, María José Zapata 6, 9, 17

capitalism: and commons theory 54–6; and sexuality 53; and the city 56; and the commons 16, 53–4
Carlson, Jennifer 71–2
Carrier, Jean-Baptiste 57
Chicago 35
Chinandega 92
citiness 34–5
city: as commons 50; and history 64–5; and knowability 51–2; material form of 51; sexual geography of 50–2
class 57, 59, 74, 83–4, 113–14, 133, 138
Colding, Johan 32, 36–7, 42
collective space 88
collectivity 2, 11–16, 85; urban 11–15, 23, 37, 42, 109–10, 118
commodification 68, 88, 156, 158–9, 164, 168
common good 154, 155, 162
common property regime 154–7, 159–60
common-pool resources 5–6, 8, 12, 59, 98, 102–3, 106; management of 25–6, 30–1, 33, 41, 96
commoners 2, 17–18, 57–9, 155–6, 161–2; human/non-human 22–3, 26, 32–3, 36–7; and power 9; urban 14–15, 43, 58
commoning 14–19, 48, 58, 68, 87, 98, 104–5, 107; economies of 155, 161; social practice of 15n6, 158; more-than-human 10, 25–7, 32–4, 39–42
commons: ambient 11; and activism 32, 48–9, 64–5; and community 154–6, 160–2; and consumption 5–8, 11, 15, 38, 107, 157; and have-nots 55, 128–31, 135–6, 138–9, 144–5; and markets 6, 17, 48–9, 54, 59, 61–2, 158–9; and property 154, 156, 160–1;

and relationality 6–13, 118–19; as sphere 8–9, 27; designing urban 109, 122; ecological interpretations of 60–1; false historical memories of 57–8; historical attributes of 47–8; historical claims about 56–8; historical evidence about 58–9; historical methods and 59; human/non-human divide 22–3, 33–4, 39, 41–4; imagined 18, 128; moral attributes of 48; new 154–6, 160, 168; open field 155, 161; producing 12, 50–4; railway station as 17, 69, 72–82, 88–9; rights in 154, 159, 161–2, 165–6; urban beach as 69, 82–9; us vs them 39, 127–8, 148; waste as 17, 94–8, 101–7; *see also* commons theory; enclosure; governing the commons; tragedy of the commons
commons theory: critiques of 64; history and 48–9; problematic uses of history in 55–60; *see also* Hardin, Garrett; Ostrom, Elinor
conviviality 26, 38–9, 42
cooperative 98, 103
Copenhagen 72–7, 80, 82, 87, 89, 153, 155, 159, 162
cosmopolitics 29, 37, 41
CPR *see* common-pool resources
critical sociology 133, 137
crowd psychology 13–14, 70
crowds 13–15, 70, 73–5, 78–9, 87
Czarniawska, Barbara 26

de-individualization 13–15
Deleuze, Gilles 27
Deleuze, Gilles 28
democracy 104, 112, 128, 156–7, 160, 165
density 1, 6–14, 16
Derrida, Jacques 145
difference 11–12, 26, 114, 115–16, 119, 122–3
diversity 11–12, 109–10, 113–17, 121–3
Durkheim, Émile 61

Edgerton, Robert B. 83–4, 89
Eisenman, Peter 113
Eizenberg, Efrat 56
Eknert, Bo 36
Elmau 27
Elmqvist, Thomas 32, 35, 42
Emanuelson, Urban 36

enclosure 58, 104, 128, 156–9, 161n3, 164, 168
entanglement 16, 22–3, 33, 39, 72, 85
entrainment 70–1
ethics 42–3, 128, 132
eugenics 3, 30, 42
exclusion *see* inclusion/exclusion
experts 17, 59, 110–12, 115, 117, 119, 122, 128

Feldman, Mark B. 41
Foster, Sheila R. 5, 32
Frankfurt am Main 17, 110–11, 113, 119–23
free-riding 5–8, 62, 127, 132, 156, 160
Frers, Lars 76, 88, 89
Freud, Sigmund 33–4

Galanakis, Michael 81–2
García, Ramón 102
Garden City 6–7, 62
Garnett, Nicole Stelle 31–2
gender 89, 115
Giddens, Anthony 62
Gillis, John 83
Global Alliance of Waste Pickers 103
Goffman, Erving 84, 115
Gothenburg 106–7
governing the commons 17, 88, 105, 116, 119, 141, 162, 168; see also Hardin, Garrett; Ostrom; Elinor
Gramsci, Antonio 61
Guattari, Félix 28
Gudeman, Stephen 154–5

Habermas, Jürgen 60, 109
Hache, Émile 40
Haeg, Fritz 40, 41
Haraway, Donna 27–8, 33–4, 37, 42–3
Hardin, Garrett 8, 11, 14–15, 19, 36, 42–3, 159–60; on overpopulation 3, 30; on tragedy of the commons 1–5; 29–33, 38, 58, 155–6, 168
Hardt, Michael 10–1, 47, 61, 63–5, 94, 110; historical flaws in arguments of 56–7
Harvey, David 6n3, 13n5, 32, 65, 105, 110–11, 158; on commoning 15n6, 17, 68, 87; on rights to the city 98, 146, 157
Heibach, Christiane 71
Heidegger, Martin 27–9
Helsinki 81

Henriques, Julian 71, 77–8
Hess, Charlotte 6, 11, 55–6
heterotopia 130, 132
hierarchy 128–9, 142, 162–3
Hinchliffe, Steve 36, 39, 41–2
Hiss, Tony 79
Hobbes, Thomas 127
homosexuality 17, 49, 50–4, 61–2, 64–5, 116
housing cooperatives 18, 153–6, 159, 162–7
Howard, Ebenezer 1, 6–8, 11, 13, 15, 62

inclusion/exclusion 1, 59, 81, 149, 159–60, 162; and humans/non-humans 23; and mobilization 101; and urban norms 75; and social status 84, 89, 94, 133, 135–36, 139; and spheres 9; see also terraine vague
informal entrepreneurs 17, 94
Ingold, Tim 72, 77, 86
Istanbul 75, 98

Jacobs, Jane 12, 26
Jeremijenko, Natalie 40–1
Jerram, Leif 6, 12, 16–17
Johansson, Magnus 32, 41
journalism 18, 128–30, 133–49

Kant, Immanuel 51, 132
Kaufmann, Jean-Claude 84–5, 89
Key West 147
Klein, Naomi 55
Koolhaas, Rem 117

La Chureca 92–106
Latour, Bruno 23, 26, 33–4, 37, 40–3
Lefébvre, Henri 118, 157
Libeskind, Daniel 113
Linebaugh, Peter 15n6, 158n2
Lisbon 59
Lobo, Michele 84
Locke, John 7
London 17, 36, 49–50, 52, 61, 82–4
Los Angeles 55, 59, 61–2, 64, 83–4, 132–3, 137, 143
Lovelock, James 37
Löfgren, Orvar 10, 17, 35
Löw, Martina 7, 17

Madrid 98
Malmö 82–4
Managua 17, 92, 95–6, 99, 103–5

marginalization 42, 56, 64, 73, 87, 158; and sexuality 54, representation in journalism 135–6, 138
Marstein, Trude 80–1
Marx, Karl 13n5, 61–2
mass suggestion 2, 13–14
Massey, Doreen 72
materialities 72, 77, 85, 95, 98
McCullough, Malcolm 11
Metzger, Jonathan 10, 16
Mezzadra, Sandro 16
Miami 132, 137, 143, 146–7
modernity 49, 62, 64, 73–4; and the city 61; hostility towards 61–2; and sexuality 64
Montreal 132–4, 138, 140–1, 145
Moreck, Kurt 50–4, 56, 60–1, 63–5
Moscow 59
Mozart, Wolfgang Amadeus 72
multitude 56–7, 114–15, 123, 127–9

Nassehi, Armin 109
Negri, Antonio 10–1, 47, 61, 63–5, 94, 110; historical flaws in arguments of 56–7
neoliberal 156, 159, 164
Németh, Jeremy 47
New Labour: and the third way 62
New York 40, 61, 79, 98, 132–3, 136, 140–1, 143–5
Nielsen, Greg M. 9, 18
Nielson, Brett 16
Nietzsche, Friedrich 28, 43
Nowotny, Helga 38

Occupy movement 48, 139
open access 68, 153, 156–7, 159–62, 164, 167
Ostrom, Elinor 1, 87, 94, 110, 154; assumptions of 3–8, 22, 25–7, 33, 36–7, 47–9; on common pool resources 5, 30–1, 33, 59, 96, 103; on design principles 4–5, 30–1, 41, 102, 105, 160; versus Garrett Hardin 3–8, 103, 156; on scaling 64; on subtractive/non-subtractive resources 5–6; reliance on historical argument 55–6, 59–60; use of historical methods 55, 59–61
Otter, Christopher 25
ownership 104, 153, 155–6, 159–62, 167

Park, Robert E. 11–13, 15
Parker, Peter 32, 41

Paris 119
participation 111
Philo, Chris 25n2, 33, 35
Philo, Chris 24
planning 11, 17, 42, 109–10, 112, 115, 117–22
Plumwood, Val 38
polis 27, 29, 35–6
political economy 155–6, 168
power 1, 10–11, 16, 103–6, 111, 155, 161–3; and subjectification 9, 13–14
prisoner's dilemma 3–4, 11
privacy 53, 84–5
privatization 8, 55, 88, 105–6, 127–9, 156–9; and housing 164, 167; Garrett Hardin on 2, 4, 38; Elinor Ostrom on 4, 30–1
property regime 156, 160
property rights 153, 160, 162
property: no one's 156; private 147, 156, 159–60, 162; public 147, 156, 160, 165
Pry, Paul 50–4, 56, 61, 63–5
public interest 110–13, 115–19, 122–3
public space 69, 110–12, 157–8, 167; commodified 88; design of 76, 109; privatized 88; segregated 74, 88
public sphere 112, 116

Raman, Bhuvaneswari 111
recycling 96, 99–100, 102, 104, 106–7
representation 110, 116–17, 122–3
responsibility 22–24, 43–4, 112
restriction of access 159
rhythm 71, 78–9, 86–7
right to the city 88, 98, 157, 162, 167
Rio de Janeiro 130
Rose, Carol 165
Rose, Deborah Bird 39
rubbish 94, 99, 102

Salgado, Marisa 100
Sao Paulo 130
Scharpf, Fritz W. 109
segregation 78, 87
Sennett, Richard 12
Serra, Richard 113
Serres, Michel 26, 38
Showalter, Elaine 45
Sidis, Boris 14
Simmel, Georg 11–12, 26, 123

Singer, Joseph William 160
Sisyphus 26
Sloterdijk, Peter 19, 23, 27–9, 38–9, 43; on spheres 2, 8–10, 14–16, 27
slum 94–6, 100–1
smell 76–8, 86–7
sociability 69, 88
social justice 155, 157, 159, 163, 165
social movements 64, 88, 103–4, 129, 157
sound 73, 76–8, 80, 86
Star, Susan Leigh 95–6
state: and the city 56; and the common 52; and commons theory 54–5; common pool resources and 59–60; moral aspects of 60
Stengers, Isabelle 27, 38, 41, 43
Stewart, Kathleen 71–2
Stockholm 23–4, 32, 36
surveillance 82, 88
Susser, Ida 87, 158
Svensson, Julia 80

Tan, Qian Hui 78
Tan, Yi-Fu 83
terraine vague 69, 72
third way, the 54, 60–3; and social criticism 49
throwntogetherness 72, 85–6
Tonnelat, Stéphane 87, 158
Toronto 131–3, 136–7, 140, 142, 145
tragedy of the commons 14–15, 22, 32, 37, 103, 127, 168; Garrett Hardin on 2–4, 29–30, 38, 58, 155–6
Tryggestad, Kjell 37
Tsing, Anna 34

Ullman, Micha 113
Urbain, Jean-Didier 84

Vancouver 131–3, 140, 143, 145–6
Venturi, Robert 12
Villa del Carmen 92

Walton, John K. 83
Warsaw 81
waste pickers 94–107
Weber, Max 61
Webster, Chris 31
welfare society 162–3, 165
Whatmore, Sarah 25–6, 36, 39–42

Whitehead, Alfred North 30
Wilbert, Chris 24
Wirth, Louis 2, 9, 11–16, 26
Wolch, Jennifer R 39
Wolch, Jennifer R. 34–5

Young, Iris Marion 116–7

Zapata, Patrik 6, 9, 17
zoning 83

University of Strathclyde
Dept of Architecture
Library

Lightning Source UK Ltd.
Milton Keynes UK
UKHW011812311018
331549UK00011B/222/P